Financial Success In a Box

Robert Bassford

DISCLAIMER

CLIMB
C CLIMBB
Incorporated

This book is dedicated to my Lord & Savior Jesus Christ,
my fabulous wife and my wonderful children—
the biggest blessings in my life.

About Robert Bassford

Robert Bassford designs practical "bridges" that allow people and organizations to get from "where they are" to "where they want to be" in a simple step-by-step way. He shows that if given a simple Success Plan, people can reach amazing levels of potential while still being themselves.

Robert Bassford has worked in the field of Talent & Organizational Development for more than 15 years. He knows what it takes to help people reach higher levels of potential in all areas of their life. His expertise in designing simple, practical "bridges" that take individuals and organizations from "where they are" to "where they want to be" has enabled his clients to reach a much higher level of potential and accomplish their goals.

Robert has a BBA and MBA and has held positions as the head of talent development for the flight test center of a private jet manufacturer, a city government, the largest retailer of sport boats and yachts in the world, and many other corporations. He has also taught a wide variety of classes for universities and colleges. He has extensive experience planning, designing, developing and delivering a wide range of training and development programs that have built individual and organizational capabilities in many industries including retail, wholesale, manufacturing, service, healthcare, universities, churches, and government entities. Robert has helped people at all levels of these organizations ranging from hourly employees, secretaries, and supervisors to computer programmers, retail phone salespeople, policemen, firefighters, pilots, former astronauts and all levels of upper management, including general managers and CEOs.

He has used his vast experience in the area of human potential to design this program into a simple step-by-step plan that will take you from where you are now to a great financial life in 10 simple steps. He has designed this program so that you can be successful just being yourself; you do not have to become a totally different person to be successful in this program. He has also included all the tools and techniques you will need to be successful. Follow the 10 simple steps one step at a time, and you will go from financial frustration to financial success and change your life forever.

Robert is dedicated to helping people reach financial success so they can live their dreams and enjoy the blessings they have received.

Robert lives with his family in the Tampa Bay area of Florida.

CONTENTS

STEP 1

10-STEP PLAN

FINANCIAL SUCCESS IN A BOX

FINANCIAL SCOREBOARD

NAME: _____   DATE: _____

STEP 1 10 STEP PLAN	I have a step-by-step plan to follow to reach financial success 1 2 3 4 5 6 7 8 9 10 No · · · Maybe · · · Yes	**1** Fill in the circles that best describe your current situation
STEP 2 WORK TOGETHER	I work together with my spouse in all areas of our finances toward common goals (if you are single, mark the 10) 1 2 3 4 5 6 7 8 9 10 Never · · Sometimes · · Always	
STEP 3 THE BASICS	I know key success factors of money, behavior change and marketing self-defense 1 2 3 4 5 6 7 8 9 10 No · · · Maybe · · · Yes	
STEP 4 GIVING	I currently give to my church, charities, etc. on a regular basis 1 2 3 4 5 6 7 8 9 10 Never · · Regularly · · 10% Gross	
STEP 5 PUT MONEY TO WORK	I currently save the following % of gross income every paycheck (includes savings, 401K, IRAs, etc) 1 2 3 4 5 6 7 8 9 10 1% or less · · 2% · · 3% Gross	**2** Connect the Dots
STEP 6 EMERGENCY FUND	I currently have the following amount in a dedicated cash emergency fund 1 2 3 4 5 6 7 8 9 10 $0 $200 $300 $400 $500 $600 $700 $800 $900 $1000	
STEP 7 PAY OFF DEBT	I currently owe the following total amount in consumer debt (Includes credit cards, student loans, etc. – everything except your house) 1 2 3 4 5 6 7 8 9 10 $20,000+ $16,000 $12,000 $8,000 $4,000 $0	
STEP 8 SURVIVAL FUND	I currently have a cash survival fund that will cover my total expenses for 1 2 3 4 5 6 7 8 9 10 1 Month 2 Months 3 Months 4 Months 6 Months	
STEP 9 PLAN RETIREMENT	I contribute to my retirement fund every month and I know I will have enough (If you are currently retired, mark 10) 1 2 3 4 5 6 7 8 9 10 No · · · Maybe · · · Yes	**3** Total the Points
STEP 10 PAY OFF HOUSE	I pay extra on my mortgage (If you do not have a mortgage, mark 10) 1 2 3 4 5 6 7 8 9 10 Never · · Regularly · · Paid Off	

If your score is less than 90, you need this program

> *For I know the plans I have for you, says the Lord, plans to prosper you and not to harm you, plans to give you hope and a future.*
>
> *Jeremiah 29:11*

	Put a check mark by each item you want
	$1,000 Cash Emergency Fund
	3-6 month Cash Survival Fund
	All debt paid off
	Automatic monthly deposits into a retirement account
	Confidence that you will have enough money to retire
	Ability to give on a regular basis
	A plan to pay your house off early
	Knowledge of the key success factors of money
	Knowledge and ability to change your behaviors
	Ability to work for a dollar once and then make It work for you
	Financial information/documents/tools in one easy to find location
	Confidence that your loved ones are protected financially
	Enough financial success to pursue your real dreams
	Working together with loved ones on common financial goals
	A positive feeling when you check your bank balance
	Knowledge/ability to teach your children to be financially strong

If you put a checkmark by any of these items, this program is for you.

10-STEP PLAN

I am so excited that you are taking this journey. I have created a Financial Success Plan for you. I will be taking you step-by-step to a wonderful place of Financial Success. I have provided everything you will need to go from Financial Frustration to Financial Success. You can be successful being yourself. I have designed this program so that you do not have to become a totally different person to be successful. This book can pay for itself thousands of times as you make your way through each step. There are 10 simple steps in this program. If you take these 10 simple steps, you can have a great financial life!

IMAGINE

Imagine having a financial life that was so great you never worried about money.

Imagine:
- Having a simple 10-Step Plan to go from Financial Frustration to Financial Success one step at a time
- Working Together with loved ones toward the same financial goals—no more arguments, no more fights
- Knowing the basics of how money works and how to change your behaviors
- Being able to give on a regular basis
- Having your money work for you to build wealth
- Having a cash emergency fund to protect you from car breakdowns, appliance repairs, and other emergencies
- Having all of your consumer debt paid off—no credit cards, car loans, etc. No monthly debt payments.
- Having a cash survival fund that would pay all of your expenses for 3 to 6 months if you lost your job
- Having a simple automatic retirement fund that would provide a strong and secure retirement
- Paying your house off years early and saving thousands and thousands of dollars—no monthly house payment
- Having important financial information, documents, and tools in one easy-to -find place—no more searching the house for information
- Having peace of mind because you have built a strong financial life
- Sleeping well at night because you know you and your family are taken care of financially
- Having the extra money to travel
- Having the money and freedom to follow your life dreams
- Being able to share these principles with your children and others

Imagine how well you would sleep at night knowing that all of the major areas of your financial life are together. It would only take about 1 hour a month to keep it on track. You can actually experience the wonderful feeling of Financial Success. If this sounds good, then you have chosen the right program.

PURPOSE

LAUNCH YOUR SUCCESS PLAN

The purpose of this program is to get you to the wonderful place we just described—a great financial life. This program contains 10 simple steps that will take you to the peaceful, stable lifestyle described above. The 10 steps are put in a particular order. Focus on one step at a time. Once you complete a step, simply move to the next step. Successful completion of one step greatly increases your chances of success on the next step. The more steps that are completed, the easier the next steps are to complete.

I have scoured the vast, complicated world of finances and boiled it down to the basic things you need to know and do to be successful. There are 10 major areas that determine the success of your financial life. These 10 steps will show you how to be successful in each of the 10 major areas.

The purpose of Step 1 is to show you your Success Plan. Your Success Plan will help determine where you are now, where you are going, and show you the 10 simple steps that will take you there.

> *All our dreams can come true—if we have the courage to pursue them.*
>
> *Walt Disney*

10 STEP PLAN

YOU ARE ONLY 10 SIMPLE STEPS FROM A GREAT FINANCIAL LIFE.

	10 STEPS	
1	**10 Step Plan**	Follow the 10 Step Plan Step by Step
2	**Work Together**	Start working together with the ones you love toward common financial goals. No more fighting or pulling in different directions
3	**The Basics**	Learn the basics of how money works, how to change your behaviors and how to win the marketing war for your dollars.
4	**Giving**	Learn to plug in to the power of Giving – learn to give as much as 10%+ of your gross income
5	**Put Money to Work**	Put 3% of your pretax gross income to work
6	**Emergency Fund**	Build $1,000 Emergency Fund
7	**Pay Off Debt**	Pay off all consumer debt using the credit cascade tool
8	**Survival Fund**	Build a survival fund that will cover your total expenses for 3-6 months
9	**Plan Retirement**	Fully fund a retirement plan – automatically putting the right amount in the right accounts every month and you know you will have enough to retire
10	**Pay Off House**	Pay Off House Early by paying extra every month to pay it off years early and save thousands and thousands of dollars

FINANCIAL SUCCESS IN A BOX

WHAT IS IT
Financial Success in a Box is a simple step-by-step program that will take you from Financial Frustration to Financial Success, one step at a time. This program is based on the very powerful principle of:

Work for a dollar once—then make it work for you!

WHY IT WORKS
1. PUTS THE BIG ROCKS FIRST
I do a demonstration at the beginning of my financial classes that illustrates the big rocks concept. I place an empty jar on the table and begin to place large rocks into the jar. I ask the audience to tell me when the jar is full. When I place the last large rock that will fit into the jar, the audience tells me that the jar is full. I ask, "Is the jar really full?" They answer, "Yes." Then I take a container of gravel and start pouring it into the jar with the large rocks. The gravel starts to fill the areas between the large rocks. I tell the audience to let me know when the jar is full. Once the gravel reaches the top of the jar, the audience tells me, "The jar is full." I ask, "Are you sure the jar is full?" They are not as confident, but they still say, "Yes." Then I take a container of sand and start pouring it into the jar with the large rocks and gravel. I ask the audience to tell me when the jar is full. When the sand reaches the top of the jar they tell me to stop: "The jar is full."

I ask them to tell me the point of the demonstration. They typically say, "You can always get more in the jar." I tell them that the real answer is, "You have to put the big rocks in first." If you are going to be successful at anything, you have to put the big rocks in first. You must do the *important* things first. The big rocks represent the important things you must do that will lead to success. The gravel and sand represent things that are not important and take up a lot of space. By the time I fill the jar with rocks, gravel, and sand, it is impossible to put another big rock in the jar.

This demonstration illustrates the current condition of many people's financial situation. Over time, they have filled their financial jar with a lot of gravel and sand and very few big rocks. Now, they are having trouble putting in the big rocks. The 10 steps in this program are the big rocks of your financial life that you need to have in your jar to be successful. The problem is that your current financial jar may be so full of gravel and sand that you will struggle to put in the big rocks. Instead of struggling to empty your current jar to make room for the big rocks, we will simply start with a brand new empty jar. As you complete each of the 10 steps it will be like placing a big rock in your new financial jar. You will build a brand new financial life one big rock at a time. As you move forward and complete additional steps you will leave your old financial jar behind. You will have a brand new financial jar with all 10 big rocks right where they should be, and you can have a great financial life.

If you want to be successful at anything, from time management to sports to financial success, you have to put the big rocks in first. You have to do the *important* things first. You will not be successful by simply trying to cram more into the jar. Put the big rocks in first, and you will be successful. In this program the 10 steps are your big rocks.

2. STEP-BY-STEP PLAN

Most financial programs will give you a list of ideas about how to manage your money, but they do not provide a path or road map for you to follow. This program provides a complete step-by-step roadmap.

3. ONLY ONE STEP AT A TIME

This program allows you to focus on one step at a time. You do not have to work on all the areas of your financial life at the same time. Each step is in a particular order to increase your chances of success and build your confidence. You will do one step at a time, and with each step you complete you will come closer to Financial Success.

4. SIMPLE AND EASY TO USE

I have taken the complex world of finances and boiled it down into simple, practical terms and tools that are easy to understand and use. Think of it as Financial Lite—twice the effectiveness with half the boring details. After all, you do not need to be an expert; you simply need to be successful.

5. START WHERE YOU ARE

No matter where you are currently with your finances, you can begin this program and move forward one step at a time.

6. WORKS NO MATTER WHAT STAGE OF LIFE YOU ARE IN

This program works if you're young or old, married or single, working or retired, man or woman, in college or not in college, with or without children, single mom or single dad, low income or high income. I have designed this program to work for people regardless of their stage in life.

7. DO THE PROGRAM PRIVATELY OR AS PART OF A GROUP

You can complete this program in the privacy of your home or you can attend a group session that provides additional moral support.

8. WORKS NO MATTER WHAT YOU CURRENTLY KNOW ABOUT FINANCES

This program is designed to help you be financially successful whether you know little about money or you are an expert. The information and tools are presented in a way that a novice will understand and an expert will appreciate.

9. WORKS NO MATTER WHAT YOUR CURRENT FINANCIAL SITUATION MAY BE

This program works if you are doing poorly in your financial life, and it works if you are doing well financially. If your financial life is not what you want it to be, this program will take you step-by-step to a great financial life. If you are doing well with your finances, then this program will help you make your financial life even better. You do not have to be in financial trouble to benefit from this program.

10. GIVES YOU A WAY TO CATEGORIZE ALL FINANCIAL TOOLS AND ADVICE

This program gives you a way to categorize and apply all the financial tools and advice you receive from other sources. If you receive advice or a new tool from another source, for example on planning for retirement, then you can put that advice in the Step 9 section – Plan Retirement.

11. EVERY CHAPTER FOLLOWS THE SAME FORMAT
Every chapter of this program has the same key elements. Each chapter has an *Imagine* section—a view of what success will look like for that step, a *Purpose* section—the specific purpose of that step, an *Action* section—gives the specific actions to accomplish that step, and a *To Do List* section—guides you through each step to success. This format makes it very simple to accomplish each step and allows you to move through the program much faster.

12. ADDRESSES THE PRACTICAL AND PERSONAL SIDE OF MONEY
This program was designed to help you be successful with the practical aspects of money as well as the emotional and psychological aspects. It is not just about dollars. It is also about you.

13. BASED ON BIBLICAL PRINCIPLES
I spent months reading every word of the Bible and highlighting all it said about money to make sure that this program is supported biblically. There are more than 2,000 verses in the Bible that reference money.

14. GO AT YOUR OWN PACE
You can go through the 10 steps at your own pace. Some of the steps will be completed very quickly and others may take longer. Decide your own pace based on your situation.

15. YOU ARE NOT ALONE
I will provide the knowledge and tools you will need to complete each step, and I will encourage and inspire you to keep you going. I will also do my best to make the journey enjoyable.

16. WORKS IN GOOD TIMES/WORKS IN BAD TIMES
The 10 steps work in good times and in bad times. If someone asked me, "With the economy being so bad, what financial advice would you recommend?" My answer would be, "The advice I would give you in good economic times is the same advice I would give you in bad economic times…You need:

A financial success plan in good times and in gad times
To work together in good times and definitely in bad times
To know the basics of money in good times and bad times
To be a giver in good times and bad times
To put your money to work in good times and bad times
A cash emergency fund in good times and bad times
To be debt free in good times and bad times
A cash survival fund of 3 to 6 months expenses in good times and bad times
A simple automatic retirement plan in good times and bad times
To pay your house off in good times and definitely in bad times

17. IT IS ABOUT BEHAVIOR
This program is designed with behavior in mind. It is not just about financial principles. I have been in the field of Talent Development and Human Potential for more than 15 years. I served as the head of Talent Development for the flight test center at Learjet, the Director of Talent Development for an entire city and head of Talent Development for a variety of small and large corporations in a myriad of industries. I have worked with a wide range of individuals including

pilots, former astronauts, engineers, military personnel, policemen, firemen, librarians, secretaries, frontline workers and top executives, including CEOs and General Managers. I have also taught many college classes and countless training sessions on many different topics. My expertise is in designing a way to *get people from where they are to where they want to be and helping them stay there.* I have designed this program to give you every chance possible to reach financial success. I know how difficult it can be to change behaviors. This program was designed to help you be successful with financial principles and behaviors.

18. BE YOURSELF AND HAVE GREAT SUCCESS

I spent years researching, designing, building, and testing this program to get it just right. It is designed so that people can have great success and still be themselves. You do not have to become a super-disciplined financial genius who watches stock quotes all day. If you will redirect a few behaviors, redefine a few things, and apply the simple powerful tools and techniques, the program will take you step-by-step from Financial Frustration to Financial Success, and it will show you how to stay there.

19. A COMPLETE KIT

Another great thing about this program is a Complete Financial Success in a Box Kit that is available with all the tools you need. If I ask you to track your spending for a week, I give you a form to track it on. If I ask you to cut up your credit cards, I even provide a pair of scissors for you to do it with. I provide every tool you will need to be financially successful in this program.

20. EVERYTHING IN ONE PLACE - THE BOX

This program helps get your finances organized once and for all. I provide a central command center to keep all financial information and documents in one easy-to-find place. Never again will you have to search the entire house for financial information. It will be right at your fingertips.

21. NO COMPLICATED BUDGETS

You can be successful without using complicated budgets or having to track every penny every month. In some situations you will even be able to spend all you have. I will show you easy ways to make success automatic so you will not have to be super-disciplined or spend a lot of time keeping things on track.

22. NO COMPLICATED GOAL SETTING

I have provided the financial goals for you and the step-by-step plan that will allow you to reach those goals. You will not spend a long time trying to identify financial goals and develop plans to reach those goals. The program is also flexible and will allow you to add additional financial goals.

23. EVERY STEP HAS A BENEFIT

You will get maximum benefit from completing all 10 steps because then you will be healthy in all 10 of the major areas of your financial life. But even if you only complete one or two of the 10 steps, your financial life will be exceedingly better.

24. IT MAKES YOU A THERMOSTAT INSTEAD OF A THERMOMETER

A thermometer tells you what the temperature is, but a thermostat does something about it. This program makes it easy for you to take specific actions to make your financial life better. You will not only know your financial temperature, you will be able to do something about it.

HOW IT WORKS

The program works by teaching you how to be successful in the 10 key areas that determine your Financial Success. You will only have to work on one step at a time. You will learn how to turn a dollar into an employee and put it to work for you. You will also learn how to put a dollar's children (interest) and the dollar's grandchildren (compound interest) to work for you for the rest of your life.

BUT I HAVE TRIED THIS BEFORE

It is stated that an elephant never forgets, but maybe that is not such a positive attribute. I heard a story about how they train circus elephants to stay in one place and not wander off. When the elephant is a baby, a rope is attached around one of his legs and connected to a large stake in the ground. The elephant pulls and pulls, but he is not strong enough to pull away from the stake and the rope. Eventually, the elephant realizes that he is not strong enough to break free, and he gives up and stops trying. As the elephant grows in size and strength, they continue to secure him with the same rope and the same stake. He remembers that he tried before and could not break free. Therefore, he believes he still cannot break free.

The elephant is the largest mammal walking the earth. This guy can grow up to be 12 feet tall and weigh over 6 tons. That is 12,000 pounds! He can live about 70 years. That one failed attempt when he was little will tie him to that little rope and stake for all of his life. That is sad.

I think a lot of people are held back by their own ropes and stakes from their past. They have tried something and were not successful so, they think they will never be able to accomplish it. Just like the elephant, they think back to the time they tried and failed and think that they still will not be successful if they try again.

If you have tried in the past to get your finances under control, to get some Financial Success in your life and were not successful, do not let that stop you from trying again— right now with this program. This program can help you grow taller and stronger just like the elephant. It will also give you the steps and the tools to break free from the rope and stake that have kept you tied down to your current financial situation for years or even generations.

Imagine how easy it would be for that 12,000-pound elephant to break free if he would just try! Imagine the great life he could live roaming free. Imagine how excited you will be when you break free of your financial rope and stake and start living a fabulous life of Financial Success and living the dreams that you are capable of achieving. Do not be like the elephant and give up just because you have tried it before and were not successful.

> *If we all did the things we are capable of doing, we
> would literally astound ourselves.*
> *Thomas Edison*

Let this program help you break free and live the full, rich life that you are capable of living.

A SUCCESSFUL JOURNEY

There are 3 things you need to have a successful journey. You need to know:

- Where you are now
- Where you want to be
- The steps to get there

I give you all three of these things. You do not have to create anything.

- **The Scoreboard.** It will tell you where you are now financially in less than 2 minutes. You do not have to do detailed analysis and assessments for a month to figure out where you are now financially.

- **Financial Destination.** The goal is a score of 10 on all 10 steps. You do not have to spend months and months figuring out your financial destination.

- **10 Simple Steps.** This program will take you step-by-step to your financial destination.

> *Do not wait for all the lights to be green before you get moving.
> Take it one light at a time.*

ACTION ITEMS

Now it is time to do the three simple action items for Step 1 to launch your Success Plan. Use the form below and place a check mark by each action item as you complete it. There is an additional To Do List at the end of each chapter to which you can add items.

ACTION ITEMS

ACTION 1 → Do Scoreboard

ACTION 2 → Understand Destination

ACTION 3 → Take the 10 Steps

The person who makes a success of living is the one who sees his goal steadily and aims for it unswervingly. That is dedication.

Cecil B. DeMille

ACTION 1

COMPLETE THE SCOREBOARD FORM

FINANCIAL SUCCESS IN A BOX

FINANCIAL SCOREBOARD

NAME: _____   DATE: _____

STEP 1
10 STEP PLAN

I have a step-by-step plan to follow to reach financial success

1 No   2   3   4   5 Maybe   6   7   8   9   10 Yes

STEP 2
WORK TOGETHER

I work together with my spouse in all areas of our finances toward common goals
(If you are single, mark the 10)

1 Never   2   3   4   5 Sometimes   6   7   8   9   10 Always

STEP 3
THE BASICS

I know key success factors of money, behavior change and marketing self-defense

1 No   2   3   4   5 Maybe   6   7   8   9   10 Yes

STEP 4
GIVING

I currently give to my church, charities, etc. on a regular basis

1 Never   2   3   4   5 Regularly   6   7   8   9   10 10% Gross

STEP 5
PUT MONEY TO WORK

I currently save the following % of gross income every paycheck
(Includes savings, 401K, IRAs, etc)

1 1% or less   2   3   4   5 2%   6   7   8   9   10 3% Gross

STEP 6
EMERGENCY FUND

I currently have the following amount in a dedicated cash emergency fund

1 $0   2 $200   3 $300   4 $400   5 $500   6 $600   7 $700   8 $800   9 $900   10 $1000

STEP 7
PAY OFF DEBT

I currently owe the following total amount in consumer debt
(Includes credit cards, student loans, etc. – everything except your house)

1 $20,000+   2   3 $16,000   4   5 $12,000   6   7 $8,000   8   9 $4,000   10 $0

STEP 8
SURVIVAL FUND

I currently have a cash survival fund that will cover my total expenses for

1 1 Month   2   3 2 Months   4   5 3 Months   6   7 4 Months   8   9   10 6 Months

STEP 9
PLAN RETIREMENT

I contribute to my retirement fund every month and I know I will have enough
(If you are currently retired, mark 10)

1 No   2   3   4   5 Maybe   6   7   8   9   10 Yes

STEP 10
PAY OFF HOUSE

I pay extra on my mortgage
(If you do not have a mortgage, mark 10)

1 Never   2   3   4   5 Regularly   6   7   8   9   10 Paid Off

1 Fill in the circles that best describe your current situation

2 Connect the Dots

3 Total the Points

_____

If your score is less than 90, you need this program

Copyright © 2010

The scoreboard is a simple and powerful tool. In less than 2 minutes you will have a clear picture of where you are now in the 10 major areas of your financial life. Simply fill out the scoreboard form. Use the blank form at the end of this section.

Step 1: On each step, fill in the circle that best describes your current situation.
Step 2: Connect the dots.
Step 3: Total your score.

In less than 2 minutes you have a picture of where you are now financially.

10 STEP PLAN

EXAMPLE AFTER DOTS ARE FILLED IN

EXAMPLE AFTER DOTS ARE CONNECTED AND SCORE IS TOTALED

ACTION 2
UNDERSTAND YOUR DESTINATION AND WHAT SUCCESS WILL LOOK LIKE

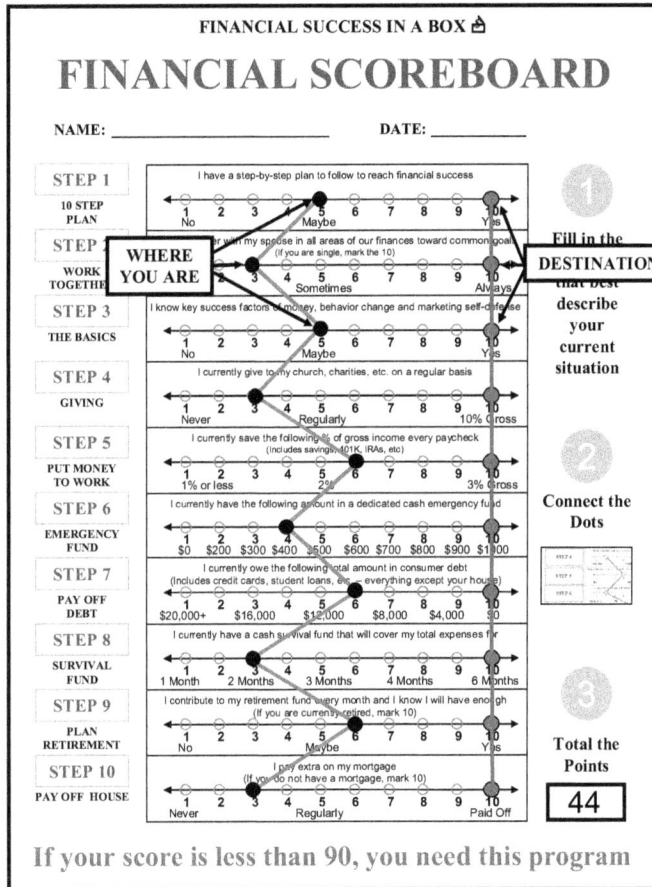

FINANCIAL SUCCESS IN A BOX

FINANCIAL SCOREBOARD

NAME: _____   DATE: _____

STEP 1	10 STEP PLAN	I have a step-by-step plan to follow to reach financial success
STEP 2	WORK TOGETHER	... with my spouse in all areas of our finances toward common goal (if you are single, mark the 10)
STEP 3	THE BASICS	I know key success factors of money, behavior change and marketing self-defense
STEP 4	GIVING	I currently give to my church, charities, etc. on a regular basis
STEP 5	PUT MONEY TO WORK	I currently save the following % of gross income every paycheck (includes savings, 401K, IRAs, etc)
STEP 6	EMERGENCY FUND	I currently have the following amount in a dedicated cash emergency fund
STEP 7	PAY OFF DEBT	I currently owe the following total amount in consumer debt (Includes credit cards, student loans, etc., everything except your house)
STEP 8	SURVIVAL FUND	I currently have a cash survival fund that will cover my total expenses for
STEP 9	PLAN RETIREMENT	I contribute to my retirement fund every month and I know I will have enough (If you are currently retired, mark 10)
STEP 10	PAY OFF HOUSE	I pay extra on my mortgage (If you do not have a mortgage, mark 10)

WHERE YOU ARE

Fill in the DESTINATION that best describe your current situation

1 Connect the Dots

2 Total the Points **44**

3

If your score is less than 90, you need this program

Copyright © 2010

No matter where your dots are, the goal of this program is to help move each dot, one at a time, to a score of 10 on the scoreboard. The farther you move each dot to the right of the scoreboard the closer you get to Financial Success. You may find that you already have a score of 10 in some of the categories.

Having a score of 10 in each of the 10 categories will give you the life we described in the Imagine section at the beginning of this chapter. If you are able to fill in the score of 10 on each of the statements on the scoreboard, you can have a great financial life. This is a destination worth working toward!

ACTION 3
TAKE THE REMAINING STEPS

FINANCIAL SUCCESS IN A BOX

FINANCIAL SCOREBOARD

NAME: _____   DATE: _____

You have now completed Step 1 and launched your Success Plan.

All you have to do is complete the remaining 9 steps.

On one piece of paper, you have all three of the critical elements to a successful journey. You know where you are now with the dots, you know where you are going with the destination—a score of 10 in all 10 categories, and you have the 10 steps that will take you there.

YOU NOW HAVE A SUCCESS PLAN
This program will help you move each of the dots, one at a time, to a score of 10. Move forward and complete the other 9 steps, one at a time.

ONE STEP AT A TIME
I want to make the point that we are only going to focus on one step at a time. If we focus on one step at a time, your chances of being successful in the whole program greatly increase. It will give you regular victories, and it will keep you from getting overwhelmed and confused. The momentum from each successful step will accumulate and carry over into the next steps. So if at times you feel overwhelmed or discouraged, remember that we will only focus on one step at a time.

In his great motivational video series, *Do Right with Lou Holtz* and *Lou Holtz Do Right! The Plan*, Lou Holtz tells the story of the year his football team set their goals, and one of those goals was to win the Orange Bowl. The first practice after the goals were set was fabulous, every player was pumped and excited to work toward the lofty goal of winning the Orange Bowl, but then Lou noticed that the next practice was not as good and the next got even worse. He realized the problem was that the big goal of winning the Orange Bowl was too far away. It was too far in the future to create daily inspiration and motivation. There were a lot of smaller goals that had to be accomplished to lead up to that big goal.

Coach Holtz decided that the team needed to work toward the big goal of winning the Orange Bowl, but they needed to *focus* on winning each weekly game. The game of that week was close enough to keep them focused and motivated, so he helped the team concentrate on the next game and then the next game. They kept their eye on the big goal of winning the Orange Bowl, but he focused their energy and minds on the immediate goals that would add up to the big goal. He used the acrostic W.I.N., which stands for **W**hat's **I**mportant **N**ow? The important thing for them each week was to do whatever it took to beat the team they faced that week, then the next week, and then the next. By accomplishing those weekly goals, they would end up accomplishing the big goal of winning the Orange Bowl.

That is how this program is designed. The ultimate goal is to have a score of 10 in all 10 of the financial categories—a great financial life. That is the big goal that we will keep our eye on. That is where we want to end up, but we will concentrate on one step at a time. We will practice the W.I.N. concept and by accomplishing each step, one at a time, we will be successful and end up accomplishing the big goal of reaching a great financial life.

I DO NOT CARE WHAT YOU KNOW—I CARE WHAT YOU DO
When I conduct seminars and teach college classes, I will start off with the statement "I do not care what you learn—I care about what you *do* with what you learn." If you learn 100 interesting, powerful things in this session but do not go out and actually *do* something with them, then you wasted your time and money. You were simply entertained. If you apply even one powerful tool from this session, then the time and money you spent will be well worth it.

IF YOU DO NOT MEASURE IT, YOU CANNOT MANAGE IT
Some financial advisors will tell you to track everything you do and use a super detailed budget that NASA would have trouble understanding. They believe you should track and measure every

minute detail. On the other end of the financial advisor spectrum are those who say you do not need to track anything. Just do a few key things and you will be a fabulous financial success!

The problem with the super-detailed budget approach is that it requires a lot of time, a lot of discipline, and a certain personality type to be successful. Most people will not be successful with this approach because it is simply too much work, and it is not much fun. Many of the most dedicated people after a while will find it not worth the effort and give up.

The problem with the do-not-track-anything approach is that it is too freewheeling for most people, and it does not tell you how you are doing. It also does not show you the areas where you could make improvements. People want to know where they are going and how they are doing.

What do I recommend? My recommendation would fall somewhere in between the two extremes above. My philosophy can be expressed in one simple statement:

Do not track everything, but track what is important.

FINANCIAL DASHBOARD

WHAT IS IT
The Financial Dashboard is a simple tool that allows you to keep an eye on the important items that show how you are doing without getting bogged down in a thousand little details.

It is a tool that will help you reach Financial Success because you can and will actually use it. It is not too detailed like the super-detailed budget approach, but it does tell you how you are doing unlike the do-not-track-anything approach. It is simple to use. I will show you what you need to know.

> *If you keep doing what you are doing, will you get where you want to go?*
>
> *Unknown*

HOW IT WORKS
The Financial Dashboard works just like the dashboard of a car. The car dashboard allows you to monitor the few key gauges that tell you how you are doing—the speed, oil pressure, temperature, battery, and fuel gauge. Every once in a while you glance at the dashboard to make sure the gauges are where they should be, and then you look back up and continue to enjoy the ride. If you glance at the gauges and one of them is not where it should be, you simply take the appropriate action.

If your speed is too fast, you slow down. If your gas gauge is too low, you get gas. If your oil pressure is low, you check the oil. If the temperature is too hot, you pull over and get it checked.

With the Financial Dashboard, you keep your eyes on the road and occasionally check the key gauges. There are thousands and thousands of things happening inside your car when you drive, but thankfully there are only a few key items that you need to monitor to have a successful trip. If anything goes wrong with one of the thousands of items, it will show up on one of the gauges. You do not have to be a highly skilled mechanic in order to be successful driving a car, and you do not have to be a great financial analyst to have Financial Success.

WHY IT WORKS

The dashboard works because it fits the way people like to operate. People want to know what is going on, but they do not want to know every detail on earth. They typically want to know just what is necessary to know to have a successful trip.

Using the super-detailed budget approach is like having a dashboard with 8,000 gauges telling you every single thing that is happening in your car as you drive down the road. Chances are that you would look at it a few times, get overwhelmed, and never look at it again, or you would be so focused on the 8,000 gauges that you would never look up at the road to make sure you were going in the right direction. Even if you successfully reached your destination, it would probably not be an enjoyable trip.

The dashboard gives a nice balance of measuring what is important without getting too detailed.

Over the next few weeks, start filling out the dashboard form at the end of this chapter. Each major category of your financial life has its own gauge—for example housing, utilities, groceries, entertainment, etc. You can record the total amount you spend each month in each category. You can also record the percentage of your monthly expenses going to that category. I have listed recommended percent ranges. This will give you the ability to see how you are doing with just a glance. It will also tell you which gauge you may want to look at closer to improve your financial life. For example, if the amount you spend on groceries every month greatly exceeds the recommended percentage range, then you could look at ways to reduce your monthly grocery bill. The dashboard lets you target your improvement efforts. The gauges that are within the recommended percent ranges may not need improvement.

You can probably fill in the dollar amounts and percentages of some of the gauges from memory. Others you may need to keep track of for a month to see how much you are spending. I have provided a list for each gauge so you can total the amount and then write it on the dashboard. One easy way to track how much you spend in each category is to have an envelope for each category. Simply put all the receipts for that month in the envelope. At the end of a month, you simply add up the receipts and that is the amount you write on the dashboard.

The goal of the dashboard is to help you watch the important elements of your financial life. You can track every single penny spent on every single item or just track enough details to fill out the gauges on the dashboard. The goal is to know where your money is going. If one of the gauges seems out of line, look at it a little closer to see what is going on and then make improvements to bring the gauge within the proper range.

COMPLETING THE DASHBOARD

Use these simple steps to complete the dashboard.

- Fill in your monthly gross income at the top of the form.
- Fill in the monthly total for each gauge. Use the detail sheet or envelopes to calculate.
- Calculate the percent for each gauge: percent = total dollars of gauge/monthly gross income. For example if your monthly gross income is $5,000 and your monthly total spent on groceries is $500, then your percent equals ($500 / $5,000 or .1 or 10percent). You are spending 10percent of your monthly gross income on groceries.
- After the percentages are filled in, see if any gauge is out of the recommended range. These gauges are where you can begin to look to improve your financial life. Some gauges you will want to decrease (the spending categories) and some gauges you will want to increase (savings and giving).
- Add up all of the dollars and percentages from each gauge and see what the total dollars and total percentages are. If your total dollars are less than your total monthly gross income and your total percentage is less than 100percent, congratulations. You have less going out than you are bringing in. If your total dollars are more than your total monthly gross income or your total percentage is more than 100 percent, then you have more going out than coming in each month. In this situation, you need to identify the gauges that are causing the problem and make changes to bring your percentages to the goal.

The dashboard also has a gauge to record how you are doing on your emergency fund and survival fund. We will discuss those in a later section.

EXAMPLE OF A COMPLETED DASHBOARD FORM

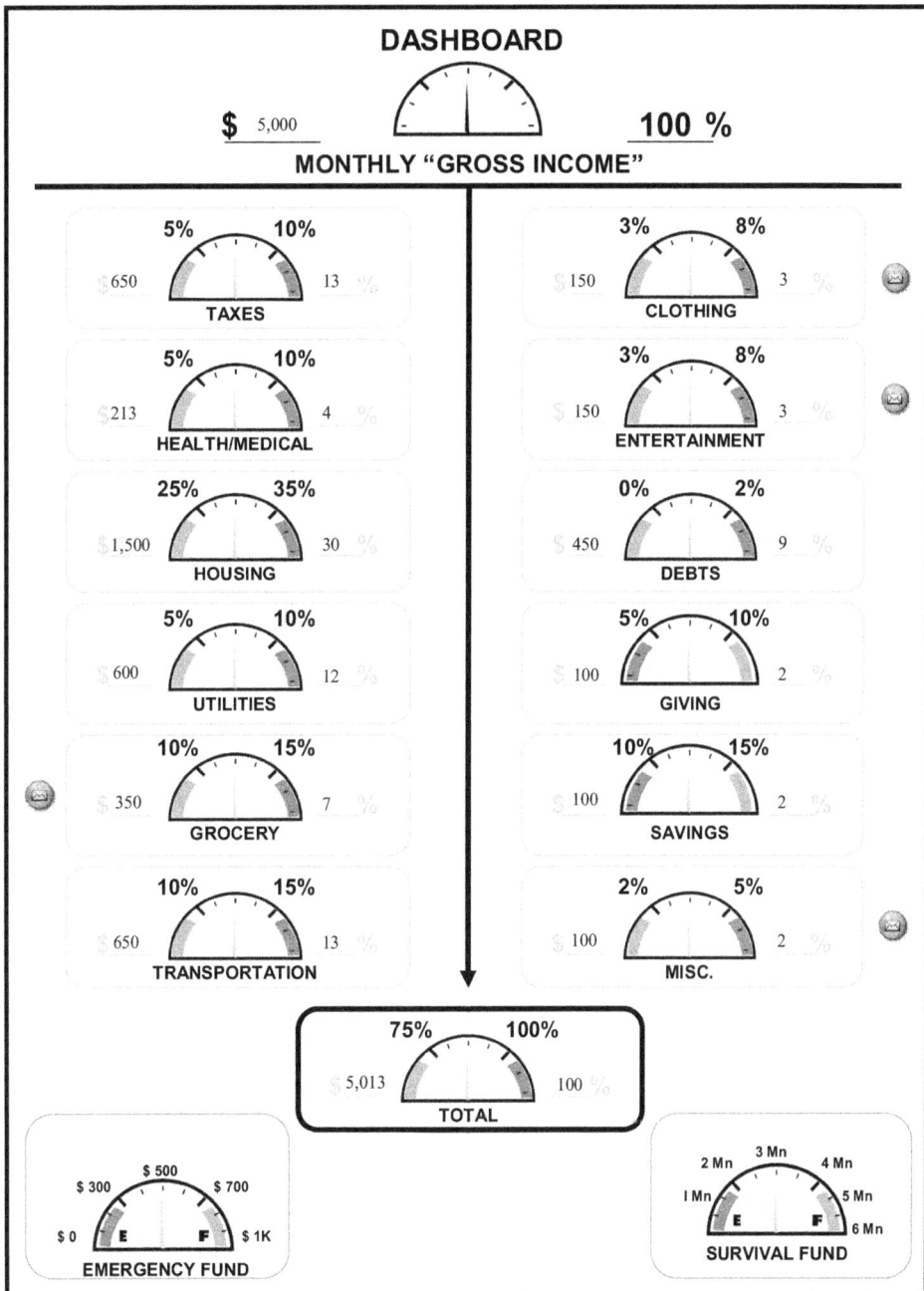

DASHBOARD

$ 5,000   100 %

MONTHLY "GROSS INCOME"

5% — 10%	3% — 8%
$650 13 % TAXES	$150 3 % CLOTHING
5% — 10%	3% — 8%
$213 4 % HEALTH/MEDICAL	$150 3 % ENTERTAINMENT
25% — 35%	0% — 2%
$1,500 30 % HOUSING	$450 9 % DEBTS
5% — 10%	5% — 10%
$600 12 % UTILITIES	$100 2 % GIVING
10% — 15%	10% — 15%
$350 7 % GROCERY	$100 2 % SAVINGS
10% — 15%	2% — 5%
$650 13 % TRANSPORTATION	$100 2 % MISC.

75% — 100%

$5,013   100 %

TOTAL

$ 300 $ 500 $ 700
$ 0   E   F $ 1K
EMERGENCY FUND

2 Mn   3 Mn   4 Mn
1 Mn   5 Mn
E   F   6 Mn
SURVIVAL FUND

Note: The envelope icon next to several of the gauges indicates that you may want to consider using the envelope system in that category. (We will discuss the envelope system later in the program.)

Below is an example of a completed detail sheet used to complete the dashboard on the previous page.

DETAIL SHEET

	5% — 10%			5% — 10%
TAXES			**UTILITIES**	
Federal	300		Electricity	250
State			Gas	80
SS	300		Water	56
Other	50		Trash	15
Other			Phone	75
Other			Cable	125
TOTAL	650		**TOTAL**	600

	5% — 10%			10% — 15%
HEALTH/MEDICAL			**GROCERY**	
Medical	133		Food	
Dental	23		Toiletries	
Eye	7		Cosmetics	
STD			Hair Care	
LTD			Pets	
Life Insur	50		Other	
TOTAL	213		**TOTAL**	350

	25% — 35%			10% — 15%
HOUSING			**TRANSPORTATION**	
1st Mort	15,00		Car Pymts	350
2nd Mort			Insurance	125
Taxes			Tags	25
Insurance			Gas & Oil	150
Maintenance			Maint	
Other			Other	
TOTAL	15,00		**TOTAL**	650

10 STEP PLAN

Below is an example of a person who is *not* overspending. Their outgo matches their income (100 percent), but they could still make improvements in three areas. The three gauges that are outside the recommended range are debt, giving, and savings. If this person will decrease the amount consumed by debt each month, they could increase the amount in giving and saving. All of the other gauges appear to be within the recommended ranges. The dashboard helps target improvement efforts.

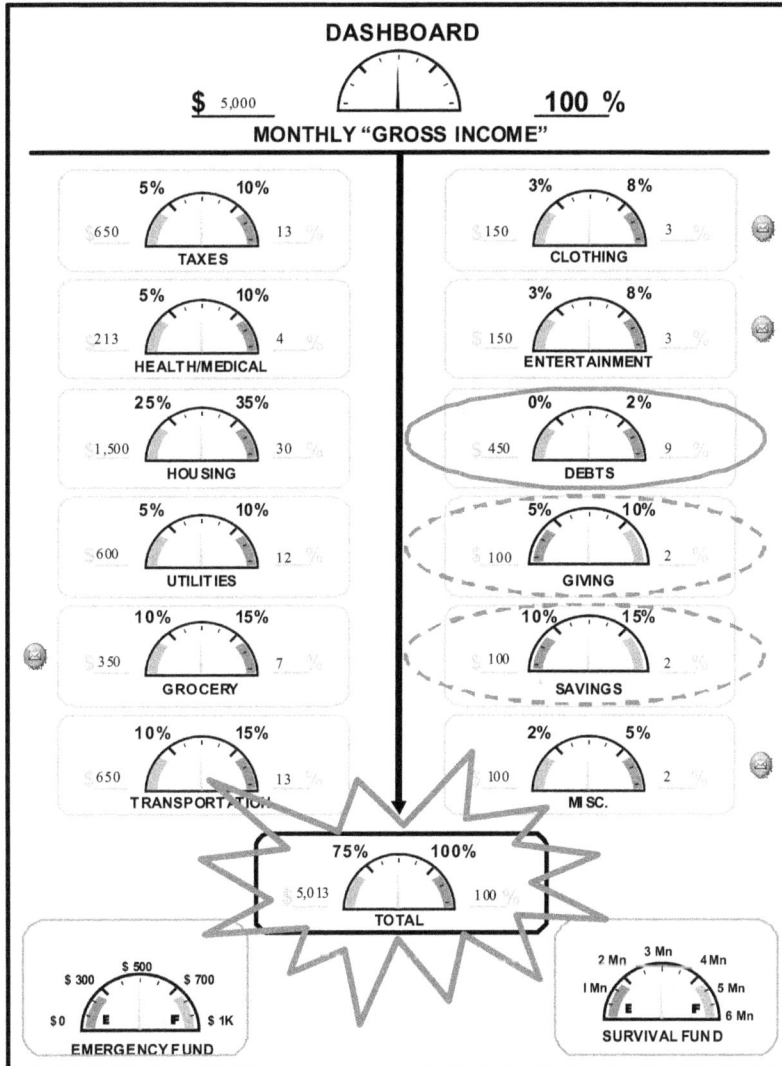

You can also improve gauges that are within the recommended ranges to become even more successful financially.

Note: Recommended percentages are a guide not an absolute. The key is to make sure that your total percentage does not exceed 100 percent of your monthly gross income.

Below is an example of a person who *is* overspending. Their outgo is 127 percent. That means they have 27% percent more money going out than they have coming in each month. This person can look at making improvements in five areas. The five gauges that are outside the recommended range are transportation, entertainment, debt, giving, and savings. If this person will decrease the amount they are paying toward transportation, entertainment, and debt they could increase the amount they are giving and saving and bring their monthly outgo to 100 percent or less. All of the other gauges appear to be within the recommended ranges. The dashboard helps target improvement efforts.

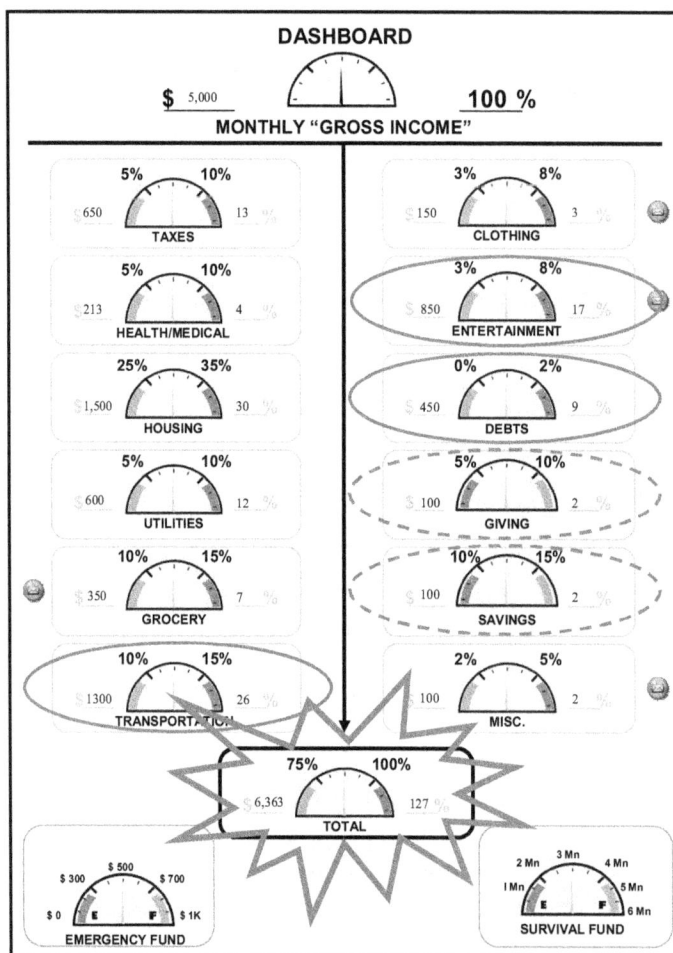

Over the next few weeks, fill out your dashboard and use it to improve your financial success in a targeted way. The dashboard works great for couples. If you are a detail person you can fill out all the details you want. If you are a carefree person you can just look at the main gauges. You can both be happy!

You can fill out your dashboard every month or you can do it every couple of months to make sure you are staying on track. You can get very detailed, or you can just watch the key gauges.

CONGRATULATIONS!

You have now begun your journey to Financial Success!

- You have completed Step 1 of your 10-Step Plan, and you have launched your Success Plan. You have taken the first of 10 steps that can take you to a great financial life. You know where you are, where you are going, and the 10 steps that will get you there.

You can now move your dot on Step 1 of the scoreboard to a score of 10.

SCOREBOARD

FINANCIAL SUCCESS IN A BOX

FINANCIAL SCOREBOARD

NAME: _____ DATE: _____

STEP 1 10 STEP PLAN	I have a step-by-step plan to follow to reach financial success
STEP 2 WORK TOGETHER	I work together with my spouse in all areas of our finances toward common goals (If you are single, mark the 10)
STEP 3 THE BASICS	I know key success factors of money, behavior change and marketing self-defense
STEP 4 GIVING	I currently give to my church, charities, etc. on a regular basis
STEP 5 PUT MONEY TO WORK	I currently save the following % of gross income every paycheck (includes savings, 401K, IRAs, etc)
STEP 6 EMERGENCY FUND	I currently have the following amount in a dedicated cash emergency fund
STEP 7 PAY OFF DEBT	I currently owe the following total amount in consumer debt (Includes credit cards, student loans, etc. – everything except your house)
STEP 8 SURVIVAL FUND	I currently have a cash survival fund that will cover my total expenses for
STEP 9 PLAN RETIREMENT	I contribute to my retirement fund every month and I know I will have enough (If you are currently retired, mark 10)
STEP 10 PAY OFF HOUSE	I pay extra on my mortgage (If you do not have a mortgage, mark 10)

Fill in the circles that best describe your current situation

Connect the Dots

Total the Points

If your score is less than 90, you need this program

Copyright © 2010

You are off to a great start! Now it is time for Step 2—Work Together. What does "work together" mean? It means learning how to work together with the ones you love toward common financial goals.

Get ready to move forward and conquer Step 2 – Work Together.

FINANCIAL SUCCESS IN A BOX 📋

FINANCIAL SCOREBOARD

NAME: _____   DATE: _____

STEP 1 10 STEP PLAN	I have a step-by-step plan to follow to reach financial success 1 2 3 4 5 6 7 8 9 10 No — Maybe — Yes	**①** **Fill in the circles that best describe your current situation**
STEP 2 WORK TOGETHER	I work together with my spouse in all areas of our finances toward common goals (If you are single, mark the 10) 1 2 3 4 5 6 7 8 9 10 Never — Sometimes — Always	
STEP 3 THE BASICS	I know key success factors of money, behavior change and marketing self-defense 1 2 3 4 5 6 7 8 9 10 No — Maybe — Yes	
STEP 4 GIVING	I currently give to my church, charities, etc. on a regular basis 1 2 3 4 5 6 7 8 9 10 Never — Regularly — 10% Gross	
STEP 5 PUT MONEY TO WORK	I currently save the following % of gross income every paycheck (Includes savings, 401K, IRAs, etc) 1 2 3 4 5 6 7 8 9 10 1% or less — 2% — 3% Gross	**②** **Connect the Dots**
STEP 6 EMERGENCY FUND	I currently have the following amount in a dedicated cash emergency fund 1 2 3 4 5 6 7 8 9 10 $0 $200 $300 $400 $500 $600 $700 $800 $900 $1000	
STEP 7 PAY OFF DEBT	I currently owe the following total amount in consumer debt (Includes credit cards, student loans, etc. – everything except your house) 1 2 3 4 5 6 7 8 9 10 $20,000+ $16,000 $12,000 $8,000 $4,000 $0	
STEP 8 SURVIVAL FUND	I currently have a cash survival fund that will cover my total expenses for 1 2 3 4 5 6 7 8 9 10 1 Month 2 Months 3 Months 4 Months 6 Months	
STEP 9 PLAN RETIREMENT	I contribute to my retirement fund every month and I know I will have enough (If you are currently retired, mark 10) 1 2 3 4 5 6 7 8 9 10 No — Maybe — Yes	**③** **Total the Points**
STEP 10 PAY OFF HOUSE	I pay extra on my mortgage (If you do not have a mortgage, mark 10) 1 2 3 4 5 6 7 8 9 10 Never — Regularly — Paid Off	

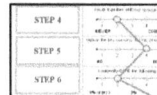

If your score is less than 90, you need this program

DASHBOARD

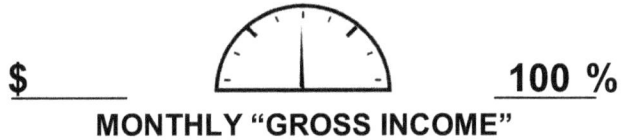

$ _____   100 %

MONTHLY "GROSS INCOME"

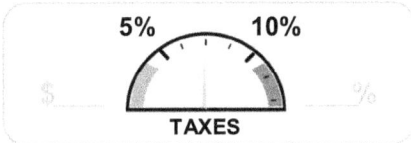

5%   10%

TAXES

3%   8%

CLOTHING

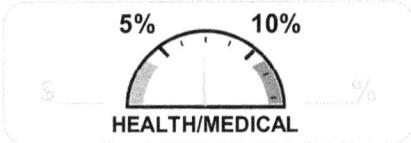

5%   10%

HEALTH/MEDICAL

3%   8%

ENTERTAINMENT

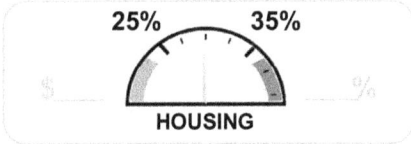

25%   35%

HOUSING

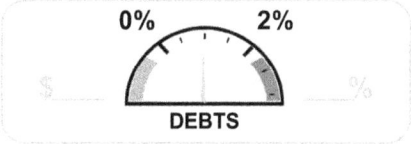

0%   2%

DEBTS

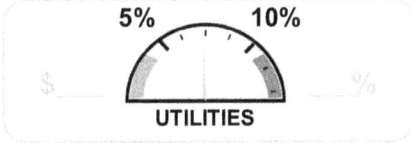

5%   10%

UTILITIES

5%   10%

GIVING

10%   15%

GROCERY

10%   15%

SAVINGS

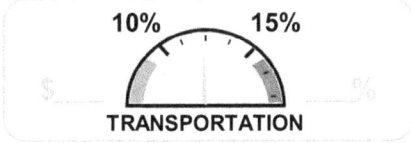

10%   15%

TRANSPORTATION

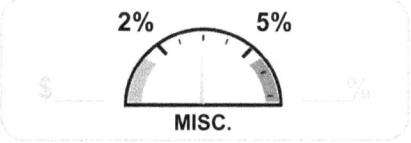

2%   5%

MISC.

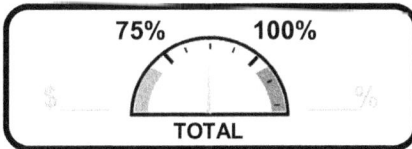

75%   100%

TOTAL

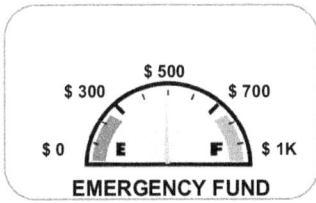

$ 500
$ 300 $ 700
$ 0   E   F $ 1K
EMERGENCY FUND

2 Mn   3 Mn   4 Mn
1 Mn   5 Mn
E   F   6 Mn
SURVIVAL FUND

TAXES
5%   10%

$ _____   _____ %

Federal	_____
State	_____
SS	_____
Other	_____
Other	_____
Other	_____
TOTAL	

UTILITIES
5%   10%

$ _____   _____ %

Electricity	_____
Gas	_____
Water	_____
Trash	_____
Phone	_____
Cable	_____
TOTAL	

HEALTH/MEDICAL
5%   10%

$ _____   _____ %

Medical	_____
Dental	_____
Eye	_____
STD	_____
LTD	_____
Life Insur	_____
TOTAL	

GROCERY
10%   15%

$ _____   _____ %

Food	_____
Toiletries	_____
Cosmetics	_____
Hair Care	_____
Pets	_____
Other	_____
TOTAL	

HOUSING
25%   35%

$ _____   _____ %

1st Mort	_____
2nd Mort	_____
Taxes	_____
Insurance	_____
Maintenance	_____
Other	_____
TOTAL	

TRANSPORTATION
10%   15%

$ _____   _____ %

Car Pymts	_____
Insurance	_____
Tags	_____
Gas & Oil	_____
Maint	_____
Other	_____
TOTAL	

3%   8%

CLOTHING

Clothes   _____

Cleaners   _____

Other   _____

TOTAL [   ]

5%   10%

GIVING

Tithe   _____

Charities _____

Other   _____

TOTAL [   ]

3%   8%

ENTERTAINMENT

Eating Out   _____

Vacations   _____

Videos & Games   _____

Personal Fund   _____

Other   _____

Other   _____

TOTAL [   ]

10%   15%

SAVINGS

Emergency Fund   _____

Survival Fund   _____

Retirement Fund _____

College Fund   _____

Other   _____

Other   _____

TOTAL [   ]

0%   2%

DEBTS

Credit Cards   _____

Student Loans _____

Finance Co.   _____

Other   _____

Other   _____

Other   _____

TOTAL [   ]

2%   5%

MISC.

-------------   _____

-------------   _____

-------------   _____

-------------   _____

-------------   _____

-------------   _____

TOTAL [   ]

10 STEP PLAN
To Do List

ITEM	COMPLETED
Complete Scoreboard	
Start Filling Out Dashboard	

_____   _____

Signature   *Date*

_____   _____

Signature   *Date*

STEP 2

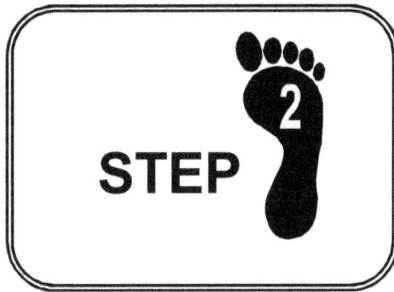

WORK TOGETHER

FINANCIAL SUCCESS IN A BOX

FINANCIAL SCOREBOARD

NAME: _____   DATE: _____

Fill in the circles that best describe your current situation

STEP 1
10 STEP PLAN

I have a step-by-step plan to follow to reach financial success

1 2 3 4 5 6 7 8 9 10
No   Maybe   Yes

STEP 2
WORK TOGETHER

I work together with my spouse in all areas of our finances toward common goals
(if you are single, mark the 10)

1 2 3 4 5 6 7 8 9 10
Never   Sometimes   Always

STEP 3
THE BASICS

I know key success factors of money, behavior change and marketing self-defense

1 2 3 4 5 6 7 8 9 10
No   Maybe   Yes

STEP 4
GIVING

I currently give to my church, charities, etc. on a regular basis

1 2 3 4 5 6 7 8 9 10
Never   Regularly   10% Gross

STEP 5
PUT MONEY TO WORK

I currently save the following % of gross income every paycheck
(includes savings, 401K, IRAs, etc)

1 2 3 4 5 6 7 8 9 10
1% or less   2%   3% Gross

STEP 6
EMERGENCY FUND

I currently have the following amount in a dedicated cash emergency fund

1 2 3 4 5 6 7 8 9 10
$0 $200 $300 $400 $500 $600 $700 $800 $900 $1000

STEP 7
PAY OFF DEBT

I currently owe the following total amount in consumer debt
(Includes credit cards, student loans, etc. – everything except your house)

1 2 3 4 5 6 7 8 9 10
$20,000+ $16,000 $12,000 $8,000 $4,000 $0

STEP 8
SURVIVAL FUND

I currently have a cash survival fund that will cover my total expenses for

1 2 3 4 5 6 7 8 9 10
1 Month   2 Months   3 Months   4 Months   6 Months

STEP 9
PLAN RETIREMENT

I contribute to my retirement fund every month and I know I will have enough
(if you are currently retired, mark 10)

1 2 3 4 5 6 7 8 9 10
No   Maybe   Yes

STEP 10
PAY OFF HOUSE

I pay extra on my mortgage
(If you do not have a mortgage, mark 10)

1 2 3 4 5 6 7 8 9 10
Never   Regularly   Paid Off

Connect the Dots

Total the Points

If your score is less than 90, you need this program

Copyright © 2010

If you are not pulling together, you are pulling apart.

IMAGINE

Imagine a lifestyle where you and the people you love worked together toward the common goal of Financial Success.

Imagine:
- No more fights about money
- No more financial surprises
- No more bringing up past hurts or failures
- No more sleepless nights worrying about money

Imagine:
- Working toward the same financial goals
- Knowing where you stand financially
- Appreciating each other's strengths
- Trusting each other to do the right thing financially
- Knowing what's going on with your money
- Celebrating your financial successes together
- Feeling like an unbeatable team

Imagine:
>Having complete Financial Success in your life

If this sounds good to you, then you are really going to like this step.

PURPOSE

WORK TOGETHER TO REACH SUCCESS

The purpose of this section is to give you the knowledge, tools, and motivation needed to reach a score of 10 in this category.

The action items will help you work together with the ones you love to reach the common goal of Financial Success and to strengthen your relationships.

> *Two are better than one because they have a good return for their labor.*
> *For if either of them falls, the one will lift up his companion. But woe to the one who falls when there is not another to lift him up. Furthermore, if two lie down together they keep warm, but how can one be warm alone? And if one can overpower him who is alone, two can resist him.*
> *A cord of three strands is not quickly torn apart.*
> *Ecclesiastes 4:9-12*

> *If everyone is moving forward together, then success takes care of itself.*
>
> *Henry Ford*

WE WORK TOGETHER
BECAUSE 1 + 1 = MORE THAN 2

An experiment was conducted to see how much a single horse could pull. It was discovered that a single horse could pull six tons. So logically, if two horses were hooked together, they could pull 12 tons. When the two horses were harnessed together, they discovered that together they could actually pull 36 tons! Their results working together were three times the sum of their individual efforts. The point is if you and the other people involved in your financial life will work together, you can achieve many times what you could achieve individually. Working together yields amazingly powerful results. By working together, 1 + 1 can equal a lot more than 2!

By the end of this section you will have the knowledge and tools to move your Working Together score to a 10 and keep it there.

> *None of us is as good as all of us.*
>
> *Ray Kroc*

YOU ARE NOT AN ISLAND
You are not an island when it comes to your finances. There are other people who have input into financial decisions, and there are definitely others who are affected by the financial decisions you make.

> *Talent wins games, but teamwork and intelligence wins championships.*
>
> *Michael Jordan*

CHOOSE THE TEAM	
INPUT	**AFFECTED**

CHOOSE THE TEAM

First, identify the people you want for your team. Use the chart above to list people who either have input into the financial decisions you make or will be affected by those decisions.

If someone else has say in how money will be made or spent, then write their name on the input side. List the names of individuals that would be affected by the decisions on the affected side.

Example: A single person, just out of college, not engaged to be married, would have their own name on the input side and no names on the affected side. A young married couple would have both of their names on the input side and no names as affected. A married couple with two children at home would have their names on the input side and their children on the affected side. A retired couple with no children at home would list their own names on the input side and would have no names on the affected side. A single parent with three children at home would have their name on the input side and the children's names on the affected side. If a grandparent is living with the single parent, the grandparent could be on the input and affected sides.

Do not let this form get complicated. There should only be a few names on the form. If you are married, you and your spouse should be on the input side, but your parents and in-laws should not be on the list. They can be advisors and give you the wisdom of their experience, but it is ultimately you and your spouse who have actual input. The input partners will need to work together. The people on the affected side of the form will need to be informed and you will need their cooperation and participation to be successful.

Going back to the story of the horses, people on the input side can be seen as the horses that will pull together. The people on the affected side will need to be supportive as the whole team makes the journey to Financial Success.

If you are not pulling together, you are pulling apart.

.

SPECIAL NOTE TO MARRIED COUPLES

> *Fifty percent of all marriages end in divorce*
> *(according to divorcerate.org)*
>
> *Fifty-seven percent of divorced couples in the U.S.*
> *cited financial problems as the primary reason for*
> *their divorce.*
> *(according to Citibank survey)*

If you really want to have a strong marriage, then work together and get your financial life in good shape. If you work together on this step, you will be eliminating one of the biggest single threats to your marriage.

If you are currently single, then getting your financial life under control before you get married will increase your chances of having a long-lasting, strong marriage from the beginning.

This is worth doing!

SPECIAL NOTE TO SINGLES

If you are single, this program will work for you. Even this chapter on working together can help you build a strong lifestyle of Financial Success. It can help you get the commitment of other family members, such as children, who can work together with you.

If marriage is in your future plans, this program can prepare you. You will want your future spouse to have a financially peaceful and stable situation before you get married. They will also be happy that you have your financial life under control and healthy.

AVOID TRANSMITTED DEBTS
A story of a typical man:

Graduates from college with $19,000 of debt.
Gets a new job and buys a wardrobe, adding $3,000 of debt to his credit cards.
Buys a new car for $24,000.
Rents an apartment and fills it with stuff to add another $10,000 to credit cards.
Has a grand total of approximately $56,000 of debt.

Meets the girl of his dreams who also has $56,000 of debt.
Their combined debt is $112,000.

They create their first debt together by charging a $28,000 wedding.
The honeymoon adds $5,000.

Next, they buy the house of their dreams creating another $200,000 of debt.

They start their life together as slaves to debt with a total burden of $345,000 that is likely to crush them.
The expenses of children have not even begun.

Imagine taking a different path than the one above. Imagine how great life would be if you and your future spouse started your new life together with a strong foundation of Financial Success. You could immediately start together in a positive way and begin to pursue your dreams of building a fantastic future together. This program can help you do that.

Do your future spouse and family a great favor. Do not bring socially transmitted debts to your marriage.

> *The best way to get the best spouse is to*
> *be the best spouse.*

ACTION ITEMS

I have consulted for many corporations, departments, and individuals. I have worked with retail organizations, manufacturing companies, government entities and a wide variety of organizations spanning many different industries. I have consulted with a wide variety of individuals ranging from hourly employees, secretaries and supervisors to computer programmers, test pilots, scientists, former astronauts, policemen, firefighters, and all levels of management.

There have been many occasions where I have helped a team work together to reach their goals. There are five action items that I share with these teams to help them work together to achieve their goals. Any team—a family, an organization, or a corporate executive committee—will be much more successful if they will use these five keys for success. They will also increase their chances of enjoying the journey. Your team can work together as a world class team.

WORK TOGETHER

ACTION 1 →
Have a
common goal.

ACTION 2 →
Combine your
strengths.

ACTION 3 →
Leave the past
in the past.

ACTION 4 →
Communicate
regularly.

ACTION 5 →
Celebrate &
praise.

ACTION 1
HAVE A COMMON GOAL

> *Where there is no vision, the people perish.*
> *Proverbs 29:18*
>
> *Begin with the end in mind.*
> *Stephen Covey*

VISION

Speaker Joel Barker made a great video series on the power of vision. It explored the positive effects that having a powerful vision can have for individuals, corporations, and even countries. He illustrated how young students, adults, organizations, and countries can attribute much of their success to the fact that they had a very powerful vision of the future—a powerful goal. He also made the point that you must add action to the equation in order to reach your vision. A vision is simply a positive goal for the future. A vision alone is not effective—there must be action to make it happen.

> *The most important thing about goals is having one.*
> *Geoffry F. Abert*

PUZZLE BOX COVER

When I consult teams, one of the first things I do is an activity that is designed to demonstrate to the team members the vital importance of having a common goal. The team members gather around a table. Then I take a bag full of jigsaw puzzle pieces and pour them on the table and say, "Get started." The team members instantly start putting the puzzle pieces together. Without even knowing what it is, they are perfectly willing to start constructing the puzzle. The teams generally struggle and do not make much progress. Early on they will yell, "That piece goes over there," or "Hey, I need that piece over here." The team members typically work against each other without success. Your financial life is probably the same—lots of voices shouting, "Put that dollar there," or "I need those dollars over here." After a few minutes of struggle, I will dump additional puzzle pieces on the table and say, "Sorry, I forgot about these pieces." They say, "Well, now we will be able to put it together," but the reality is that the addition of more pieces slows them down even more.

Finally, after they have struggled long enough, I stop them, hold up the puzzle box cover, and say "Would anyone like to see the box cover?" They instantly say, "Yes!" and grab the box cover. From that point on, the puzzle goes together smoothly and quickly. Every member looks to the box cover for guidance, and since they know what the ultimate vision looks like, it is much easier and more enjoyable to construct the puzzle properly. At this point the team also starts to work together a lot better. They can check their progress using the box cover and know how well they are doing, and they can celebrate because with every completed piece of the puzzle they are getting closer to their goal.

What amazes me is that in the countless times I have conducted this activity, only twice has anyone asked for the box cover. The puzzle I use is not typical; there are no straight edges. It is a cutout of a space shuttle with modular sections that show the interior. No one would ever suspect the final picture. They have faith that it will all work out okay. Many people are the same way in their financial life. They are perfectly willing to work hard and not have a clue as to what their ultimate financial picture will look like.

The puzzle activity is a powerful illustration of how a single common goal, the box cover, can help people work together to accomplish their goals in an effective, fun way.
That is why I have given you a financial box cover.

YOUR BOX COVER

I have provided the box cover for your Financial Success—a score of 10 on all 10 steps of the scoreboard. Your puzzle has 10 key pieces, and I will show you how to put them together one piece at a time so that your life can be a great picture of Financial Success.

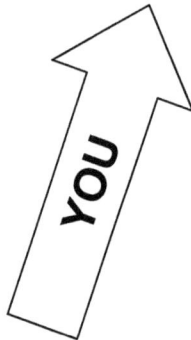

Working toward the same goal will not only increase your chances of success, it will bring you closer together. Agree on a score of 10 on all 10 steps of the scoreboard as the common goal. When you work toward the same common goal, a lot of the things you used to have conflict about simply go away.

ACTION 2
COMBINE YOUR STRENGTHS

> *Every kingdom divided against itself will be ruined,
> and every city or household divided against itself will
> not stand.*
>
> *Matthew 12:25*

OPPOSITES ATTRACT

How many of you would say you are different than your spouse when it comes to managing money? I would bet that most couples are different when it comes to finances. One is more detail-oriented than the other; one is more organized than the other. One is more of a saver, while the other is more of a shopper. The fact that you are different is good. Most people have not been taught how to appreciate their differences and use them in a powerful way.

> *Coming together is a beginning.
> Keeping together is success.*
>
> *Henry Ford*

DIFFERENT IS GOOD

There is a good chance that as a couple working as a team, you already have what it takes to be successful financially. You just need to combine your strengths and release the power of your relationship.

When I started my Training and Performance Development career, the common approach was this: measure all areas, find weaknesses, and then work almost exclusively on building up and improving the weak areas. Then I discovered a different approach— build strengths and manage weaknesses.

If a football coach had an all-star quarterback who was not good at tackling, the coach would be crazy to spend all of his time trying to make the quarterback a great tackler. He may need to know how to tackle in case he throws an interception, but he does not need to be the world's best tackler. The team would be much better off if the quarterback worked on developing his throwing and running strengths and let the other members of the team use their strengths for tackling.

You cannot ignore your weaknesses because they could take you over a cliff if allowed to run free, but you should not spend all of your resources trying to be the best at everything.

I once consulted a Vice President of Marketing who had fantastic visionary skills, but was so unorganized he could not make it to meetings on time. If he did have an agenda you could bet your life that he would not follow it. It was driving his staff crazy and affecting the performance of his department. I could have approached that situation thinking, "I am going to make him the most organized person in this company," and we could have spent all of our time and effort trying to make him someone he was not. Instead, we decided to build his strengths and manage his weakness. We simply teamed him up with an administrative aide who had fantastic organizational skills. Every morning she would give him his agenda for the day that told him where to be at what time and what to bring with him. All he had to do was follow it. The results: He remained a great visionary—which was his strength. He got credit for being very organized, which was his administrative aide's strength. His staff was very happy, and as a team they were much more productive. He, the visionary, and his administrative assistant, the organizer, made a very powerful team and were able to use their gifts to be successful. If we had tried to turn him into "Mr. Organized" we probably would have lost him as a very valuable asset to a competing company.

Ask if your relationships are combining skills as a team and helping each other manage weaknesses or blaming each other for weaknesses and working against each other. One of the fastest ways for a team to fail is to fight against each other. If you will view yourself and the special ones in your life as a team with a variety of strengths that as a whole make a very strong team, you will have stronger relationships, be more successful, and have a lot more fun doing life together.

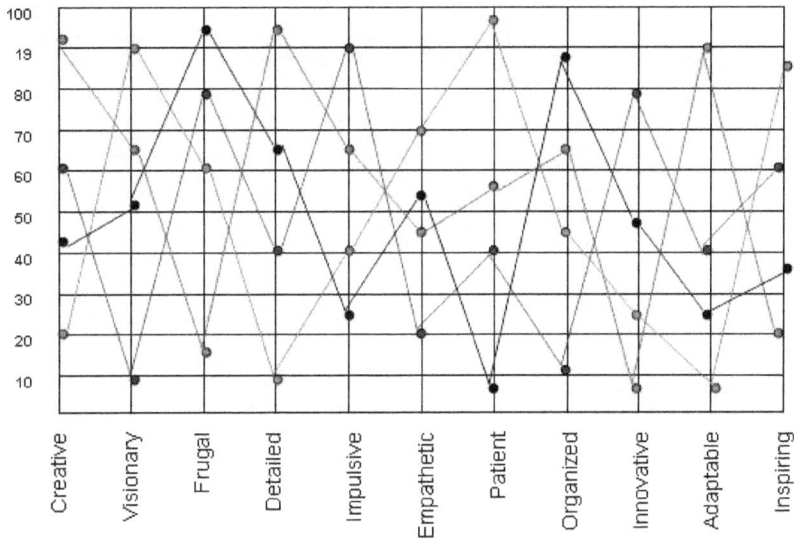

COMBINE YOUR STRENGTHS

View the Team, Not the Individuals

This tool, the S&W (strengths & weaknesses) Chart helps teams work together to reach their goals. The strengths and weaknesses for each individual are plotted and then the dots are connected. They assess each member and put a dot on the scale for each category. This "picture" tells a lot about that individual.

This is similar to the scoreboard tool. It is a great way of taking tons of information and putting it into a picture on one sheet of paper.

When I use this tool for corporations, I create a line for each person, and we show it to the group. Typically the members of the group say, "Yeah, that's Jack," or "You really nailed John." After I show each line individually, then I show all of the lines at the same time on the same chart. That is when I am likely to hear, "What a mess!" or "No wonder we don't get along," and "We are all so different." At first glance, it does look like a mess, but this is where the team can have a great breakthrough, and so can you.

If you look at this as a bunch of individuals, it looks like a mess, but if you look at it as a team, it looks powerful and unbeatable. As a team, it has every strength necessary for success. I would want to be on that team.

The team illustrated in the graph above is a very strong team. The team has high scores in all of the different strengths. The team is made up of very different individuals, but as a team they have all the strengths they need for success.

The team illustrated in the graph below is a team of individuals who are exactly alike. They have the same strengths and the same weaknesses. As a team, they are weak in five of the eleven strengths listed. This team is alike, but weak. I would not want to be on this team.

During the civil war, Abraham Lincoln stated that a house divided against itself cannot stand.

My wife and I are very different.
I am a visionary: "What is the 10-year plan?"
She is practical: "What is going on today?"
I am very "big picture."
She is very detailed.
She can do 10 things at the same time.
I have trouble listening to her when I am putting on my socks!

We are very different individuals, but when we combine our strengths we become a powerful team.

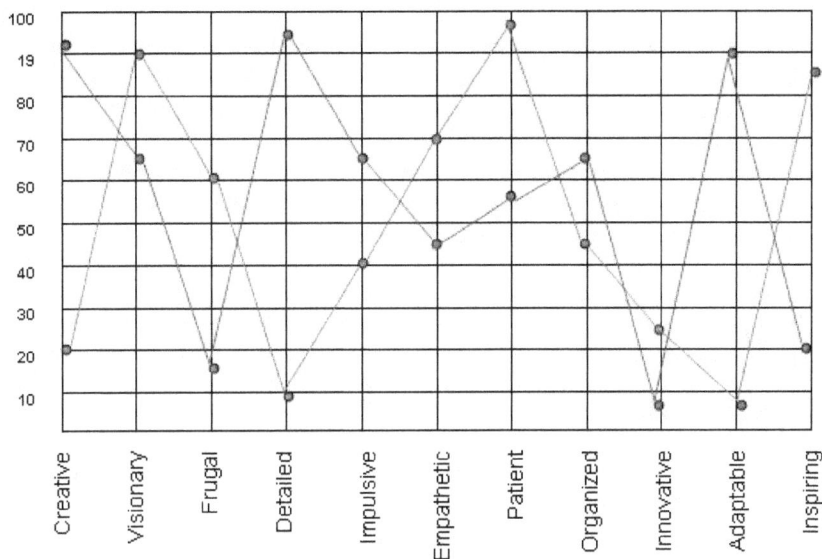

MY STRENGTHS + YOUR STRENGTHS = POWERFUL TEAM
God gives each person special gifts.

Look at the couple in the chart above. These people have very different scores in almost all of the attributes on the chart. At first glance, they look as if they would not get along or agree on anything. They look like an argument waiting to happen. If you look at them individually, you would doubt that they could ever be successful financially, but if you look at them as a team, it appears differently. As a team, they have high scores in almost all of the attributes. They look like an unbeatable team. That is the secret to using each other's strengths. If you will use the strengths that each of you have, you can increase your chances greatly of reaching great Financial Success.

ACTION 3
LEAVE THE PAST IN THE PAST AND FORGET THE REARVIEW MIRROR
This step is not easy to do. How many times have you thought of something that happened in the past, and it upsets you again or it keeps you from moving forward in a positive way?

How many times have you been in the middle of a disagreement and one of you says, "Well what about this thing or that thing" that happened a long time ago and the other replies with, "Remember when you…" and that person brings up something that happened even longer ago? The arguing continues until no one can remember what originally started the disagreement.

How many of you are still upset or could get upset about something that happened years ago? You must agree with your loved ones that *this* is a new beginning and that you will focus on the road ahead and stop looking in the rearview mirror all the time. There is a reason that the windshield is 85 times larger than the rear view mirror. Imagine what kind of a trip you would have if you reversed the size of the windshield and the rearview mirror. You would crash in no time, and you would keep on crashing.

Everybody has had failures and made mistakes in their past. People make mistakes— forgive, forget, and move on!

TOSS THE BAGGAGE

A friend told me a great story about her grandparents who were first generation immigrants from Russia. Her grandparents had gathered all of their worldly belongings into suitcases and were on a dock, waiting in a long line to board a ship that would take them to America.

Her grandparents noticed a family they knew working their way back from the front of the line. As the family passed by them, her grandfather asked, "What is wrong? What are you doing?" The father of the other family replied, "They won't let us take our luggage," and they continued to work their way back through the crowd and disappeared.

Her grandfather instantly grabbed their suitcases and threw them into the water and said, "Nothing is going to keep us from going to America!"

Her grandfather decided that nothing would stop his family from reaching their goal. All of the stuff from their past life had become baggage that would keep them from moving to a wonderful new life full of unlimited possibilities. He decided to leave the past in the past and move on to a great future. A man, his family, and future generations were changed because in the moment of a critical decision, this man had a goal and did not waiver. This story perfectly illustrates this point.

Make a commitment that you will not let baggage from the past stop you from being financially successful. Determine that you will not let the past hold you back on your journey to Financial Success.

I hope that you will decide that the past is the past, and you are going to leave it behind and move on to your great new future.

ACTION 4
COMMUNICATE REGULARLY

When my oldest son was about five years old we went to a lake for a picnic. It had the typical campground bathroom facilities: a concrete building with no plumbing or running water—just a toilet with a deep well in the ground. The place had not been cleaned in decades. It had spider webs, stuff on the floor, and the smell created an actual physical barrier that you could feel as you entered. I am sure that new life forms could be discovered by conducting experiments on the stuff that covered the floor. It was horrible, but guess what? We had to go to the bathroom, and this was the only civilized option. Besides, we were macho guys, and I was sure we could hold our breath for at least two minutes. We could do this! So we prepared for entry. I had one simple command for my son: "Don't touch anything!" We took a deep breath and stormed the building like a Navy Seals Special Forces team that must accomplish its vital mission in less than two minutes and extract the entire team without losing anyone while keeping injuries to a minimum. My son went into the stall, and I stood guard just outside the stall door. Time passed, more time passed, and even more time passed. I did not hear anything going on inside the stall—only an eerie silence. I became concerned that we would not make our two-minute mission limit. I decided to find out what was happening. I knew if I opened my mouth to say anything, I would have to breathe and risk a life-threatening disease entering my body, but better to lose one team member and accomplish the mission than to lose the entire team. So I went for it and said, "Marshall, what are you doing?" Instantly, he replied, "How am I supposed to undo my belt if I can't touch anything?" He was standing there frozen, literally obeying my order: "Don't touch anything." Bless his heart—he was trying to figure out how he could accomplish our mission and still obey my order. Did I really mean "Don't touch anything?" No. I really meant "Don't touch anything associated with the building that would most likely give you a terminal disease of some kind." What did he hear? He heard, "Don't touch anything!" We could still be standing in that nasty building right now. Fortunately, we identified our communication problem, corrected it, and the mission was successful with only minimal injuries. We have both moved on to live full and productive lives. This is an illustration of what happens to all of us when we try to communicate with each other. Communicating clearly is not easy!

> *Disagree without being disagreeable.*

If you think communicating clearly is easy, check this out. Even churches struggle to communicate clearly. These are items that appeared in actual church publications.

Church Bulletin Bloopers

Bertha Belch, a missionary from Africa, will be speaking tonight at Calvary. Come hear Bertha Belch all the way from Africa.
Ladies, don't forget the rummage sale! It's a chance to get rid of those things not worth keeping around the house. Don't forget your husbands.
Potluck supper Sunday at 5:00 pm – prayer and medication to follow.
For those of you who have children and don't know it, we have a nursery downstairs.

The insurance industry also struggles to communicate clearly.

"Coming home, I drove into the wrong house and collided with a tree I don't have."
"I thought my window was down, but I found out it wasn't when I put my head through it."
"The indirect cause of the accident was a little guy in a small car with a big mouth."
"I was on my way to the doctor with rear end trouble when my universal joint gave way causing me to have an accident."

Even advertisers struggle to communicate clearly. Check these out.

Tired of cleaning yourself? Let me do it!
Great Dames for sale.
Four-poster bed, 101 years old. Perfect for antique lover.
For sale: Antique desk suitable for lady with thick legs and large drawers.

I have compiled a few tools that you can use to help you communicate clearly and on a regular basis. These tools will help you be successful in reaching your goal of Financial Success, and they will also make the journey a lot more enjoyable.

THE TOOLS
- The scoreboard
- Plus delta (+/Δ)
- Start/Stop/Continue
- Check-in amount
- Surprise income

FINANCIAL SUCCESS IN A BOX

FINANCIAL SCOREBOARD

NAME: _____ DATE: _____

STEP 1 10 STEP PLAN	I have a step-by-step plan to follow to reach financial success. 1 No — 2 — 3 — 4 — 5 — 6 — 7 — 8 — 9 — 10 Yes (Maybe)	**Fill in the circles that best describe your current situation**
STEP 2 WORK TOGETHER	I work together with my spouse in all areas of our finances toward common goals. (If you are single, mark the 10) 1 Never — 2 — 3 — 4 — 5 — 6 — 7 — 8 — 9 — 10 Always (Sometimes)	
STEP 3 THE BASICS	I know key success factors of money, behavior change and marketing self-defense. 1 No — 2 — 3 — 4 — 5 — 6 — 7 — 8 — 9 — 10 Yes (Maybe)	
STEP 4 GIVING	I currently give to my church, charities, etc. on a regular basis. 1 Never — 2 — 3 — 4 — 5 — 6 — 7 — 8 — 9 — 10 (Regularly) 10% Gross	
STEP 5 PUT MONEY TO WORK	I currently save the following % of gross income every paycheck (includes savings, 401k, IRAs, etc) 1 1% or less — 2 — 3 — 4 — 5 — 6 — 7 — 8 — 9 — 10 (2%) 3% Gross	**Connect the Dots**
STEP 6 EMERGENCY FUND	I currently have the following amount in a dedicated cash emergency fund. 1 $0 — 2 $200 — 3 $300 — 4 $400 — 5 $500 — 6 $600 — 7 $700 — 8 $800 — 9 $900 — 10 $1000	
STEP 7 PAY OFF DEBT	I currently owe the following total amount in consumer debt (Includes credit cards, student loans, etc., everything except your house) 1 $20,000+ — 2 — 3 $16,000 — 4 — 5 $12,000 — 6 — 7 $8,000 — 8 — 9 $4,000 — 10 $0	
STEP 8 SURVIVAL FUND	I currently have a cash survival fund that will cover my total expenses for 1 Month — 2 Months — 3 Months — 4 Months — 6 Months	
STEP 9 PLAN RETIREMENT	I contribute to my retirement fund every month and I know I will have enough (If you are currently retired, mark 10) 1 No — 2 — 3 — 4 — 5 — 6 — 7 — 8 — 9 — 10 Yes (Maybe)	**Total the Points**
STEP 10 PAY OFF HOUSE	I pay extra on my mortgage (If you do not have a mortgage, mark 10) 1 Never — 2 — 3 — 4 — 5 — 6 — 7 — 8 — 9 — 10 (Regularly) Paid Off	**44**

If your score is less than 90, you need this program

Copyright © 2010

THE SCOREBOARD

WHAT IS IT
The scoreboard is a great tool to help you quickly assess where you are on the 10 steps. In less than two minutes, you can find where you are on the 10 key elements of Financial Success. You are able to see your status in all 10 areas on one piece of paper. The scoreboard is simple, easy to use, and very effective.

HOW IT WORKS
Every few months after you have reached a score of 10, fill out a scoreboard form to make sure that you are maintaining that score on each of the 10 steps. If you discover that any of the scores are slipping below a score of 10, go back and review the lesson for that step and make adjustments that are required to bring you back to a score of 10.

Plus	Delta
Week of _____	
+ Things that are working well	**Δ** Things that could be improved

PLUS/DELTA FORM

WHAT IS IT

The Plus/ Delta form is a great tool to help you identify what is working and what could be improved. When I was the head of Talent Development for the Flight Test Center at Learjet, I learned about this valuable tool. The test pilots conducted a debriefing after every flight to identify what went well and what needed to be improved. The Flight Test Center was very serious work. These pilots and engineers flew uncertified aircraft to and beyond their limits in order to make sure they were safe for public use.

These guys' idea of a great day was flying 200 feet off the ground with one engine out or flying around the globe to find icing conditions so they could see how the plane operated as a block of ice. Every flight had the potential for major trouble or even death. I was impressed that the entire crew would conduct a detailed debriefing after every flight. It was a great way to identify things that worked and things that needed to be improved while they were still fresh in their minds. I started using this technique after each development session and eventually after each meeting. I was amazed how effective it was. We would sit down and list what worked, the pluses, to make sure we continued to do those items. Then we would list what needed to be improved, the deltas, for the next time. You will be amazed how much you can improve something if you use this simple tool to debrief after each event.

HOW IT WORKS

Each week list the things that have been working on your journey through this program and also list the things that could be improved for the next week. This will provide a fabulous way to make sure you know what is working and continue to do it. It will also show the things that are not yet working as well as you would like that need to be improved or the things that are not working at all and can be eliminated.

START/STOP/CONTINUE FORM

Date	START	STOP	CONTINUE

START /STOP /CONTINUE FORM

WHAT IS IT

The Start/Stop/Continue form is much like the Plus/Delta form. It allows you to identify the things that are working and the things that are not working to help you be successful in your journey to Financial Success.

HOW IT WORKS

Each week list the things that you need to begin doing to help you become successful in the Start column. List the things you need to stop doing, because they are not helping you be successful, in the Stop column. List the things that have been working on your journey to Financial Success in the Continue column. This will provide a way to add new positive behaviors and habits, stop negative destructive behaviors and habits, and continue the positive behaviors and habits that are working.

CHECK-IN AMOUNT

In order to reach our financial goals,
we agree to check with each other

BEFORE

spending any amount over

$ _____

CHECK-IN AMOUNT

WHAT IS IT

The check-in amount is a great tool to help you avoid disagreements and regrets. The check-in amount is a particular dollar amount that you agree on with your spouse that you will not exceed on a purchase without checking in with each other. These are purchases outside of your normal monthly expenses such as groceries, car payments, utilities, etc.

HOW IT WORKS

The check-in amount is a simple tool to use. You simply choose a dollar amount that you and your spouse (or you individually, if you are single) would like to be aware of before it is spent. For example, my wife and I decide that we will check in with each other before we spend more than $50 on a particular item. We do not want to know about every $5, $10, or $25 purchase that each other makes, but to avoid disagreements caused by surprises, we need to agree to check in on purchases above $50.

So before I spent $100 dollars to have the car detailed, I would let my spouse know what I was planning. We could decide together whether that was what we wanted to do with the $100. If I were single, I would spend time seriously considering if that was how I wanted to use the $100 or if there were a better use for it.

> *Choosing a goal and sticking to it*
> *changes everything.*
> *Scott Reed*

The check-in amount you choose could be $20 or it could be $1,000. It depends on your personal situation. The check-in amount should not be used to oppress or totally restrict freedom—that would only cause more disagreements and unhappiness. It is not a tool to require permission from the other person. The check-in amount should be chosen so that it allows freedom to a certain dollar amount, but encourages cooperation or serious consideration above that dollar amount. Try your check-in amount for a month to see how it is working. You may need to adjust the amount. The check-in amount should create a healthy balance between freedom and cooperation.

This tool can help you work better together to avoid disagreements, or if you are single on your own to avoid regrets. It can help you reach your goal of Financial Success much faster.

> *Obstacles are those frightful things you see when you*
> *take your eyes off your goal.*
> *Henry Ford*

SURPRISE INCOME
Whether you are single or married, determine what you will do with unexpected income *before* you receive it!

WHAT IS IT
The surprise income form is a great tool to help you decide the best way to use any unexpected income in the most powerful, constructive way *before* you receive it.

HOW IT WORKS
A married couple in one of my classes practically got into a fight over $2,000 dollars they had received unexpectedly. He wanted to pay off debt; she wanted to take a vacation. If they had agreed in advance what they would do, they would have avoided an argument. I recommended that they divide the money. If they were working on Step 6 - emergency fund (saving toward a $1,000 emergency fund), they could put 30 percent of it toward that, 30 percent toward paying off debt, another 30 percent toward a vacation, and the last 10 percent toward celebrating. Remember that one of the major keys to this program is to Put Your Money to Work. When you receive unexpected money it can be very exciting and emotional. That is not the best time to make decisions on how it should be allocated. If you decide how unexpected funds will be distributed before you receive them, then you have a much better chance of making the optimum use of those funds. Allocate at least a certain amount toward a celebration and another amount to each individual to spend however they want. You need to update this sheet every few months because

the steps you are working on will change, and other things will also change over time that may drive different allocation percentages. This is a fabulous way to make the most of unexpected funds and to enjoy the blessing without arguing.

The percentages must add up to 100 percent and all of the funds must be allocated. One reason this tool works really well is because it uses percentages. You can allocate the money in portions without even knowing the amount of the unexpected money.

SURPRISE INCOME	
Any unexpected money we receive will be spent in the following way	
Assign %	Calculate Actual Dollars
_____% on Giving	= $_____
_____% on Taxes	= $_____
_____% on _____	= $_____
_____% on _____	= $_____
_____% on _____	= $_____
_____% on _____	= $_____
= 100%	Total Received $ _____

ACTION 5
CELEBRATE AND PRAISE

BRING MOMMA UP ON DECK
Remember the story I shared earlier about the grandparents who immigrated to the United States from Russia? The stories that the grandfather shares about the journey to the United States are very different from the stories that the grandmother shares. The men were required to stay on the deck of the ship while the women and children were required to stay below deck for safety reasons. The grandfather tells stories of the glorious sunrises and inspiring sunsets, and the wonderful taste of the wind as it blew the fresh ocean air across the deck. The inspiring conversations on the deck were about the great opportunities that lay ahead.

The grandmother tells stories from below deck of sea sickness, foul smells, extreme temperatures, darkness, crowded conditions, and the noise of crying children. They were both on the same ship going to the same great destination, but their experiences were vastly different.

The journey to Financial Success can sometimes be the same way. One person is excited because they are dreaming about how great life will be—and it will be, but the other person may feel like they are in the bowels of the ship, and it is not a fun journey.

The point of this story is to bring mama up on the deck once in awhile. If grandma had been brought up on deck occasionally, she could have seen the beautiful sunsets and smelled the sweet winds of opportunity, and the journey would have been exciting and positive for both of them. Do not wait until you can see the Statue of Liberty before you bring your loved ones up on deck.

That is why regular celebration is so important. Make sure that you celebrate, in an inexpensive way, when you complete each of the 10 steps, when you successfully redirect a negative behavior, and when you make progress and are successful reaching goals together. Celebrating regularly will make the journey just as enjoyable as reaching the final destination of Financial Success.

Start off with simple celebrations as you move closer and closer to Financial Success. As more and more pieces of your financial life come together, your celebrations can get larger and more elaborate. Instead of picnics you can go on vacations and cruises. You will be able to fully enjoy the vacation or cruise because you did it right. You are not worried the whole time because you charged it on a credit card. As your 10 steps improve, do not automatically bump up your celebrations. I have been to some of the best restaurants in the world. Some have $25,000 bottles of wine, meals that cost several hundred dollars, and great views, but no restaurant in the world can ever compare with the $15 picnic dinner that my wife and I shared sitting on the beach watching the sun set on the Gulf of Mexico.

In today's fast-paced culture, it is easy to move from one project or accomplishment to the next without stopping to celebrate. I highly recommend that you stop and celebrate when you accomplish something significant that brings you closer to your wonderful goal of Financial Success.

Here are a few ideas of inexpensive ways to celebrate:
- Borrow a movie from the library and have a movie night.
- Make dinner into a picnic and take it to the best natural setting close to you— beach, park, mountains, etc.
- Eat at a special restaurant, but use coupons to keep the price down or even just go for an appetizer or dessert.
- Watch the sunrise while having a picnic breakfast.
- Watch the sunset while having a picnic dinner.
- Make a special dessert.
- Do a small project to update the house—paint a room, etc.
- Do something pampering—a manicure, etc.

THE POWER OF PRAISE

Praise is one of the most powerful forces in the world. It is typically inexpensive and simple to do, yet it is greatly underutilized. If praise is done regularly and properly it can release great potential and raise relationships to new levels. Think of the last time you received a compliment through an email or praise from your spouse or a friend. It probably made you feel really good. Most people love to receive praise, but few people praise others as much as they could. So if praise is powerful, inexpensive and simple, why is it not used more often? I believe there are two reasons.

1. People do not think to do it.
2. People are not comfortable doing it.

The solution to #1 is to make praise a regular habit in your life. Make it a habit to compliment at least one person every day. Compliment your spouse every day.

The solution to #2 is that people are uncomfortable because they do not know how to praise another person. They do not know how because they have never been taught how to praise.

Most people spend 12 years in school and another 4-6 if they go to college, and they are never taught something as important as complimenting another person. I conducted a leadership class where I was teaching the power of praise, and I realized that the leaders in the class were hesitant to give compliments to their employees. I asked each one of them to give the person next to them a compliment. I was horrified—these fabulous leaders had no idea how to praise another person. They mumbled, avoided eye contact, forgot names, and were insincere.

I decided right there that I was going to formally teach them how to give a compliment.

HOW TO PRAISE

PRAISE OFTEN

Make it a habit to compliment the people in your life on a regular basis. There is a story of a couple who had been married for 25 years and had gone to a counselor because they were having relationship troubles. The wife said, "You never tell me you love me!" The husband said, "I told you I loved you the day we got married. If I change my mind I will let you know." That is not good enough. Compliments are fuel for a relationship. You do not fill the gas tank on your car once when you buy it and expect it to run smoothly forever. Relationships are the same way. You need to fill the praise tank on a regular basis.

BE TIMELY

Do not wait too long to give a compliment because the more time that passes between the praiseworthy behavior and the compliment, the less value the compliment will have. A good example of this is the annual performance appraisal that most people have at work. If your boss waits until the end of the year to praise and compliment you, it will not be as powerful as if they praise and compliment you throughout the year as you perform these worthy tasks.

BE SPECIFIC

Your compliment needs to be specific so the person will know what to continue doing. "You are the best wife ever" is certainly nice to hear and will surely make her feel great, but "I bet every husband on earth wishes he had a wife that supports him even in the tough times like you did during my layoff from work," is a lot more specific and will mean even more to her.

BE SINCERE

Every person on earth has a built-in bologna meter. If you do not mean it, then do not say it. People can tell when someone is not being sincere.

LOOK THEM IN THE EYE

When giving a compliment in person, make eye contact. It will mean a lot more if you make eye contact during the compliment.

USE THEIR NAME

People love to hear their name. State their name, and then deliver the compliment. Caution: If you do not remember their name, do not try to fake it. I remember a time when I forgot a name and tried to be clever asking, "How do you spell your last name"? They replied, "J-O-N-E-S." If you do not remember their name just say, "I don't remember your name, but I do want to remember it. Can you tell me again?"

Here are some examples of compliments:
- I really appreciate the way you balance the checkbook every month. It helps to know where we are financially.
- Thanks for working so hard to provide for the family.
- Thanks for all the work you did to reduce our grocery bill.
- Thank you for caring enough to get this program. I cannot wait for us to reach Financial Success.

> *It doesn't matter where you are coming from.*
> *All that matters is where you are going.*
> *Brian Tracy*

HOW TO ACCEPT A COMPLIMENT

Another thing I discovered while conducting leadership classes was that there are many people who find it difficult to *accept* a compliment. A woman would compliment another woman on her lovely dress, and the woman in the dress would reply, "Oh, it's nothing. I got it at the Salvation Army store for $5." Why would she say that? One person would tell another person, "That was a great job," and the person would reply, "It was nothing." Some people who find it difficult to accept a compliment will say something that deflects or flat out refutes the compliment.

Here is your crash course in how to accept a compliment:

Look at the person and say, "Thank you," and then resist any temptation to say anything else. If you struggle with accepting compliments, then you will find that this technique will help you be courteous and not refute the compliment while keeping your discomfort to a minimum.

If you are not used to praising others and giving them compliments, then you need to practice so you do not sound insincere. Start small and use the tips listed above to release the potential in your relationships.

> *There is no man living that can not do*
> *more than he thinks he can.*
> *Henry Ford*

RELATIONSHIP BANK
MAKE DEPOSITS EARLY AND OFTEN
If I could give you a tool that would make all of your relationships stronger, richer, and more enjoyable, would you be interested? This is a tool that allows you to know exactly where you stand at any particular time in any of your relationships—a tool that allows you to make sure you are always in good standing. This tool is the relationship bank.

This invisible banking system has existed since God created Adam and Eve and will continue as long as people interact with each other.

You can see this invisible banking system and understand the basic principles of how it works. Use it to strengthen and enrich all of your current and future relationships. As you begin to understand its principles, you may have flashbacks to times in past relationships and understand why it went well or why it went badly.

THE BASICS
An invisible banking system exists.
The system is at work every minute of every day whether you like it or not.
Every person on earth is a banker and is participating.
Most people are not even aware of the system.
Every person has an account for every other person they know.
Accounts are being opened. Accounts are being closed.
Deposits and withdrawals are being made all of the time.

When you meet a person for the first time, your banking account is opened. If your friend introduces you to someone and that person is genuinely interested to meet you, tells you they have heard many good things about you, and they even invite you to an upcoming event, then that person has a positive balance with you because they treated you well. They made a deposit in their newly opened account with you. On the other hand, if while you were being introduced the other person acted completely disinterested in you, looked at other people as they passed by, and could not wait to move on to the next thing in their day, then that person made a withdrawal from their just-opened account with you. They are overdrawn and will stay that way until they make a deposit equal to or greater than the withdrawal they just made.

I had a student who tried to make a deposit in his wife's account by giving her flowers. When she asked why he gave her flowers he responded, "I had to do it. It was homework." He made a great deposit and immediately made a larger withdrawal.

I could mention the name of anyone you know and you could tell me if they have a balance or they are overdrawn. They could also tell you what your balance is at any particular time. Over the next week, be observant and you will notice people making deposits and withdrawals. It is as if you have been given a special pair of glasses and now you can see the invisible banking system at work all around you.

Make regular deposits and maintain a positive balance in each other's account. This will help you work better together as a team.

You now know the tools necessary to work together to reach Financial Success. When you work together you not only increase your chances of success, you make the journey much more enjoyable.

> *Goals are dreams with deadlines.*
> *Diana S. Hunt*

SPECIAL ASSIGNMENT
DECLARE WAR ON YOUR BILLS

WHAT IS IT
Declaring war on your bills is a systematic way of reducing the amount of your bills.

HOW IT WORKS
To declare war on your bills, simply take each bill one at a time and identify ways to reduce the amount that you pay in the future. When the amount of the bills reduces, the amount of money going toward building your wealth can increase.

You can use the war on bills form at the end of this section to start this process.

EXAMPLE

\multicolumn{5}{c}{}

WAR ON BILLS

Take each monthly bill to see how much you can reduce it. Record the results on this form.

Bill	Current Amount	Action Taken	New Amount	Yearly Savings
Cable TV	$150 Month	Called for new customer special + one month free	$122 Month	$366
Car Insurance	$1,400 Year	Called for analysis – found unnecessary item	$1,000 Year	$400
P.O. Box	$30 Month	Cancelled Service	$0 Month	$360

The form is simple to use:
- List the name of the bill
- List the current amount of the bill
- Take action to reduce the amount
- List new amount of the bill
- List yearly savings amount

This activity can save huge amounts of money.

EXAMPLES
My wife and I decided to declare war on our bills. Here are the results of that decision:

CABLE TV

Monthly cost before	**$150**
Monthly cost after	**$122**
Yearly savings	**$336** (Plus received 1 month free/2 movie channels)

The first bill we decided to attack in our war on bills was our cable bill. We were paying $150 a month for cable TV, Internet, and phone service. Our goal was to see how much we could reduce the bill. Our cable provider had a radio advertisement special of $99 a month for new customers. Since I had been a loyal customer for four years, I thought I deserved that special rate. I called the cable company and told them I would like to have the $99 a month special promotion. They asked me if I was a current customer. I told them I did not want to talk about that; I just wanted to get the $99 special. The customer service representative told me that the $99 special promotion was only for new customers, and as a current customer I was not eligible. I spent several minutes discussing how unfair this was, and that I was very disappointed that a loyal customer of four years got less respect than a brand new customer. I said I was willing to check the competition to see if I could get a better deal. I tried everything I could think of to convince him that I was worthy of the $99-a-month special. He did not waiver.

I decided to act as if I were in a war and really try to win this battle. I went for the nuclear option. As there were no disconnect or reconnect fees, I told him to disconnect all of my services, and I would call back next week as a new customer for the $99-a-month special. He was silent. Then he said, "Just a moment." The next thing I knew I was speaking to another person in the Saves Department. The customer service representative in the Saves Department greeted me, and he said that I could have the $99-a-month special as well as two movie channels for the next year for free. He also informed me that I did not need to pay the next month's bill because they would give it to me for free. It was like I had been transferred to a fantasy land where everything I asked for was granted and even more.

The reason this call was successful was because I was willing to fight for a discount. The first representative I spoke with was probably trained to tell existing customers that they are not eligible for the $99 promotion. He was also trained that if a customer were actually going to cancel their services or go to the competition, he was to transfer the customer to the Saves Department. They did not want to give existing customers the deal because they would lose income, but they absolutely did not want to lose someone totally as a customer. You need to be willing to change to a competitor or cancel the service if you really want to reduce the amount you pay. In tough economic times companies are more willing to give discounts just to keep customers. They are trying to survive.

INSURANCE

Yearly cost before	**$1,400**
Yearly cost after	**$1,000**
Yearly savings	**$ 400**

The second bill we decided to attack in our war on bills was our car insurance bill. We were paying $1,400 a year for car insurance. Our goal was to see how much we could reduce the bill.

We had received a letter in the mail from a competing car insurance company inviting us to call them for a quote. I got a print out of our current coverage and gave them a call. I told them that my reason for calling was to get the lowest price possible on the same amount of coverage I currently had. He asked me how much I was paying currently for my coverage, and I told him I did not want to share that information; I just wanted to see what their best price was for the same coverage. If he knew the amount I was paying, he was likely to calculate a price just under the current payment instead of going as low as possible. He started calculating and came up with a price about $50 less than we were currently paying. I told him that it was not low enough to justify changing companies—could he find a way to reduce it any further? He ran more numbers and asked more questions, but was unable to give me a significant reduction in my payment. I thanked him for his time, and we parted ways.

I was disappointed. My first battle with the cable company had gone so well. This battle seemed to end in failure. I decided I was not going to give up yet. Surely there was some way to reduce that bill.

I called my current provider and told them I was reducing the amounts of all of my bills, and I wanted to explore ways to reduce this bill. I told the customer service representative that I was very happy with their service; I just wanted to find a way to reduce the amount I was paying. She reviewed the coverage I currently had and asked a few questions. She ran some numbers and told me that she really did not see any way to reduce the amount. She informed me that the only way to reduce the amount was to eliminate part of the coverage. I asked her to identify any item that I did not absolutely need. She scanned my policy and said, "You really don't need this particular item's coverage. If you have this on your employer insurance, then this is really duplicate coverage." I cancelled that part of the coverage and immediately reduced our car insurance by $400 a year.

This call was successful because I did not give up after speaking with the first company. If my current company had not been able to reduce the bill, then I could have contacted another competitor and tried to get a better deal with them. When you declare war on bills, act like you are in a war and do what it takes to win each battle.

P.O. BOX

Monthly cost before	$ 30
Monthly cost after	$ 0
Yearly savings	$ 360

The third bill we decided to attack in our war on bills was our post office box bill. We were paying $30 a month for a post office box. Our goal was to see how much we could reduce the bill.

This bill was pretty easy to reduce. My wife and I discussed it and decided that we did not really need the post office box. We received very little mail in it each month, and we could have that mail routed to our house. We simply canceled the box and saved $360 a year.

This tool is very powerful. Reduce your bills in a systematic way. Starting this week, attack one or two of your bills each week and see how much you can reduce the amounts. Any reductions in spending can be put to work building your future wealth.

Use the bill titles listed on the dashboard form in Step 1. The dashboard form will help ensure the identification of all bills for reduction.

> *Vision without Action = Dream*
> *Action without Vision = Passing the Time*
> *Vision with Action = Change the World*
> *Joel Barker*

DECLARE WAR ON YOUR BILLS
TIME FOR ACTION

You now know what to do, but that is only half of the success equation. The other half of the equation is to do what you know—to take action. There is a to-do list at the end of this section. The items are in the order to be accomplished. Once all of the items are completed, celebrate the successful completion of another step toward Financial Success – Work Together.

You have a vision. When you add action, you can change the world. You can definitely change your financial world!

> *I can accept failure, everyone fails at something, but I can't accept not trying.*
> *Michael Jordan*

CONGRATULATIONS!

You have now completed Step 2 – Work Together.

You are making great progress!

- You have completed Step 1 – 10-Step Plan, and you are following the simple 10-Step Plan.
- You have completed Step 2 – Work Together, and you are working together toward the same financial goals and using each other's strengths.

You can now move your dot on Step 2 of the scoreboard form to a score of 10.

SCOREBOARD

Next is Step 3 – The Basics

What does "The Basics" mean? It means you will learn:
The basics of how money works
The basics of behavior
The basics of marketing self-defense

Step 3 will help you prepare for the remaining 7 steps, and it will equip you with the tools and techniques needed for fabulous financial success.
Move forward and conquer Step 3.

CHOOSE THE TEAM	
INPUT	**AFFECTED**

Strength & Weakness Assessment

Individual Score – A

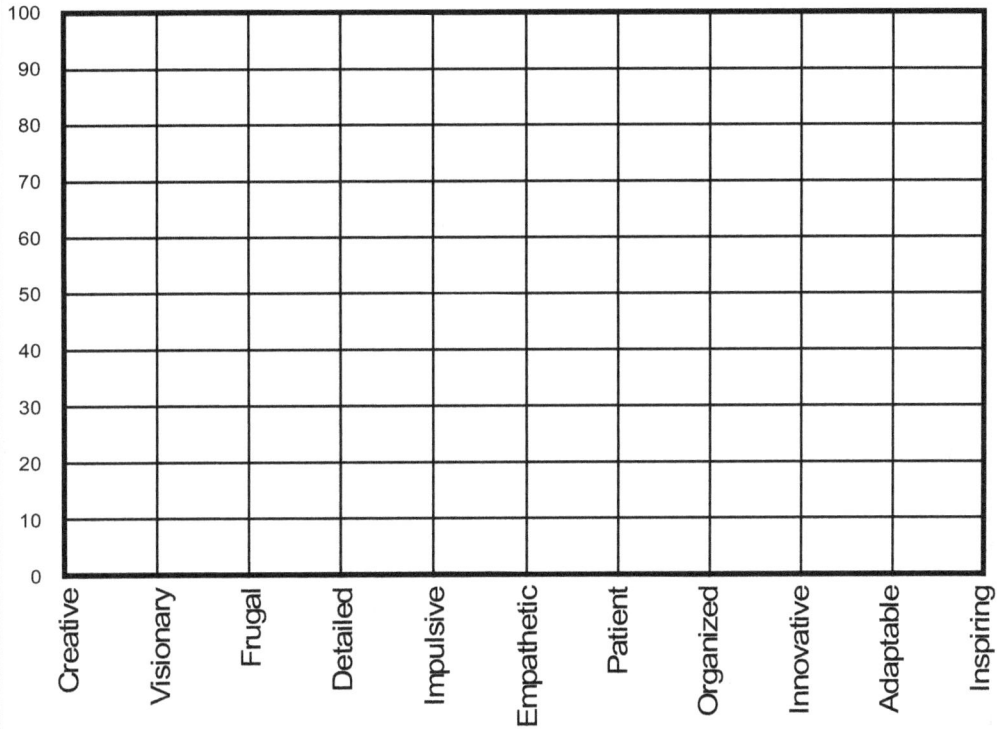

	Creative	Visionary	Frugal	Detailed	Impulsive	Empathetic	Patient	Organized	Innovative	Adaptable	Inspiring
100											
90											
80											
70											
60											
50											
40											
30											
20											
10											
0											

Strength & Weakness Assessment

Individual Score – B

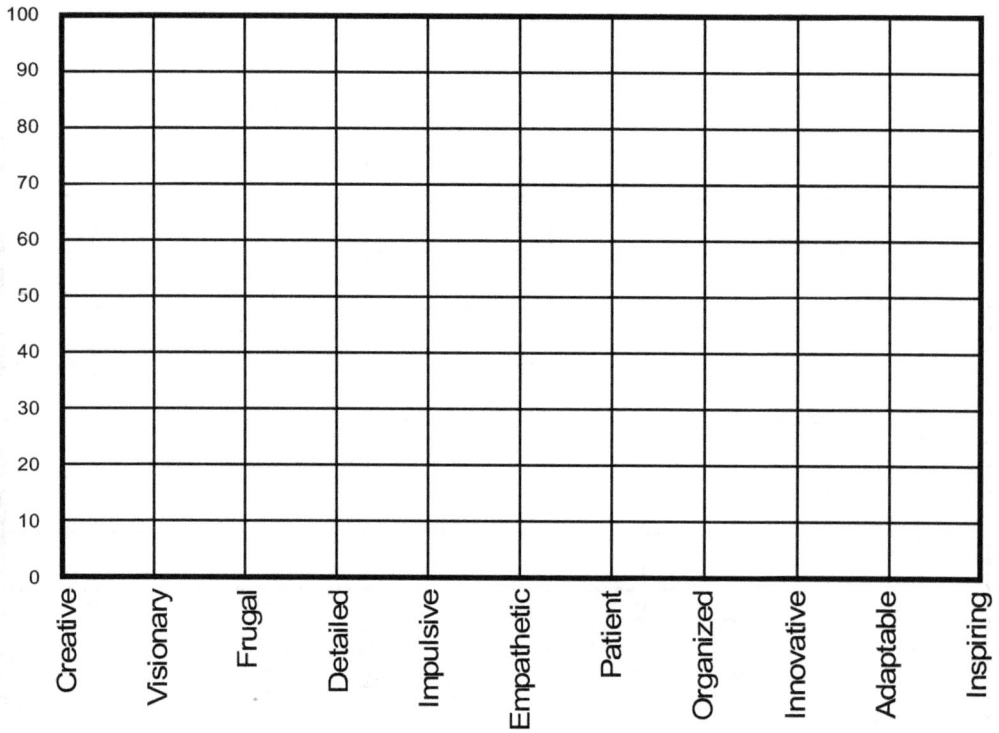

100										
90										
80										
70										
60										
50										
40										
30										
20										
10										
0										

Creative — Visionary — Frugal — Detailed — Impulsive — Empathetic — Patient — Organized — Innovative — Adaptable — Inspiring

Strength & Weakness Assessment

Team Score – A & B
Chart both scores on this sheet

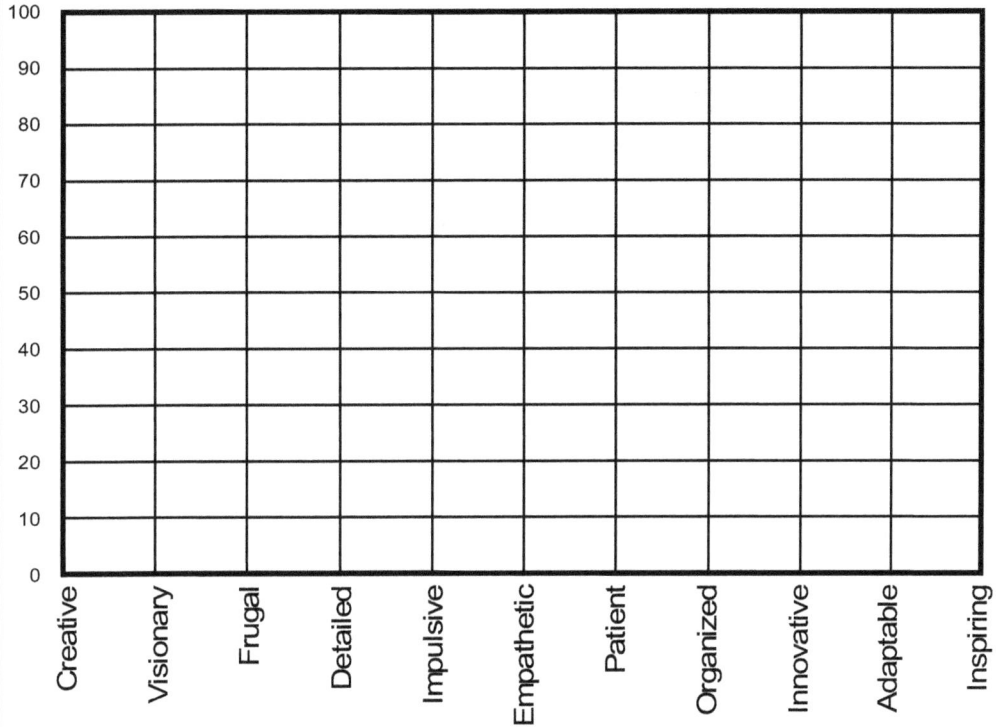

	Creative	Visionary	Frugal	Detailed	Impulsive	Empathetic	Patient	Organized	Innovative	Adaptable	Inspiring
100											
90											
80											
70											
60											
50											
40											
30											
20											
10											
0											

CHECK-IN AMOUNT

In order to reach our financial goals,
we agree to check with each other

BEFORE

spending any amount over

$_____

SURPRISE INCOME

Any unexpected money we receive will be spent in the following way

Assign %	Calculate Actual Dollars
_____% on Giving	= $_____
_____% on Taxes	= $_____
_____% on _____	= $_____
_____% on _____	= $_____
_____% on _____	= $_____
_____% on _____	= $_____
= 100%	Total Received $ _____

START/STOP/CONTINUE FORM

Date	START	STOP	CONTINUE

FINANCIAL SUCCESS IN A BOX

FINANCIAL SCOREBOARD

NAME: _____   DATE: _____

STEP 1 10 STEP PLAN	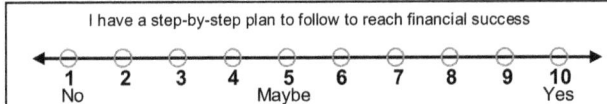
STEP 2 WORK TOGETHER	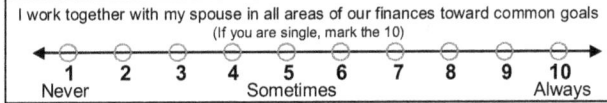
STEP 3 THE BASICS	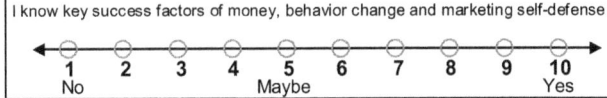
STEP 4 GIVING	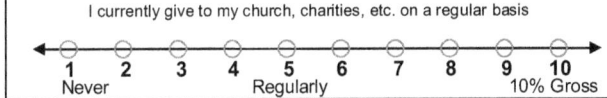
STEP 5 PUT MONEY TO WORK	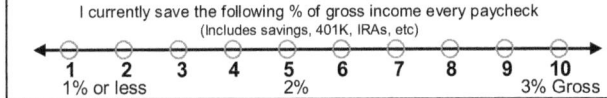
STEP 6 EMERGENCY FUND	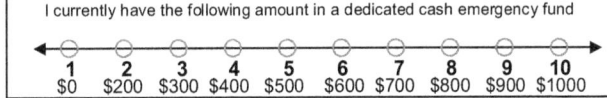
STEP 7 PAY OFF DEBT	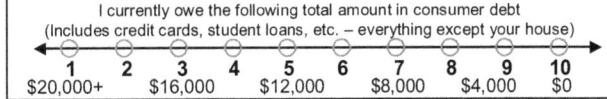
STEP 8 SURVIVAL FUND	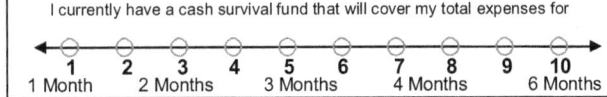
STEP 9 PLAN RETIREMENT	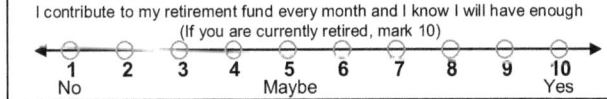
STEP 10 PAY OFF HOUSE	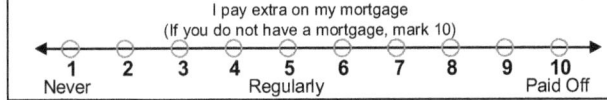

1 Fill in the circles that best describe your current situation

2 Connect the Dots

3 Total the Points

☐

If your score is less than 90, you need this program

Copyright © 2010

WAR ON BILLS

Take each monthly bill to see how much you can reduce it. Record the results on this form.

Bill	Current Amount	Action Taken	New Amount	Yearly Savings

WORK TOGETHER
To Do List

ITEM	COMPLETED
Complete Team Form	
Complete Scoreboard	
Complete Plus/Delta Form	
Complete Start/Stop/Continue Form	
Complete Check-In Amount Form	
Complete Surprise Income Form	
Complete War On Bills	

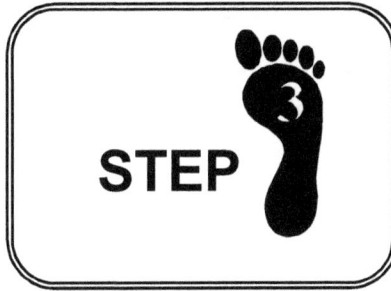

STEP 3

The Basics

FINANCIAL SCOREBOARD

NAME: _____   DATE: _____

STEP 1 — 10 STEP PLAN
I have a step-by-step plan to follow to reach financial success
1 2 3 4 5 6 7 8 9 10
No / Maybe / Yes

STEP 2 — WORK TOGETHER
I work together with my spouse in all areas of our finances toward common goals
(If you are single, mark the 10)
1 2 3 4 5 6 7 8 9 10
Never / Sometimes / Always

STEP 3 — THE BASICS
I know key success factors of money, behavior change and marketing self-defense
1 2 3 4 5 6 7 8 9 10
No / Maybe / Yes

STEP 4 — GIVING
I currently give to my church, charities, etc. on a regular basis
1 2 3 4 5 6 7 8 9 10
Never / Regularly / 10% Gross

STEP 5 — PUT MONEY TO WORK
I currently save the following % of gross income every paycheck
(Includes savings, 401K, IRAs, etc)
1 2 3 4 5 6 7 8 9 10
1% or less / 2% / 3% Gross

STEP 6 — EMERGENCY FUND
I currently have the following amount in a dedicated cash emergency fund
1 2 3 4 5 6 7 8 9 10
$0 $200 $300 $400 $500 $600 $700 $800 $900 $1000

STEP 7 — PAY OFF DEBT
I currently owe the following total amount in consumer debt
(Includes credit cards, student loans, etc. – everything except your house)
1 2 3 4 5 6 7 8 9 10
$20,000+ $16,000 $12,000 $8,000 $4,000 $0

STEP 8 — SURVIVAL FUND
I currently have a cash survival fund that will cover my total expenses for
1 2 3 4 5 6 7 8 9 10
1 Month / 2 Months / 3 Months / 4 Months / 6 Months

STEP 9 — PLAN RETIREMENT
I contribute to my retirement fund every month and I know I will have enough
(If you are currently retired, mark 10)
1 2 3 4 5 6 7 8 9 10
No / Maybe / Yes

STEP 10 — PAY OFF HOUSE
I pay extra on my mortgage
(If you do not have a mortgage, mark 10)
1 2 3 4 5 6 7 8 9 10
Never / Regularly / Paid Off

1 Fill in the circles that best describe your current situation

2 Connect the Dots

3 Total the Points

If your score is less than 90, you need this program

If I had one hour to cut down a tree, I would spend 45 minutes sharpening my axe.
Abraham Lincoln

IMAGINE

Imagine how successful you could be financially if you knew the few key principles that control the world of money, behavior, and marketing.

Imagine
- Having full knowledge of the 5 key principles that control the world of money
- Being able to put money to work for you to build a fortune

Imagine
- Having full knowledge of the key principles that control the world of behavior
- Being able to actually do the behaviors that lead to financial success

Imagine
- Having the tools and techniques to win the marketing battle for your dollars
- Knowing how to get the best deal on everything you buy

PURPOSE

TEACH THE BASICS

The purpose of this section is to prepare you for the journey to Financial Success by teaching you the basics of how money works, the basics of how to have the right behaviors, and the basics of how to defend yourself in the marketing battle for your dollars.

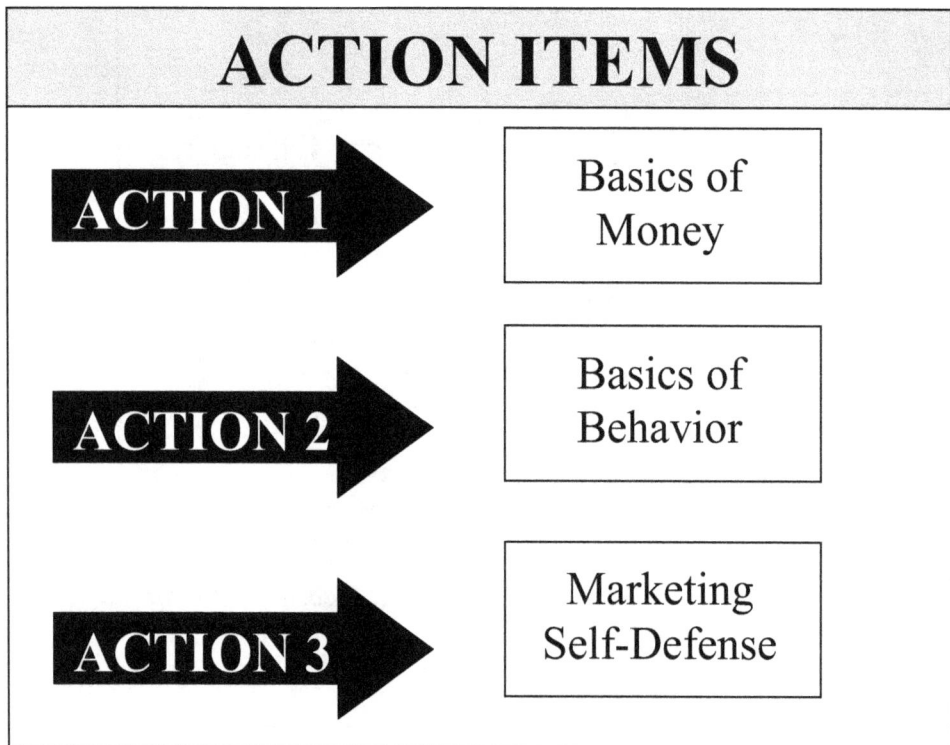

ACTION ITEMS

ACTION 1 →	Basics of Money
ACTION 2 →	Basics of Behavior
ACTION 3 →	Marketing Self-Defense

> *"By failing to prepare, you are preparing to fail."*
> *Benjamin Franklin*

Now that you have successfully completed Step 1 of the 10-Step Plan and Step 2, Working Together, it is time to move to Step 3, The Basics. Step 1 was critical because you need a 10-Step Plan to follow. Step 2 was critical because it is important that you work together to reach the goal of Financial Success. This step is equally important because it will prepare you for the rest of the journey. In this step I will give you the basic tools and techniques needed for success and teach you how to use them. These basic tools and techniques will give you what you need to reach high levels of success in the remaining 7 steps of your journey. These are tools you will use throughout the rest of this program and the rest of your life. A little time spent now in preparation will go a long way to help ensure your long-term financial success. Look at some powerful quotes about taking time to prepare:

> *First prepare your fields…then build your house*
> *Proverbs 24:27*
>
> *Everyone has the will to win. Few have the will to prepare to win.*
> *Bobby Knight*
>
> *Be Prepared.*
> *Boy Scouts of America*

> *You do not have to know everything about something to be successful at it.*
>
> *You only need to know the few key basics that create financial success.*

THE 80/20 RULE

Before we jump into learning the basic principles of money, behavior, and marketing, I would like to share a powerful tool called the 80/20 rule.

The 80/20 rule, also known as the Pareto Principle, was named after the Italian economist Vilfredo Pareto who in 1906 noticed that 80 percent of the wealth in his country was owned by 20 percent of the people. He created a mathematical formula to describe this unequal distribution of wealth.

In the 1930s and 1940s, Dr. Joseph Juran, a pioneer of TQM (Total Quality Management) called it the "Vital Few and Trivial Many." What does it mean? How can you use it? It means that in many situations in life, 80 percent of your outcomes are from 20 percent of your inputs. The 80/20 rule is a very powerful tool that keeps your focus on the few key things that will make you successful and will help you not get bogged down by the 80 percent that waste your time.

EXAMPLES

Eighty percent of the work is performed by twenty percent of the employees.
Eighty percent of the sales are made by twenty percent of the sales people.
Eighty percent of absenteeism is from twenty percent of the staff.
Eighty percent of the problems are caused by twenty percent of the staff.

We are about to learn the basics of the financial world. There are thousands and thousands of products, consultants, etc. It is so vast and complicated that it could literally take you years to understand all of its aspects. It is also so vast and complicated that there are many individuals and companies that make a living trying to explain it.
The good news is that you do not have to know *all* of this information to be successful with your money. I have researched the vast world of money and boiled it down to the few keys for success that you will need.

Those few key principles will be responsible for 80 percent of your financial success.

The 80/20 rule will help you learn the most important items you will need. There are only a few key principles at work in the world of money; the thousands of products and details are simply different ways of using these key principles.

If I could teach you five or six key principles that would help you become extremely successful in all the major areas of managing your money, would you be interested?
If I could teach you five or six key principles that would allow you to instantly assess any product or service no matter how complicated it is to see if it is right for you, would you be interested?

The reason I am sharing the 80/20 rule with you is to make the point that you do not have to be intimidated by the complicated world of finance. You do not need to know everything! You only need to know a few basic principles and you can be very successful financially.

HIT THE TARGET

Here is a story that illustrates the 80/20 Rule. I wanted to take up the sport of shooting sporting clays. In this sport, the shooter yells, "Pull!" The clay target is propelled into the air, and the shooter blasts it with a shotgun. Sporting clays is a pretty complicated sport. It is set up a bit like an obstacle course with about fifteen different stations. Each station simulates a different challenge. Station One might propel the clay target from a tower in front of you. You must shoot it as it travels over your head. Once successful at Station One, you move to Station Two that throws the clay target so that it travels across in front of you from left to right. Station Three will throw the clay target from behind a clump of bushes. Station Four throws the clay target straight up into the air above your head. At Station Five, the clay target bounces across the ground in front and you shoot it as it skips along the ground.

I did not have a lot of experience with shotguns, so I decided to take lessons. I arrived at the shooting school very early on a snow-covered Saturday. In the waiting area I watched a training video while waiting for the instructor. The training video made a very complicated sport seem simple. There are three basic keys to success in shooting sporting clays: stance, mount, and target acquisition. The video taught that if you will learn these three keys, you will be successful at this sport. The shooting instructor came and took me into the gun room, and we started my first lesson. He told me the same thing the video taught. You need to learn three keys to success: stance, mount, and target acquisition. He handed me a shotgun and proceeded to teach me how to take the proper stance (placement of my feet). Once I practiced that a little while, he showed me how to properly mount the gun (bring the gun up to my shoulder). I practiced taking the proper stance and mounting the gun together for a while. Then he moved me on to target acquisition. All three steps were simple and made perfect sense. We spent less than an hour learning and practicing these three basic keys to success.

The instructor took me to the course to begin the real shooting. Surely it could not be that simple. Surely I was not ready for the real deal after learning only three simple principles. We proceeded out to the course, and the instructor explained how the different stations along the course would throw clay targets into the air in a wide variety of ways. He told me that if I would do the three keys he taught, I would be successful no matter where the target came from or what direction it was traveling. "How could three simple techniques make me successful in so many different, unpredictable situations?" I thought. At Station One, I took my stance. He hit the switch and the clay target flew out of a huge tower, toward me high over my head. I mounted the gun to my shoulder and started the process of target acquisition. I squeezed the trigger, and boom! I missed the target. The instructor said, "You had the right stance, you did target acquisition properly, but you did not mount the gun to your shoulder properly. So he gave me a quick refresher on proper mounting of the gun, and we set up to try again. I took my stance, and he hit the switch and another clay target flew over my head from the high tower. I mounted the gun to my shoulder, acquired the target, and squeezed the trigger. The target blew into a million pieces. I was completely surprised. There was no way that I had just hit a fast-moving, small target with less than one hour of training. Maybe it was just luck. We moved to the next station on the course, and the instructor informed me that this station would throw the target in a completely different way, but if I would use the same three keys to success, I would be successful. I took my stance, he hit the switch, and a clay target flew into the air up and away from me. I mounted the gun to my shoulder the same way I had on Station One. I acquired the target, the same way I had on Station One. I squeezed the trigger. Once again, the target exploded into a million pieces. Was it possible that this instructor was right? Was it possible that my success would depend on three simple keys? Was it possible that 80 percent of my success would be dependent on 20 percent of what I do? The instructor said, "Good job," and we moved to the next station. Each station presented a different situation and created a unique challenge. At each station, I applied the same three keys to success: stance, mount, and target acquisition, and I was very successful. No matter what situation or challenge I encountered, the three keys worked. It was amazing.

My first time out in a very complicated sport, I was able to hit 80 to 90 percent of the targets. My success was not based on my great experience or skill. It was based on doing the three simple keys to success that this master instructor taught me and the fact that I was teachable. I could have spent 10 to 20 years trying to figure the sport out on my own, never figuring out the keys to success. I could have spent a lot of money on guns, equipment, and time learning things that were not important to my success. Instead, by learning the few basic keys to success at the very beginning I was able to have success from the start in a very efficient way.

DRIVING A CAR
What if you had to know everything there is to know about a car before you could drive it? That would be ridiculous. There are thousands and thousands of mechanical things going on in a car when you are driving it. Spark plugs are firing, gears are turning, oil is circulating, fans are turning, electricity is flowing, and gauges are monitoring the activities. It would take years and years of study and work to understand all of the things happening when you drive a car.

The good news is that you do not have to understand all of that to be a successful driver. There are only a few key principles you need to know. You need to know how to start, stop, go forward, backward, turn, and that is about it. There are only a few key things you need to know to keep it between the curbs.

The financial world is very similar to driving a car. There are thousands and thousands of things going on, but you only need to know a few key principles (basics) to drive your financial vehicle and successfully arrive at your destination of Financial Success. Later on, after you have mastered the basics, you can pop the hood and learn more about how the details work if that interests you. For now we will stick to the basics that will ensure your success.

So jump in, buckle up, and let's learn the basics of money!

ACTION ITEMS

ACTION 1 →

| Basics of Money |
| Basics of Behavior |
| Marketing Self-Defense |

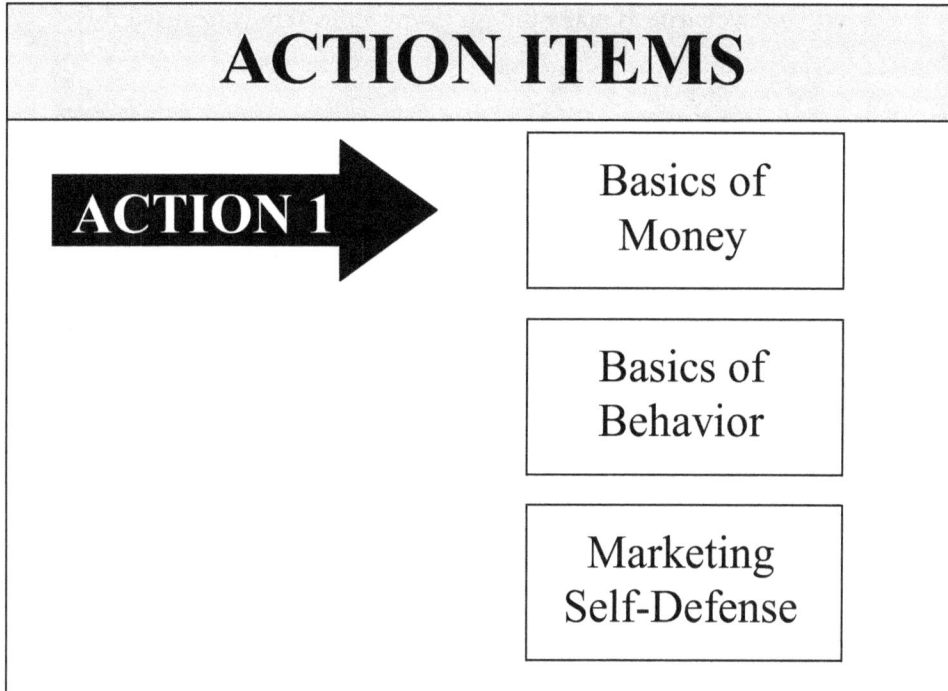

> *The future belongs to those who are prepared.*
> *Unknown*

THE BASICS OF MONEY
THE PARABLE OF THE TALENTS
Note: A "talent" was worth more than a thousand dollars.

"Again, it will be like a man going on a journey, who called his servants and entrusted his property to them. To one he gave five talents of money, to another two talents, and to another one talent, each according to his ability. Then he went on his journey. The man who had received the five talents went at **once and put his money to work and gained five more. So also, the one with the two talents gained two more.** But the man who had received the one talent went off, dug a hole in the ground and hid his master's money.

"After a long time the master of those servants returned and settled accounts with them. The man who had received the five talents brought the other five. 'Master,' he said, 'you entrusted me with five talents. See, I have gained five more.'

"His master replied, 'Well done, good and faithful servant! You have been faithful with a few things; I will put you in charge of many things. Come and share your master's happiness!'

"The man with the two talents also came. 'Master,' he said, 'you entrusted me with two talents; see, I have gained two more.'

"His master replied, 'Well done, good and faithful servant! You have been faithful with a few things; I will put you in charge of many things. Come and share your master's happiness!'

"Then the man who had received the one talent came. 'Master,' he said, 'I knew that you are a hard man, harvesting where you have not sown and gathering where you have not scattered seed. So **I was afraid and went out and hid your talent in the ground**. See, here is what belongs to you.'

"His master replied, **'You wicked, lazy servant!** So you knew that I harvest where I have not sown and gather where I have not scattered seed? Well then, you should have put my money on deposit with the bankers, so that when I returned I would have received it back with interest.

"'Take the talent from him and give it to the one who has the ten talents. For everyone who has will be given more, and he will have an abundance. Whoever does not have, even what he has will be taken from him. And throw that worthless servant outside, into the darkness, where there will be weeping and gnashing of teeth.'"

(Matthew 25:14-30, (New International Version)

As you can see from the Parable of the Talents, the two servants who put the money to work were rewarded and the one who did not put it to work had the money taken away. He was punished for not at least putting the money in the bank to earn interest.

The questions you need to answer when it comes to money are:

- Do you want to work for money, or do you want your money to work for you?

- Do you want to be rewarded as a good and faithful servant or punished as the lazy servant was?

This program is based on:

WORK FOR A DOLLAR ONCE – THEN MAKE IT WORK FOR YOU
Thousands of products and details comprise the world of money and finance. It can seem very complicated, and most people think that in order to be financially successful they need to know all of the sophisticated language. But I have good news. Becoming successful in the world of money is just like becoming a successful driver. Know the basics.

MONEY BASICS

Basic #1	Everything is either **input** or **outgo.**
Basic #2	Put as much of the **outgo to work** as possible.
Basic #3	Use the **Big 3** to build wealth.
Basic #4	**Compound interest** is a powerful ingredient.
Basic #5	**Do not touch it**—let it grow.

> *Capital isn't scarce; vision is.*
>
> *Sam Walton*

BASIC #1

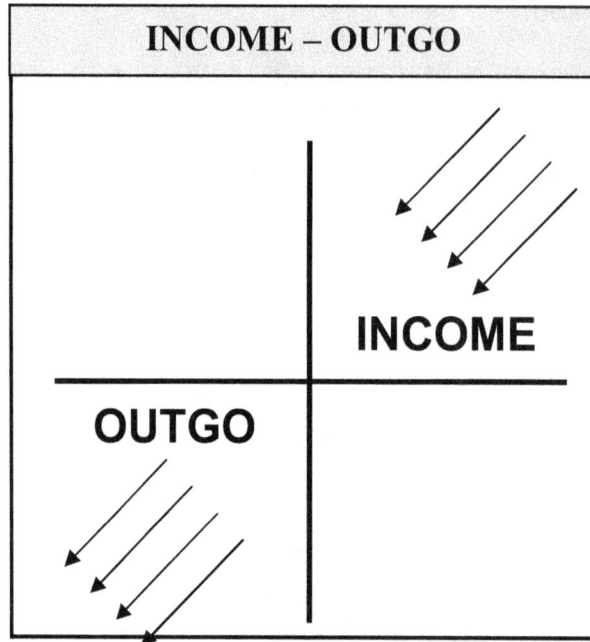

INCOME – OUTGO

INCOME

OUTGO

Here is the good news! Everything in the vast, complicated world of money and finance boils down and fits into one of two categories. Everything in the world of money and finance, in relation to you, is either coming in (income) or going out (outgo).

The reason that it is good news is because it gives you three simple choices on how you can improve your financial situation.

>   1. Improve the income.
>   2. Improve how you manage the outgo.
>   3. Improve both.

In this program we will spend most of our time improving the outgo category. Most of our lives, we are taught how to make an income. We are told when we are young to study hard so we can get a good job and make a lot of money. We spend our years in school preparing to get a good job. We spend our working years working hard to get raises and promotions. We take additional school and training so we can make more money. Our whole culture is designed to teach us how to make and increase our income.

The issue is not the income as much as it is the outgo. The average person spends countless hours and dollars learning to make money, yet they spend almost no time or money learning how to manage their money once they earn it. In the classes I have taught, I ask the participants to raise their hand if they were formally taught how to manage their money. Only one or two in 100 will raise their hand. Very few people are taught anything about how to manage their money and be financially successful. It is not taught in school, and few parents know how or what to teach their children when it comes to the basic key success factors that will lead to Financial Success. My guess is that you too have spent a lot of time learning and preparing to make money, but very little time learning or preparing how to manage it and make it grow once you receive it.

In this program, we will spend 99 percent of our efforts on choice #2, improving outgo. I do not want you to even consider increasing your income until you have a great handle on how to manage the outgo.

I am convinced that when your income increases, you will have more of what you have now. So, if you currently make $50, 000 a year and are in a financial mess, then at $100,000 a year you would simply have twice the mess you have now. It is a fantasy to think that having more money will solve your financial troubles. The reality is that more money will give you more of what you have now.

He who is faithful in a very little thing is faithful also in much; and he who is unrighteous in a very little thing is unrighteous also in much. **Luke 16:10**

Wanting to increase your income when your outgo is out of control is like stepping on the gas when your car is out of control.

THINGS WILL ONLY GET WORSE!
Get the car (outgo) under control and going in the right direction first—then you can step on the gas (increase income).

If you currently make $50,000 a year, and you are doing fabulous financially, then it is a good bet that with a $100,000 annual income, you would be twice as financially successful as you are now.

Let us get to the goal of a great financial life by teaching you to be a world-class success on the outgo, and then you can explore ways to increase your income. Focus on the outgo.

> *Tell your money what to do.*
> *Do not ask it what it did.*

BASIC #2

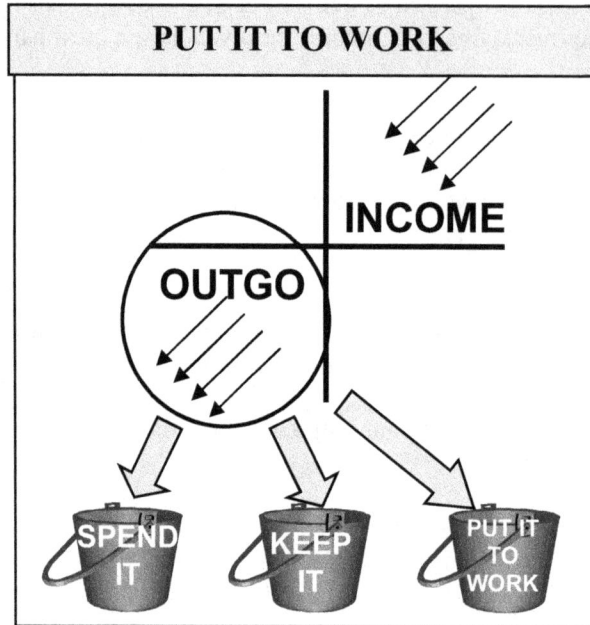

MONEY CYCLE

Bucket # 1 – You spend it.
Bucket # 2 – You keep it.
Bucket # 3 – You put it to work.

Here is some more good news—everything you do in the outgo fits into one of three categories. With every dollar you receive, you spend it, keep it or put it to work.

These three simple categories help you understand in simple terms what is going on with your money and how to manage it so you can improve your financial situation.

One of the main goals of this program is to help you develop and maintain the right balance of these three categories. It will help you get the right amount of dollars in the spending, keeping, and putting to work categories. If you get these three categories where they should be, you can build a great financial life.

Bucket # 1: Spend it.

These are dollars that you spend to live your life. You spend them on consumable things like food, utilities, credit card interest, etc., that will not increase in value or make you additional dollars. These are dollars that are spent so when they are gone, they will never return.

Bucket # 2: Keep it.

These are dollars that you do not spend, but you have not put them to work for you. They are sitting in jars and drawers around your house, sitting in checking accounts at the bank that are not earning interest, or sitting in a savings account that is earning so little interest that when you consider inflation you are actually losing money. It is good that you have these dollars. You did not spend them, but it would be better if they were working for you to earn more dollars.

Bucket # 3: Put it to work.

These are dollars that are working for you to make more dollars. They are in your 401(k) plan working for you 24 hours every day, 365 days a year, year after year to make more dollars for you. These are dollars you have invested in assets that increase in value or generate income for you. In a nutshell, they are dollars that make more dollars.

BUCKET GOALS

Bucket # 1: Spend it.

The goal for this bucket is to reduce the amount of dollars you spend without changing your lifestyle too much and then move the dollars saved into the Put It To Work category. There are many ways to reduce your spending without dramatically changing your lifestyle.

Every dollar that you are able to move from the Spend It category to the Put It To Work category can become an employee that will work for you 24/7/365. The exciting news is that these dollars' children (interest) and grandchildren (compound interest) and all their generations to come can work for you for the rest of your life. Every dollar you can move from the Spend It category into the Put It To Work category can have a powerful effect on your financial future.

Bucket # 2: Keep it.

The goal is to make sure you have the right amount in this bucket. There is a certain amount of money that you will want to maintain in this category. For example, Step 6 - Emergency Fund and Step 8 - Survival Fund will be kept in this category. The dollars in these funds are there to protect you in cases of emergency and survival situations. Their main duty is to protect you, not to build great wealth as fast as possible. They will need to be accessible if you need them and will typically earn less return than the dollars in the Put It To Work category. Our goal in this category is not to move all of the funds from this bucket to the Put It To Work bucket, but to make sure you have the correct amounts in each bucket.

Bucket # 3: Put it to work.

The goal for this bucket is to get as many dollars as you can working for you at the highest return possible for as long as possible. This is the category that will help you reach your goal of a great financial life by building wealth 24/7/365. This program will help redirect dollars from the Spend

It and Keeping It buckets to the Put It To Work bucket so you can turn your dollars into employees. They can help you build the fabulous financial future you want.

When you increase this category, you are increasing your income without having to get a better job or an additional job that could take you away from your family. The goal is to put your money to work.

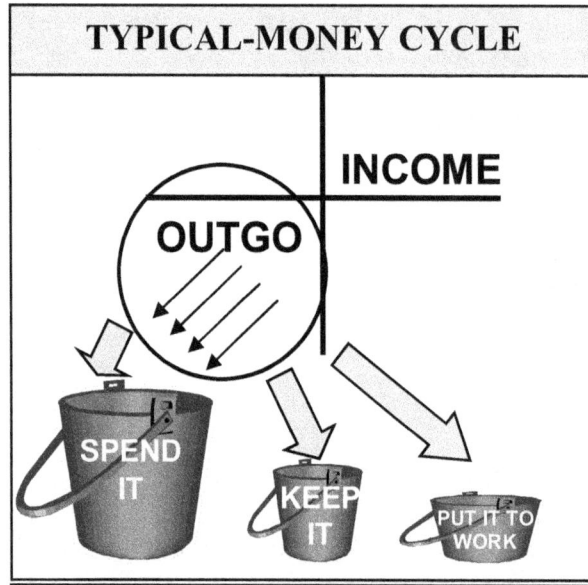

TYPICAL-MONEY CYCLE

The illustration above shows how money flows in the typical person's life. Income flows in, and then it flows out into the three buckets of outgo. For the typical person in today's culture, almost all of the income flows out through the Spend It bucket and never returns. In many cases, people spend even more than they make by using credit cards and other debt vehicles. If people are spending all of their income, then they can not keep it or put it to work. I will show you how to move some of the money you are spending to the Keep It and Put It to Work buckets. Then you will be well on your way to a great financial life.

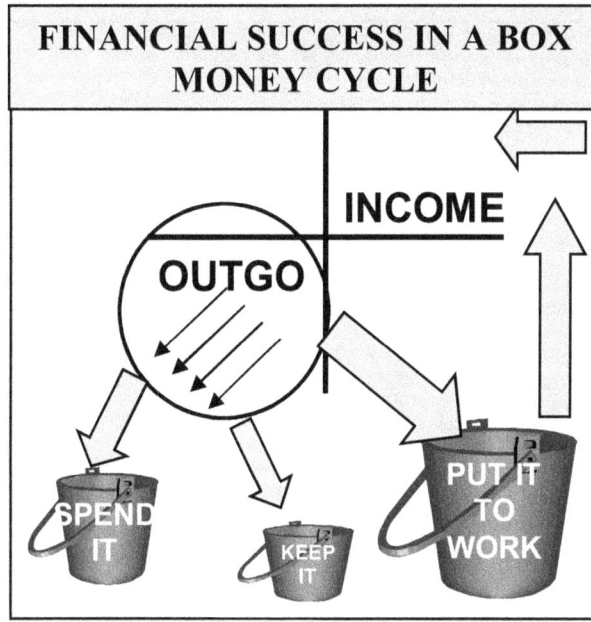

FINANCIAL SUCCESS IN A BOX
MONEY CYCLE

The illustration above shows how you want your money to flow. Income flows in and then it flows out into the three buckets of Outgo just as it did in the previous illustration. But in this illustration the proportions that flow into each of the three buckets are different. Instead of most or all of the money flowing into the Spend It bucket, some of the money has been redirected to the Keep It and Put It To Work buckets. As more and more money is *redirected* from the Spend It bucket to the Keep It bucket and the Put It To Work buckets, you begin to generate additional income from the money you have put to work, and suddenly your income begins to grow without having to work any additional hours or any harder. This program will show you step-by-step how to redirect money from the Spend It bucket to the Put It To Work bucket. You will be amazed how financially successful you can become by doing that over time.

Next, I will introduce you to the Big 3 of money. Once you understand the Big 3, you will understand why getting the proper balance between these three categories is important. You will understand why it is so important to get as many dollars as possible working for you in the Put It To Work bucket.

BASIC #3

THE BIG 3

TIME

AMOUNT   INTEREST

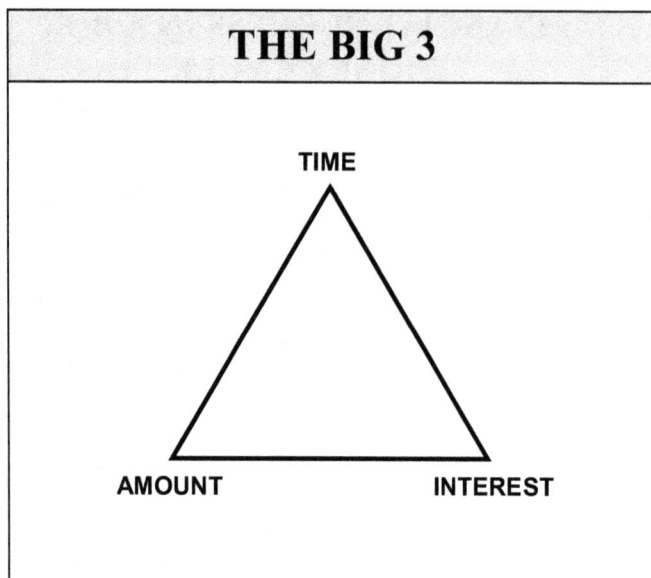

The Big 3 are the three key elements you need to make money grow. The Big 3 of the world of money are amount, interest, and time. Amount is the amount of money you put to work, interest is the rate of return your money makes, and time is the length of time you put it to work. The Big 3 are the main forces working in the world of money. If you can learn how to harness the power of these three forces and put them to work for you, you can reach amazing levels of Financial Success.

> How to turn $100 per month into $1 million dollars? How to turn $100 per month into $76 million dollars? *Use the awesome power of the Big 3.*

THE BIG 3 AT WORK

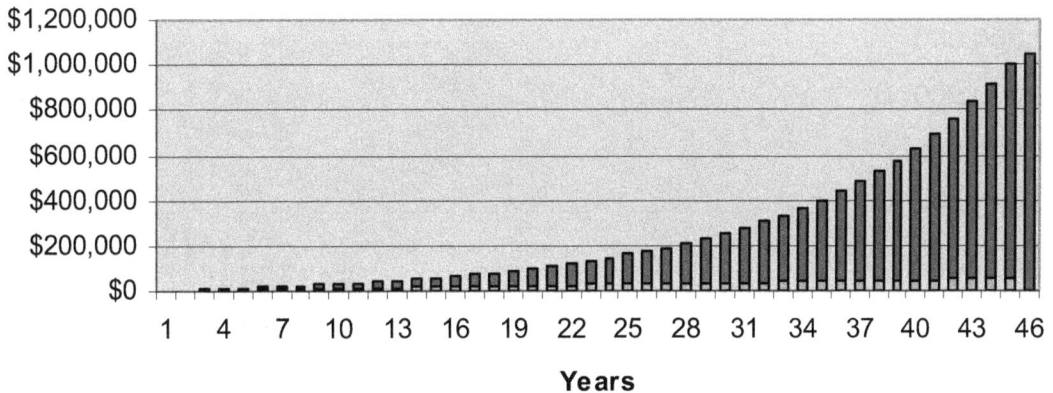

In the graph above, you can see the Big 3 at work. This graph illustrates a person putting $100 a month to work with a return rate of 10 percent for 46 years.

Amount	$100 per month
Return	10%
Time	46 years
Total	**$1,045,170**

The Big 3 work together to generate a total of $1,045,170.
Contribution: $55,200 ($100 x 12 mo x 46 yrs).
Amount of interest generated = $998,970

The Big 3 worked together to turn $55,200 into $1,045,170. That is very powerful. Now you can see why Rule #1 is Put Your Money To Work.

QUESTION: Which of the Big 3 is the *most* powerful?

A. Amount
B. Return
C. Time
D. They are all equally powerful.

One way to find out which of the Big 3 is the most powerful is to double each one and see how the final amount is impacted.

DOUBLE THE AMOUNT

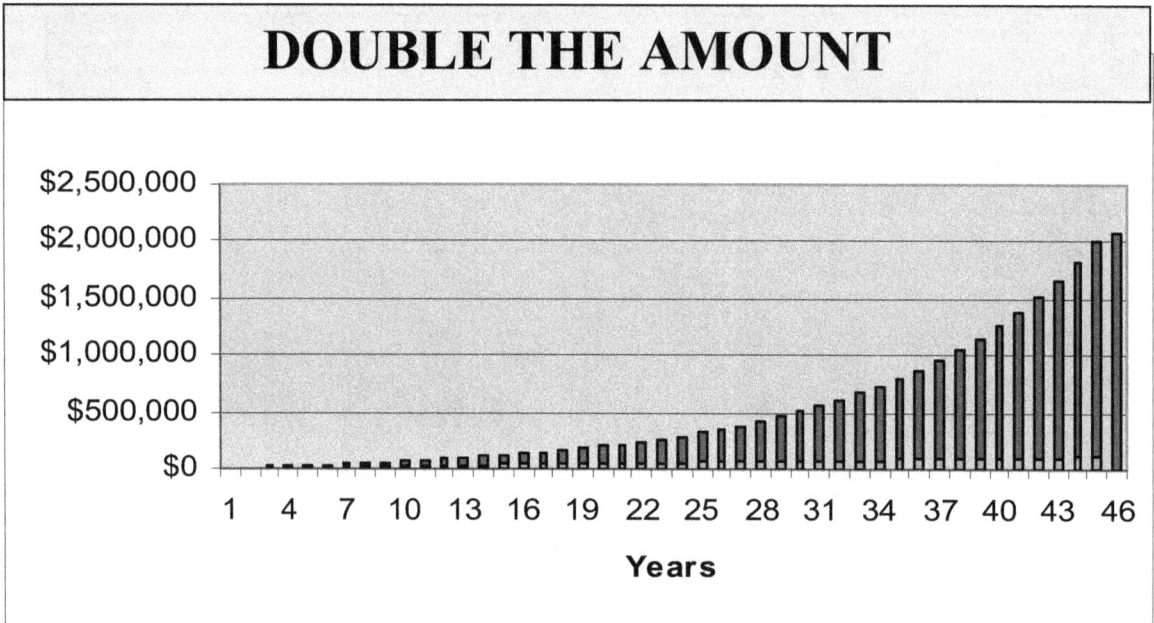

DOUBLE THE AMOUNT

$2,500,000 —
$2,000,000 —
$1,500,000 —
$1,000,000 —
$500,000 —
$0 —

1   4   7   10   13   16   19   22   25   28   31   34   37   40   43   46

Years

Double the amount and compare this to the final amount generated. In the diagram above the amount contributed is doubled to equal $200 per month. The return rate remained at 10 percent and the time remained at 46 years.

Amount	$200 per month
Return	10%
Time	46 years
Total	**$2,090,340**

As you can see, the total amount at the end of the 46 years has also doubled from **$1,045,170** to **$2,090,340.**

If you double the amount contributed, you will also double the total amount you have at the end. Remember, we kept the return rate and time the same.

DOUBLE THE RETURN RATE

DOUBLE THE INTEREST

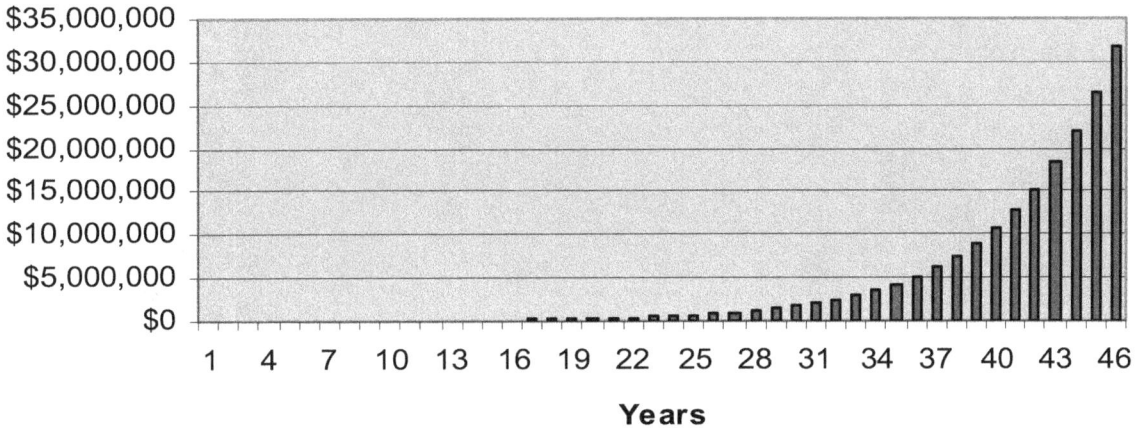

Now, double the return rate and see how it impacts the total amount generated. As you can see, the return rate doubled from 10 percent to 20 percent, but the amount and time stayed the same.

Amount	$100 per month
Return	20%
Time	46 years
Total	**$31,591,544**

The result of doubling the return rate from 10 percent to 20 percent is astonishing. You are still contributing $55,200 over the 46-year period, but the total amount you have at the end is $31,591,544. That is 30 times more than the total amount of $1,045,170 at 10 percent.

So in this example, if the return rate is doubled, the total amount generated is increased 30 times. That is an amazing increase! The return rate increased by 100 percent, but the total amount generated increased by 3,000 percent from $1,045,170 to $31,591,544.

By increasing the return rate from 10 percent to 20 percent, you allow the Big 3 to work even harder and turn $55,200 into $31,591,544.

The return rate that your money gets has a huge impact on your future financial success. That is why it is so important that you do not keep a lot of your money in a bank account earning a measly 1 to 3 percent. Your money needs to be earning the highest return rate possible that you determine to be safe and prudent.

DOUBLE TIME PERIOD

DOUBLE THE TIME PERIOD

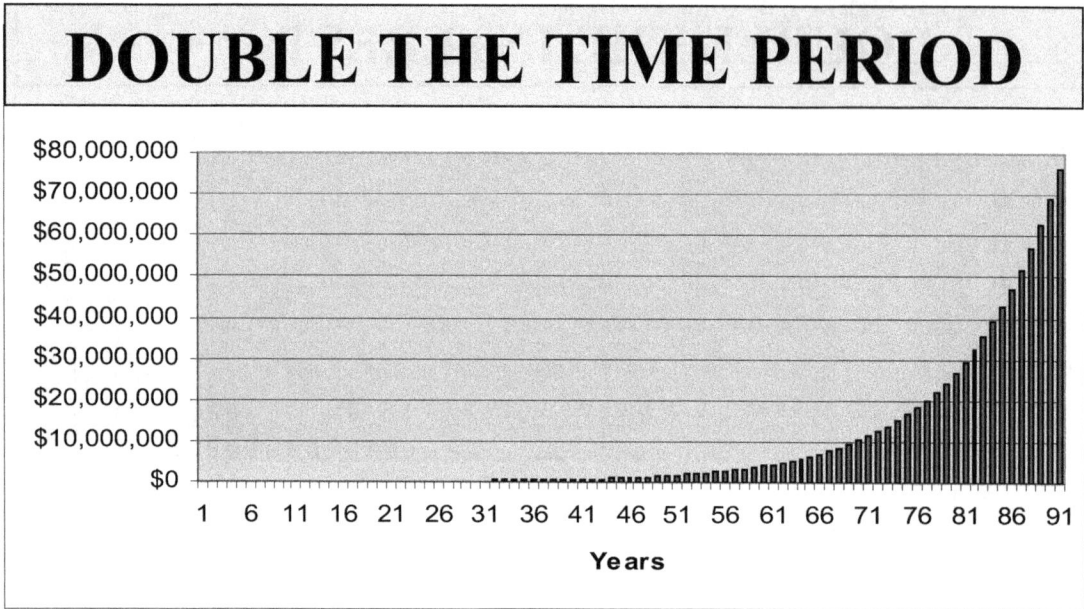

The graph above shows the results of increasing the time period to 91 years. The time period is increased from 46 years to 91 years, but the amount and return rate stay the same—an amount of $100 per month contributed for only 46 years. Then you stop making deposits and it grows on interest alone. Yes, 91 years is possible—think generationally. This is how generations keep their wealth.

Amount	$100 per month (46 years)
Return	10%
Time	91 years
Total	**$76,182,933**

The result of increasing the time period from 46 years to 91 years is staggering. You are still contributing $55,200 with a return rate of 10 percent, but the total amount you will have at the end is $76,182,933. That is 72 times more than the total amount of $1,045,170 at 46 years.

In this example, if you double the time period you increase the total amount generated 72 times. That is an amazing increase. The time period increased by 100 percent, but the total amount generated increased by 7,200 percent from $1,045,170 to $76,182,933.

By increasing the time period from 46 years to 91 years, you allow the Big 3 to work even harder, and they turned $55,200 into $76,182,933.

IN SUMMARY

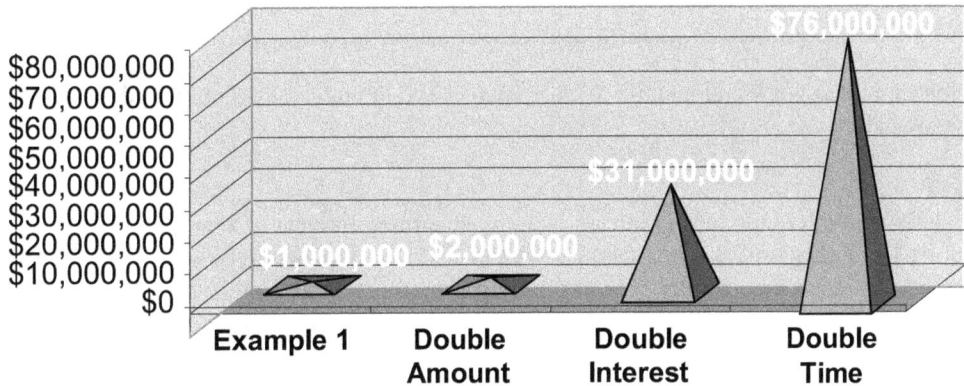

THE BIG 3
Which is the most powerful?

As you can see in the illustration above:

If you double the amount, the outcome increases 2 times.
If you double the return rate, the outcome increases 31 times.
If you double the time, the outcome increases 72 times.

QUESTION: Which of the Big 3 is the most powerful?

        A. Amount
        B. Return
        C. Time
        D. They are all equally powerful.

If you answered C, you were correct. When it comes to the Big 3, time is the most powerful, followed by return rate, then amount.

> *The line between failure and success is so fine that we scarcely know when we pass it; so fine that we are often on the line and do not know it.*
> *Elbert Hubbard*

BASIC #4
COMPOUND INTEREST

> *The most powerful force in the universe is*
> *compound interest.*
> *Albert Einstein*

When you put money to work and it starts to earn interest and the interest is compounded, it is like a financial snowball.

WHAT IS IT
The simple definition of compounding interest is interest earning interest. Compounding is a financial snowball. Every time the financial snowball rolls over, it picks up more snow (interest) and gets bigger. The next time it rolls over, it picks up even more snow (interest) and gets even bigger because the snow picked up on the last roll picks up even more snow on each additional roll. Over time, the snow (interest) picked up on the way down the hill is much more than the original snowball with which you started.

HOW IT WORKS
If you take $ 10,000 and invest it (put it to work) in a money market fund earning 10 percent annual interest and the 10 percent interest is reinvested each year for 45 years, the interest earns more interest and grows to $728,905.

COMPOUND INTEREST

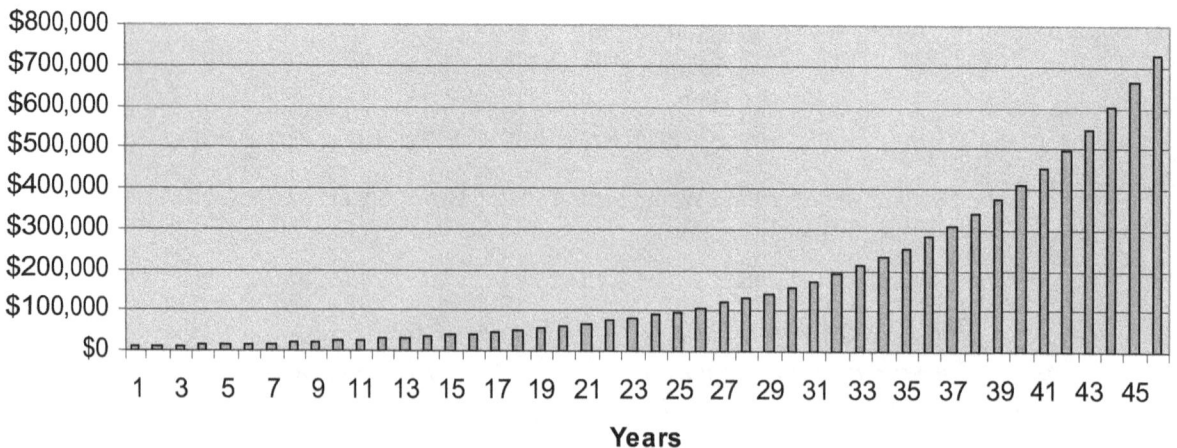

Here is what it would look like as a financial snowball.

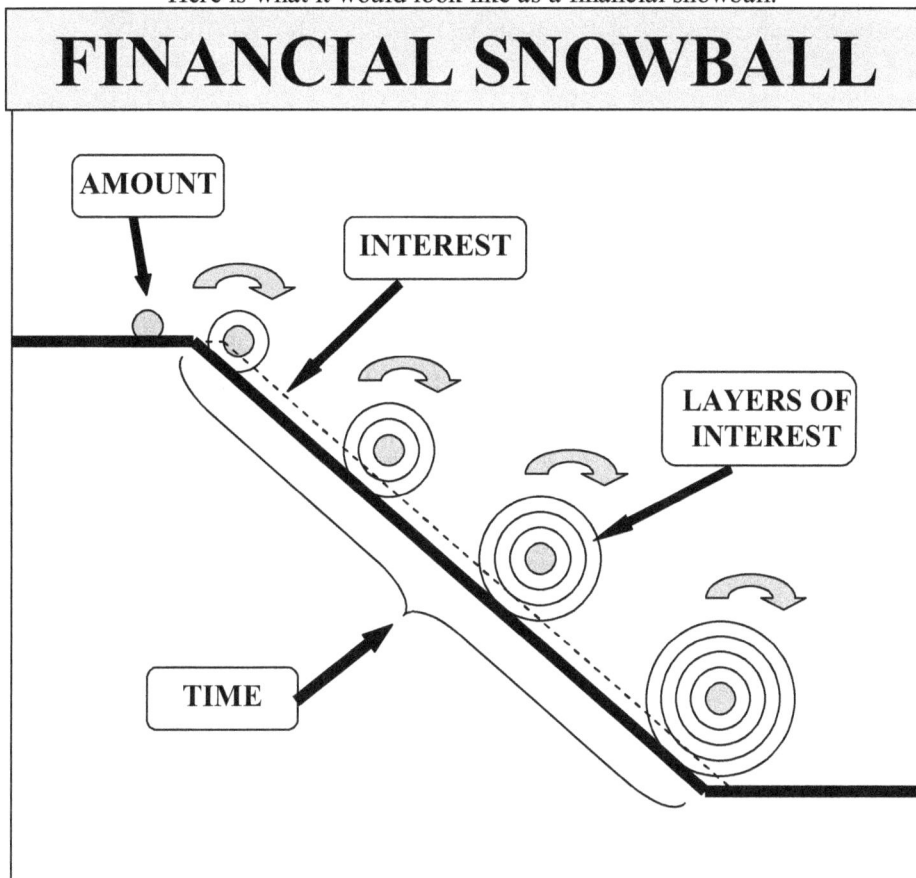

FINANCIAL SNOWBALL

AMOUNT

INTEREST

LAYERS OF INTEREST

TIME

FINANCIAL SNOWBALL

Picture standing on the top of a hill. The $10,000 is the initial snowball that you will be rolling down the hill. The depth of the snow on the hill is the interest rate—the higher the interest rate, the deeper the snow on the hill. A snowball rolling down a hill with a 10 percent layer of snow on the hill will pick up more snow, grow faster, and become bigger than a snowball rolling down a hill with a 4 percent layer of snow. The length of the hill to the bottom is how many years you want the snowball to roll. If you arc 20 years old, your snowball can roll for more years than if you are 40 years old (not considering generational wealth).

Every time this financial snowball rolls over, it picks up more snow (interest) and gets bigger. The next time it rolls over it picks up even more snow (interest). Every bit of snow (interest) you pick up on this roll will pick up even more interest on the next roll. If you let this snowball roll and grow, it can become an avalanche.

The Big 3 are the three key ingredients you need to make money grow. Add the fourth ingredient of compounding, and money will grow extremely fast. There are several keys to making the biggest snowball possible.

- **Amount** – This is the size of the initial snowball (principal). The bigger the initial snowball, the more snow it will begin to pick up as it rolls down the hill.

- **Interest** – This is the return rate. The depth of the snow (interest rate) determines how much snow it will pick up on each roll. The higher the interest rate, the deeper the layer of snow on the hill. The deeper the snow, the more it will pick up on each roll and the bigger it will get. You want your snowball on the slopes with the deepest snow. Bank savings accounts are like rolling your snowball down a hill with very little snow. It can even start losing snow when you consider inflation.

- **Time** – This is the number of years to roll. The snowball makes one roll every year. The more years it can roll, the bigger it will get.

You can add to the principal as it is rolling down the hill in addition to the snow (interest) it is picking up on each roll. You can make contributions to make the snowball bigger, and it will pick up even more snow on the next roll.

Do not ever take snow off the snowball. If you make the snowball smaller by withdrawing money, it will pick up less snow on the next roll.

When you start your 401(k), you are pushing a snowball over the edge. Every month you are making a contribution that makes the snowball bigger. Every time it rolls over, it picks up more snow (interest) and gets bigger and bigger with every roll. Your employer and the government add snow to the snowball as well.

When you fund an IRA or a Roth IRA, you are pushing a snowball over the edge. It rolls and rolls and with each roll picks up another layer of snow (interest) and it gets bigger and bigger and bigger.

The powerful wealth-generating principle of compounding interest is the major reason that Put It To Work is early in this Step by Step process. I want your snowball (401(k)) to be rolling down the hill getting bigger while you complete the other steps.

The Big 3 will work *for* you or *against* you. It is up to you.

In Step 5 - Put It To Work, we will put the powerful Big 3, with the added power of compounding interest, to work. We will get your first financial snowball rolling down the hill and growing bigger and bigger each year.

THE POWER OF COMPOUNDING

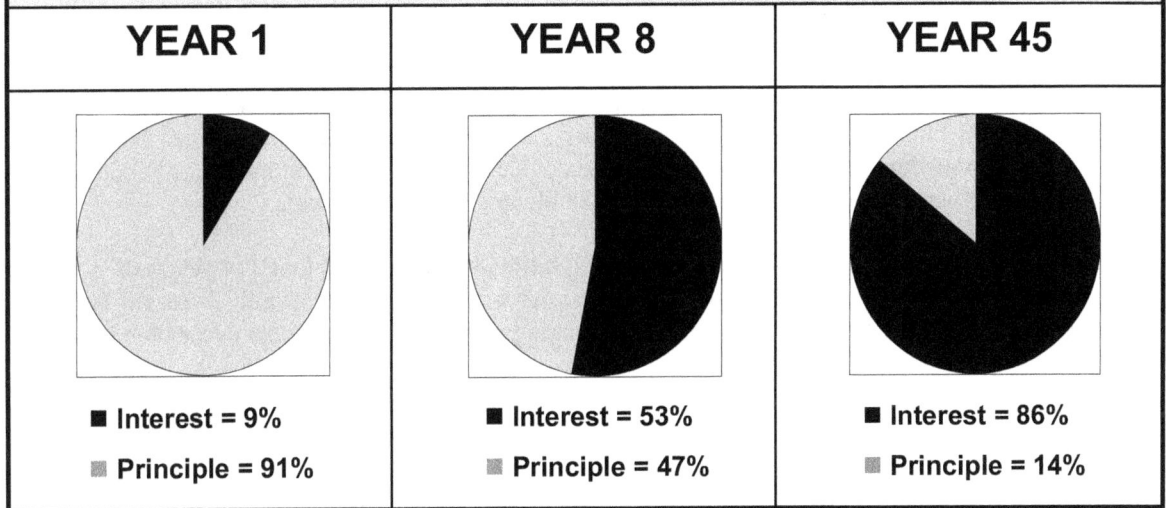

YEAR 1	YEAR 8	YEAR 45
■ Interest = 9%	■ Interest = 53%	■ Interest = 86%
▒ Principle = 91%	▒ Principle = 47%	▒ Principle = 14%

How does $10,000 turn into $728,905 without adding any money to it? The answer is that the Big 3 working together are turbocharged by the power of compounding.

In the diagram above, at the end of year 1 the original $10,000 principal has earned (picked up) $1,000 of interest. The $1,000 of interest earned in Year 1 will generate interest in Year 2. The interest generated in Year 2 will begin to generate interest in Year 3, and it will continue to grow larger and larger every year for as long as it rolls down the hill. The original $10,000 (principal) will continue to generate $1,000 (10 percent) interest every year as it rolls down the hill, but the amount of interest generated by interest will grow larger every year until it becomes much larger than the original $10,000 principle with which you started.

At the end of Year 8, the amount of interest has grown larger than the original $10,000 principle. The total is now $21,436, and interest is now 53 percent of the total. The financial snowball has more than doubled in size by the end of Year 8. Again, the original $10,000 principal will continue to generate another $1,000 in interest each year, but the amount of interest generated by interest continues to get larger each year.

At the end of year 45, the total amount of the financial snowball has reached $728,905. The amount of interest is $718,905. The interest generated now makes up 86 percent of the total snowball. The original $10,000 principle you started with makes up only 14 percent of the total.

If the interest were not compounded, you would end up with a total of only $55,000 at the end of 45 years ($10,000 principle + [$1,000 interest x 45 years] = $55,000). But when you compound the interest and interest earns more interest, you end up with a whopping $728,905. Compounding added a staggering $673,905 to your total!

This example illustrates the incredible power of compounding interest and shows you why it is so important to put your money to work.

THE RULE OF 72

The Rule of 72 is a simple tool that will help you quickly calculate how fast your financial snowball will double in size with compounding interest. The Rule of 72 states that in order to find out how many years it will take for your money (snowball) to double in size, you simply divide the interest rate into 72.

For example, if you want to know how long it will take your money to double in size at 10 percent interest, divide 10 into 72 and the answer is 7 (years). Your snowball will double in size every 7 years. To calculate how long it will take money to double in size at 5 percent interest, divide 5 into 72 and you get 14 years. The snowball will double in size every 14 years.

A money snowball rolling down a 5 percent interest hill will take twice as long (14 years) to double in size as the same money snowball rolling down a 10 percent interest hill (7 years). The money snowball on the 10 percent interest hill is picking up twice as much snow every time it rolls over.

The Rule of 72 is a very simple, useful tool that will allow you to quickly estimate how long it will take your money snowball to double in size.
[Interest rate divided into 72 = numbers of years to double]

BASIC #5
DO NOT TOUCH IT

Once you put your money to work, you need to make sure that you do not touch it. If you are continually taking money out of the financial snowball you have created, you will stifle its growth and drastically reduce the total amount that you have years later. In Step 6 – Emergency Fund, I will show you how to build an emergency fund to protect yourself from taking money from the snowball when the car or furnace needs repair. In Step 8 – Survival Fund, I will show you how to build a survival fund that will protect you and your family from major emergencies such as the loss of a job. The survival fund will pay your living expenses for extended periods of time (3 to 12 months) so you will not be tempted to take money from your financial snowball. It is a great feeling to get on the other side of a major financial crisis and be able to say, "I am so glad I did not have to touch the financial snowball to make it through. The snowball continued to grow at full speed and is continuing to grow."

Putting your money to work is a long term strategy to build wealth. You need to make a commitment that you will not touch your financial snowball—no matter what!
It is important to remember these basics of money as we move forward in this program. They will be key factors when we begin to build your financial future. It will also be important to understand how the basics work against you when you owe money in the form of credit cards, home mortgages, and other types of debt.
So let us end with a quick review.

THE BASICS OF MONEY

Basic #1	Everything is either **input** or **outgo.**
Basic #2	Put as much of the **outgo to work** as possible.
Basic #3	Use the **Big 3** to build wealth.
Basic #4	**Compound interest** is a powerful ingredient.
Basic #5	**Do not touch it**—let it grow.

Just like the clay target illustration and the driving the car illustration, if you will learn and apply these five basic principles as we move forward on our journey to a great financial life, you can be very successful in the world of money.

> *Talent alone won't make you a success. Neither will being in the right place at the right time, unless you are ready. The most important question is: Are you ready?*
>
> *Johnny Carson*

HOW BIG CAN THE BIG 3 GROW?

Use the table on the next page to see what the total will be of your Big 3. Example 1: $3.33 per day or $100 per month will be worth $21,037 at the end of year 10. Example 2: $10.00 per day or $300 per month will be worth $1,073,256 at the end of year 35.

(All amounts are based on a 10 percent return compounded, which is historically a common calculation to use over time.)

Per Day	3.33	5.00	6.66	8.33	10.00	16.66
Per Month	$100	$150	$200	$250	300	$500
Year 1	$1,320	$1,980	$2,640	$3,300	$3,960	$6,600
	$2,772	$4,158	$5,544	$6,930	$8,316	$13,860
	$4,369	$6,554	$8,738	$10,923	$13,108	$21,846
	$6,126	$9,189	$12,252	$15,315	$18,378	$30,631
Year 5	$8,059	$12,088	$16,117	$20,147	$24,176	$40,294
	$10,185	$15,277	$20,369	$25,462	$30,554	$50,923
	$12,523	$18,785	$25,046	$31,308	$37,569	$62,615
	$15,095	$22,643	$30,191	$37,738	$45,286	$75,477
	$17,925	$26,887	$35,850	$44,812	$53,775	$89,625
Year 10	$21,037	$31,556	$42,075	$52,594	$63,112	$105,187
	$24,461	$36,692	$48,922	$61,153	$73,383	$122,306
	$28,227	$42,341	$56,455	$70,568	$84,682	$141,136
	$32,370	$48,555	$64,740	$80,925	$97,110	$161,850
	$36,927	$55,390	$73,854	$92,317	$110,781	$184,635
Year 15	$41,940	$62,910	$83,879	$104,849	$125,819	$209,698
	$47,454	$71,180	$94,907	$118,634	$142,361	$237,268
	$53,519	$80,279	$107,038	$133,798	$160,557	$267,595
	$60,191	$90,286	$120,382	$150,477	$180,573	$300,955
	$67,530	$101,295	$135,060	$168,825	$202,590	$337,650
Year 20	$75,603	$113,404	$151,206	$189,007	$226,809	$378,015
	$84,483	$126,725	$168,967	$211,208	$253,450	$422,416
	$94,252	$141,377	$188,503	$235,629	$282,755	$471,258
	$104,997	$157,495	$209,994	$262,492	$314,990	$524,984
	$116,816	$175,225	$233,633	$292,041	$350,449	$584,082
Year 25	$129,818	$194,727	$259,636	$324,545	$389,454	$649,091
	$144,120	$216,180	$288,240	$360,300	$432,360	$720,600
	$159,852	$239,778	$319,704	$399,630	$479,556	$799,260
	$177,157	$265,736	$354,314	$442,893	$531,471	$885,786
	$196,193	$294,289	$392,386	$490,482	$588,578	$980,964
Year 30	$217,132	$325,698	$434,264	$542,830	$651,396	$1,085,661
	$240,165	$360,248	$480,331	$600,413	$720,496	$1,200,827
	$265,502	$398,253	$531,004	$663,755	$796,506	$1,327,509
	$293,372	$440,058	$586,744	$733,430	$880,116	$1,466,860
	$324,029	$486,044	$648,058	$810,073	$972,088	$1,620,146
Year 35	$357,752	$536,628	$715,504	$894,380	$1,073,256	$1,788,761
	$394,847	$592,271	$789,695	$987,118	$1,184,542	$1,974,237
	$435,652	$653,478	$871,304	$1,089,130	$1,306,956	$2,178,261
	$480,537	$720,806	$961,075	$1,201,343	$1,441,612	$2,402,687
	$529,911	$794,867	$1,059,822	$1,324,778	$1,589,733	$2,649,555
Year 40	$584,222	$876,333	$1,168,444	$1,460,555	$1,752,667	$2,921,111
	$643,964	$965,947	$1,287,929	$1,609,911	$1,931,893	$3,219,822
	$709,681	$1,064,521	$1,419,362	$1,774,202	$2,129,042	$3,548,404
	$781,969	$1,172,953	$1,563,938	$1,954,922	$2,345,907	$3,909,845
	$861,486	$1,292,229	$1,722,972	$2,153,715	$2,584,457	$4,307,429
Year 45	$948,954	$1,423,432	$1,897,909	$2,372,386	$2,846,863	$4,744,772

You have learned the basics of money. Now it is time to learn the basics of behavior.

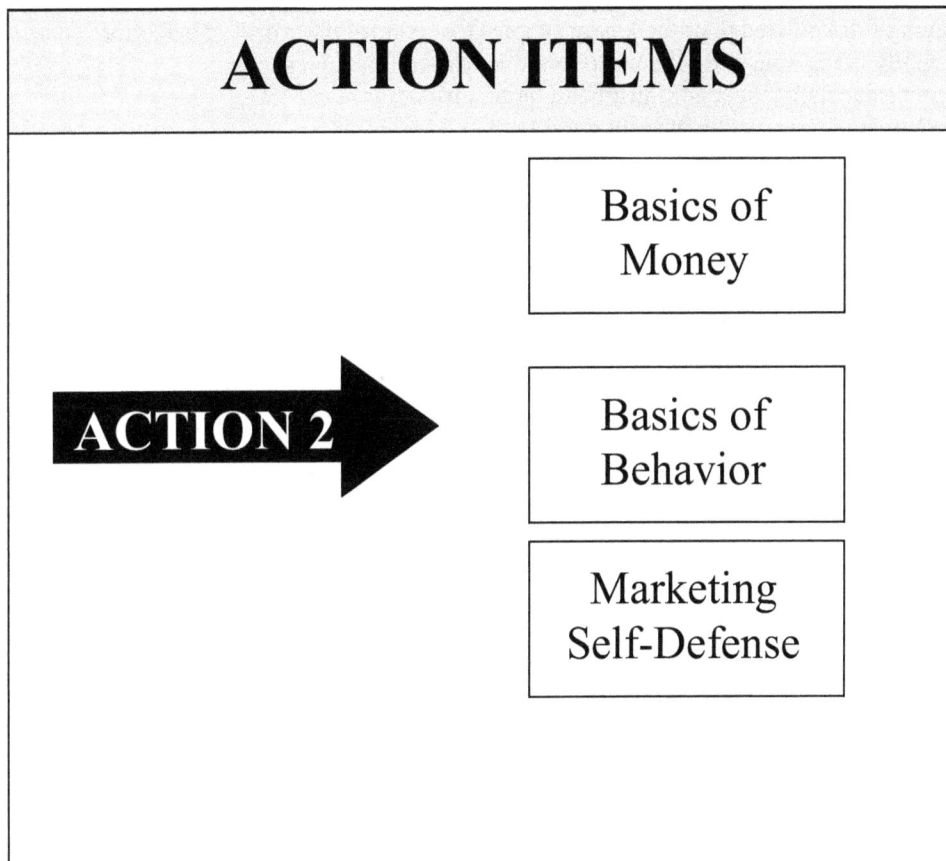

ACTION ITEMS

Basics of Money

ACTION 2 →

Basics of Behavior

Marketing Self-Defense

We are what we repeatedly do. Excellence, then, is not an act, but a habit.

Aristotle

IMAGINE

Imagine
- Having full knowledge of the key principles that control the world of behavior
- Actually being able to do the behaviors that lead to financial success
- Being financially successful just being yourself
- Turning bad financial habits into good financial habits
- Being able to do the right behaviors without even having to think about it

Behavior is what you do—the actions you take. There are certain things you must do and things you must not do to be financially successful. People who have financial success in their lives do the things that result in financial success. People who are financially frustrated have been doing those things that result in financial frustration.

Having the correct behavior is responsible for 80 percent of your financial success. What you know is responsible for only 20 percent of your financial success. It is all about the behavior.

> *80% BEHAVIOR*
> *20% KNOWLEDGE*

In this section I will teach you the basics of behavior. I will show you how behavior works and give you the simple tools and techniques to turn bad behaviors into good behaviors. I will show you how to actually do the things you need to do to be successful financially and reach a great financial life.

BEHAVIOR BASICS

Basic #1	Have a powerful goal.
Basic #2	It is right or wrong.
Basic #3	Keep the right; stop the wrong.
Basic #4	Make it a habit.

BASIC #1
A POWERFUL GOAL

Having a powerful goal is very important when it comes to the subject of behavior. A powerful goal gives you the reason and the motivation to have the right behavior. It gives you the reason to change wrong behaviors into right behaviors.

I have provided a powerful goal for you. It is the goal of a great financial life. Your powerful goal is the wonderful lifestyle you will have when you have accomplished the 10 simple steps in this program.

There is a radio channel that every person listens to on a very regular basis. It is called WII – FM. It stands for **What's In It For Me?** So what's in this for you? Why should you go through the trouble of changing your behavior? Here is what's in it for you:

Imagine how great your life will be when you reach a great financial life and have a score of 10 on all 10 steps.

You will:

- **WORK TOGETHER** with loved ones toward common financial goals
- Know the **BASICS of MONEY, BEHAVIOR and MARKETING**
- **GIVE** on a regular basis
- Have a cash **EMERGENCY FUND** of $1,000 or more
- Have a cash **SURVIVAL FUND** to pay your living expenses for 3 to 12 months
- Have a simple **RETIREMENT PLAN** that is automatically growing bigger and will be large enough for a great retirement
- **PAY YOUR HOUSE OFF** years early and save tens of thousands of dollars
- Have zero **CONSUMER DEBT**
  - No credit card debt
  - No student loan debt
  - No furniture payments
  - No car payments
  - No debt payments of any kind (except house payment)
- Have all financial information, documents, and tools in one **EASY-TO-FIND** location
- Have confidence that your loved ones would be **PROTECTED** if something happened to you
- Have a **GREAT FINANCIAL LIFE** to pursue your real dreams
- Know how to **TEACH YOUR CHILDREN** to be financially strong.

The great financial life is your powerful goal. It is a powerful reason to adopt the right behaviors and change your wrong behaviors. Stop for a few minutes and really think about how nice it will be when you reach this destination. A great financial life is a powerful thing to have.

DRIVE THE STAKE

I was told the story of a young boy who was watching his grandfather plow a field. This was back before tractors when they used horses to pull the plow. He asked his granddad, "How do you get the rows so straight?" His grandfather told him, "The secret is to take a wooden stake and drive it into the ground at the end of the field. Then I get behind the plow, and I start toward the stake. I never take my eyes off of the stake. I may fall down, I may hit a rock, but no matter what happens, I never take my eyes off of that stake, and I never give up moving toward it. With determination and focus, I reach that stake."

The great part is once you get the first row completed the rest of the rows are easy—you do not even need the stake. You just let the first row guide you. If you do not drive that stake, you could end up wandering all over the field, and it would end up a mess. That stake determines how the entire field will end up. This story illustrates the way I want you to think about the 10 steps. The 10 steps are your stake.

Plow one row at a time. The rows before make the next rows easier. You may stumble, you may hit a few rocks, you may even fall down, but if you will keep your eyes on the stake of a great financial life and keep moving, you can make it.

> *The secret of getting ahead is getting started.*
> *The secret of getting started is breaking your*
> *complex overwhelming tasks into small manageable*
> *tasks, and then starting on the first one.*
> *Mark Twain*

BASIC #2
RIGHT OR WRONG

> *IF YOU KEEP DOING WHAT YOU ARE DOING*
> *WILL YOU GET WHERE YOU WANT TO GO?*

The good news is that all behaviors fall into one of two categories. Every behavior is either right or wrong in relation to whether it takes you toward your goal or takes you away from it. This is powerful news, because there are millions of different behaviors. The fact that you can put them in one of two categories gives you a simple place to start in your efforts to keep doing the right behaviors and stop doing the wrong behaviors.

The first step is to ask: "Is this behavior taking me toward my goal or is it taking me away from my goal?" If the behavior is taking you toward your goal it is a right behavior, and you should keep doing it. If it is taking you away from your goal then it is a wrong behavior, and you need to stop doing that behavior or replace it with a right behavior that will take you toward your goal.

WRONG BEHAVIORS
(Take you away from your goal)

EXAMPLES

- Spending $6.00 a day in the vending machines at work
- Only making minimum payments on your credit cards
- Using shopping as entertainment
- Spending more than you make each month
- Buying lotto tickets

RIGHT BEHAVIORS
(Take you toward your goal)

EXAMPLES

- Making automatic deposits to your 401(k) every month
- Paying cash
- Not using credit cards
- Shopping for good deals when you buy
- Paying extra on your house payment every month

JOURNEY FROM WRONG BEHAVIOR TO RIGHT BEHAVIOR

If I could give you a tool that would take you step-by-step and help you turn bad habits into good habits, would you be interested? This is a tool that helps turn any bad behavior into a good behavior.

THIS TOOL CAN HELP YOU CHANGE

Smoking	to	Not smoking
Overeating	to	Eating properly
Not exercising	to	Exercising
Overspending	to	Not overspending
Fighting with your spouse	to	Working together
Not doing money basics	to	Doing money basics
Not giving	to	Giving
Not saving	to	Saving
No emergency fund	to	Emergency fund
No survival fund	to	3- to 6-month survival fund
Not saving for retirement	to	Saving for a strong retirement
Not paying extra on house payment	to	Paying your house off early
Not teaching others about money	to	Sharing money tools with others

BEHAVIOR CURVE

Some of the best advice I have ever received was "Expect people to be themselves and you will rarely be wrong." This program has been designed so you can be successful just being yourself. The behavior curve will help you be successful. I want to share a very powerful tool with you that I call the behavior curve. It is based on a theory called the four stages of learning introduced by Abraham Maslow in the 1940s, and it can help you turn a wrong behavior or habit into a right behavior or habit. I will first describe the behavior curve, then I will show you how to use it to help you be successful in your journey to a great financial life.

In this program as well as in life, it is what you *do* not what you *know* that makes all the difference. You could know and understand every fact and concept in this entire program, but unless you actually do them, you will not make progress. You will stay right where you are financially. If you *do* what you learn, you can move confidently toward and ultimately reach your wonderful goal of a great financial life.

To reach a great financial life, there are certain things you must *do* (behaviors). The behavior curve will help you *do* the behaviors you will need to do to be successful.

> *Motivation is what gets you started.*
> *Habit is what keeps you going.*
>   *Jim Rohn*

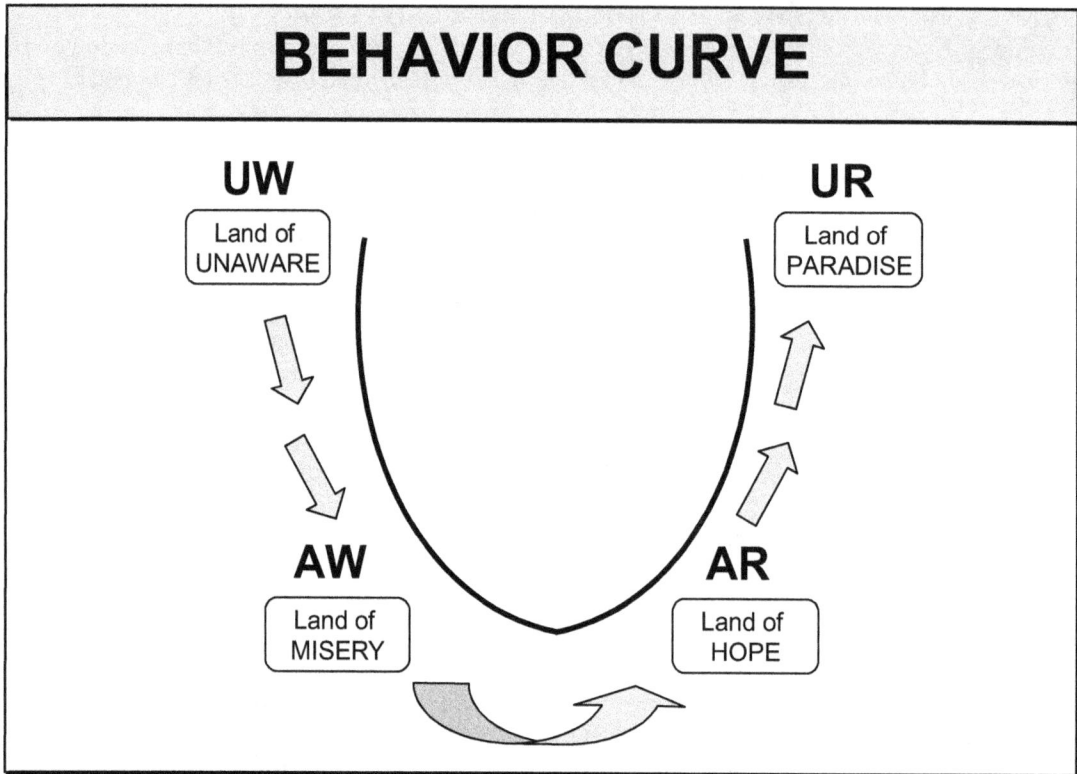

BEHAVIOR CURVE

UW
Land of
UNAWARE

UR
Land of
PARADISE

AW
Land of
MISERY

AR
Land of
HOPE

WHAT IS IT
Use the diagram above to follow the explanation of the behavior curve.

The behavior curve is a path that will take you from a wrong behavior to a right behavior. There are four major stations along the curve.

UW
The first station is called UW. This stands for unaware/Wrong. This is the place where a person is doing the wrong behavior, and they are unaware that it is wrong.

EXAMPLE 1
A preteen who smokes and is unaware of the long-term negative consequences.

EXAMPLE 2
The guy living on junk food who is unaware of the negative impact on his health.

EXAMPLE 3
The 22-year-old who is not saving and is really unaware of the negative retirement consequence.

They are unaware/Wrong. They are unaware they are doing something wrong, and they are content.

> *Habit is habit and not to be flung out of the window by any man, but coaxed downstairs a step at a time.*
> *Mark Twain*

AW

The second point on the behavior curve is AW. This stands for aware/Wrong; this is the place where someone becomes aware that their behavior is wrong.

EXAMPLE 1
The smoking preteen who sees the pictures of cancer-filled lungs.

EXAMPLE 2
The junk food guy gets a checkup and is told of heart problems—very scary.

EXAMPLE 3
The 22-year-old is given a presentation at work about retirement and realizes there is no way he will be prepared for it.

They are aware/Wrong; they are now aware that their behavior is wrong.
Now they are not content, but uncomfortable. The thing that makes you aware is called a trigger event.

AR

The third point on the behavior curve is AR. This stands for aware/Right. This is a place where a person is doing the right thing, but they have to try to do it. They have to be aware and make a conscious effort to do the right thing.

EXAMPLE 1
The smoker joins a stop-smoking group, gets medication to help him stop, etc.

EXAMPLE 2
The junk food guy buys healthy food and takes walks.

EXAMPLE 3
The 22-year-old writes a check for $500 each month to his 401(k) account.

They are aware/right; they are able to do the right behavior, but they have to be aware and make a conscious effort each time they do it.

UR

The fourth point on the behavior curve is called UR, which stands for unaware/right. This is the place where a person is doing the right behavior, and they are unaware they are even doing it. They do the right thing naturally. It has become a habit and they do not have to make a conscious effort to do it.

EXAMPLE 1
The smoker who has not smoked for years and rarely thinks about it.

EXAMPLE 2
The junk food guy now consistently eats well and exercises regularly without even thinking about it.

EXAMPLE 3
The 22-year-old has set up an automatic deposit every month into his retirement account, and he never even thinks about it.

They are unaware/right; they are able to do the right behavior without even being aware they are doing it.

At the point of UR the person has created a right habit. They naturally do the right thing without even being conscious of it.

Each of these four points is located in one of four areas.

- The point UW exists in area 1, which I call the Land of the Unaware. This is where a person is doing something wrong and is not even aware of it.

- The point AW is located in area 2, which I call the Land of Misery. This is where a person is now aware that they are doing something wrong, but has not yet changed the behavior. This area can be miserable.

- The point AR is located in area 3, which I call the Land of Hope. This is where a person is doing the right thing, but they have to consciously try to do it. This area can be difficult, but it is the Land of Hope because you are actually doing the right behavior now. You are seeing victories.

- The point UR is located in area 4, which I call Paradise. This is where the person is doing the appropriate behavior without even thinking about it. They have developed a right habit. The Land of Paradise is where you want to live. This program will help you get there, one behavior at a time.

> *My problem lies in reconciling my gross*
> *habits with my net income.*
> *Errol Flynn*

HOW IT WORKS
EXAMPLE 1

BEHAVIOR
Spending $6 a day in the vending machines at work.

BEHAVIOR POINT
UW - The person is doing this unconsciously and is not really aware that it is wrong. They put $6 in the vending machines every day without really even thinking about it. They are unaware of the total daily amount that they spend—the Land of the Unaware.

TRIGGER EVENT
This person takes this program and realizes that the $6 they are spending in the vending machines could become a fortune if put to work for 30 or 40 years. They become aware that their behavior is wrong. They also learn from this program that the per-unit-price (P.U.P.) on vending machines is sky high, and they could easily buy their snack items for a lot less and bring them to work. They have now moved to the AW point. They are now aware that they are doing something wrong. Every time they put money in the vending machine, they are conscious that the money could be growing into a fortune if put to work, and they feel a little miserable. They are now in the Land of Misery. They can stay in the Land of Misery, or they can decide to do the right behavior. They can move on to the AR point where they would be doing the right behavior.

DECISION POINT
What if this person is tired of being miserable and would love to have the fortune in 30 years or 40 years? What should they do?

NEW RIGHT BEHAVIOR
Right behavior-They go to the discount store and buy their snacks for a fraction of the vending machine cost and bring them to work. This person decides to direct the $6 to long-term savings. They have now moved to the AR and are doing the right behavior—spending less on snacks. They are doing the right behavior, but they have to consciously do it. They are in the Land of Hope.

If they will consciously continue to do the right behavior (bring their snacks), after a while they will do it without even thinking about it, and they will move to the point UR where they will be doing the right behavior without even having to think about it. They will have changed a wrong behavior of wasting a fortune on vending machines to a right behavior of putting the money to work to build a fortune and not even have to think about it. It is their new good behavior. They have reached the Land of Paradise.

BEFORE
UW (Unaware/Wrong): Spending $6 a day on vending machine snacks

AFTER
UR (Unaware/Right): Putting $6 a day to work every year to become wealthy

So this person went from UW to UR and has turned a wrong behavior into a powerful wealth-generating force, and they still get to have their daily snacks at work! That is powerful!

EXAMPLE 2

BEHAVIOR
Every year at Christmas, this person puts $1,000 on credit cards, and they start the New Year with additional debt. They end up spending the next year or two paying it off. They also pay a lot more than the $1,000 by the time they pay all of the interest.

BEHAVIOR POINT
UW (Unaware/Wrong): They have done this every year for a long time. They do it unconsciously without even thinking about it.

TRIGGER EVENT
They see a demonstration in one of these modules that shows that using credit cards to purchase items and then paying the minimum payments will take them many years to pay off. They will end up paying two to three times as much, and they realize their Christmas-buying behavior is wrong. They realize that they are not spending $1000. They are probably spending close to $2000 or $3000 including interest. They have now reached the AW point. They are now aware that they are doing the wrong behavior. They are a little miserable realizing that they are paying 2 to 3 times more than they thought. The newest iPod™ they thought was such a steal at $250 does not seem like such a great deal at $750.

DECISION POINT
Once they are at the AW point, they always have a choice. Are they going to stay in the Land of Misery, or are they going to make a decision to move to the AR point and start doing the right thing. This person decides that they will never again charge a Christmas gift on a credit card and pay two to three times what it should have cost.

NEW RIGHT BEHAVIOR
This person decides that they will replace the wrong behavior of putting Christmas presents on a credit card with the new right behavior of putting $85 into a special Christmas savings account every month ($85 x 12 months = $1,020). By doing this she will save the money in advance and will be able to pay cash to buy Christmas presents. Every year she will have $1,020 in cash to spend on Christmas gifts, and she will not have to even think about it. She will be doing the right behavior. She has moved to AR. She is doing the right behavior, but she has to consciously make herself do it each month. If she continues to do the right behavior long enough, she will move to UR and it will become a permanent habit. She will be doing the right behavior, unaware she is even doing it.

BEFORE
UW: Charging $1,000 on credit cards to buy Christmas presents.

AFTER
UR: Saving $1,000 in advance and paying cash for Christmas presents.

> *Chains of habit are too light to be felt until*
> *they are too heavy to be broken.*
> *Warren Buffet*

EXAMPLE 3
BEHAVIOR
Every day at work I buy a soda out of the vending machine.

BEHAVIOR POINT
UW: I buy soda after soda all day long without really even thinking about it.

TRIGGER EVENT
One day a coworker says, "How much are you spending every day on soda? You could bring it from home and save a fortune." I decide to track it for one day. I got an index card and wrote down the amount I spent every time I bought a soda throughout the day.

$1.16 at 7/11
60¢ vending
60¢ vending
60¢ vending
And on and on until it totals $9.00 per day.

I had now moved solidly to the AW. I became very aware that I was doing the wrong behavior. Nine dollars times 30 (days per month) = $270 per month or $3,240 per year. Two hundred-seventy dollars per month in a 401K becomes $586,257 in 30 years and $1,577,400 in 40 years. I had definitely entered the Land of Misery. I was doing the wrong behavior, and I was fully aware of it now.

DECISION POINT
The question is always the same! Do you want to stay at AW or do you want to move out of the Land of Misery and start doing the right behavior? I decided that I wanted to move out of the Land of Misery and start doing the right behavior.
New right behavior: I went to the discount store and bought cans of soda for 25 cents each instead of 60 cents each in the vending machine. I took them to work.

I am now at AR. Once I have done this for several months, I will be at UR. I will do the right behavior without even thinking about it.

> *Train up a child in the way he should go, even when he*
> *is old, he will not depart from it.*
> *Proverbs 22:6*

BEFORE
Spending $ 3,240 a year on soda

AFTER
Spending much less on soda a year and putting the difference to work to build a fortune.

WHY IT WORKS
This tool is powerful for several reasons:
- It helps you see that there is a process (road map) to changing a behavior.
- It tells you where you are on the road map.
- It tells you the steps to take.
- It gives you a goal.
- It gives you a way to actually talk about behavior.
- It gives you hope.
- It can help you actually change a wrong behavior to a right behavior.
- You can use it to help others.
- You can use it to help yourself.
- You can change one behavior at a time.

In this program, I will do more than just make you aware of a wrong behavior. I will tell you what the right behavior is and help you go from the land of the UW (Unaware/Wrong) to the land of the UR (Unaware/Right) and stay there. I will be your behavior coach.

Note: It is very powerful to raise your children with financial right behaviors from the start. If your children start in the UR, the Land of Paradise, they will not have to make the painful journey around the behavior curve later in their life. Do you wish you had been living your financial life in the UR, Land of Paradise, doing the right behaviors naturally without having to think about it? Do you wish you had been practicing right financial habits since you were young? If you start children at the UR point, there is a very good chance they will stay there. They will live their life doing the right financial behaviors without even thinking about it.

BASIC #3
WRONG TO RIGHT

> *For what I am doing, I do not understand; for I am not practicing what I would like to do, but I am doing the very thing I hate.*
>
> *Romans 7:15*

The verse above illustrates how difficult it can be to do what is right – to have the right behaviors. Knowing the basics of behavior can help you have the right behaviors.

I believe every person is disciplined, diligent, and dedicated. The problem is we are often disciplined, diligent, and dedicated to the wrong behaviors. I bet that if you tracked your behavior, you would find that there are things you do every single day. Some things you do everyday, and you are not even consciously aware of it.

For example, brushing your teeth, the route you drive to work, buying coffee on the way to work, and buying a snack from the vending machine at work are habits. All of us are creatures of habit. There are things we do on a regular basis.

So when it comes to behavior, the question is not "How do I become disciplined, diligent, and dedicated?" Chances are you are already disciplined, diligent, and dedicated. The real question is "How do I become disciplined, diligent, and dedicated in the right behaviors?"

WAYS TO CHANGE A WRONG BEHAVIOR
- **Stop it**
- **Redirect it**
- **Redefine it**

STOP IT
How do you stop a behavior? The fastest way to stop the negative effects of a wrong behavior is to simply stop doing it. Most people find it difficult to stop a wrong behavior. If you have the discipline and self control to stop doing a wrong behavior, congratulations! You have a very valuable ability. Once you realize that a behavior is wrong (it is taking you away from your goal), the fastest way to improve your situation is to just stop the behavior. If you are able to use this option, then just stop the wrong behavior and move forward.

EXAMPLE
You discover that every time you withdraw money from the ATM at work you are charged a $3 fee because the ATM is not part of the network of your bank. You withdraw $20, and the ATM charges you a $3 fee. You give away 15 percent of your money every time you withdraw $20. You are paying the bank 15 percent to access your own money! You decide that the fee is ridiculous and you simply stop using these ATMs. You have stopped a wrong behavior.

Note: If you are using the ATM twice a week, then you are paying $6 a week in fees.
Six dollars a week equals $312 a year ($6 x 52 weeks).
Six dollars a week invested with a 10 percent return compounding annually would be:

$10,904	in 15 years
$56,454	in 30 years
$151,897	in 40 years

Using that ATM is a very expensive behavior!

If you are not able to stop the wrong behavior, then you may want to try one of the other two options, redirect or redefine.

REDIRECT IT

Redirecting a behavior is when you take the power of a wrong behavior and redirect it into a right behavior. That power can be redirected to constructive activities that will build your strong financial future.

How do you redirect a behavior? The best way to explain it is to give you an example.

EXAMPLE 1

I lost 30 pounds by redirecting a behavior. I had the habit of eating junk food throughout the day—a candy bar here, a cupcake there. I decided I wanted to be healthier and lose weight. Instead of completely quitting cold turkey, I decided to redirect the behavior. I got a pack of breath mints to carry in my pocket. When I got the urge to have a snack, I ate a mint. I had a mint instead of a 270-calorie candy bar. In the middle of the afternoon when I wanted some junk food from the vending machine, I had a mint instead. I did not give up the behavior. I simply redirected it to the mints. I still had the same behavior. I had snacks throughout the day. I just redirected to something (mints) that had fewer calories and was less damaging to my health. I basically had the same snacking behavior, but by redirecting it to mints, I was able to reach my goal and lose 30 pounds. I traded 270 calories for 5 calories. Take this four times a day and I traded 1,080 calories for 20. Over a week it was 7,560 calories for 140. Over a month, I traded 30,240 calories for 560. That was a lot of fat I did not gain. As you can see, small things can add up to very large amounts over time.

EXAMPLE 2

Let's say you are paying the minimum amount on your credit cards every month. You add it up and discover that you are paying $150 in interest every month to the credit card companies. That is $150 that is going out through the spending category we discussed earlier—$150 going out every month and it is gone. It will never come back. In Step 5, I am going to show you how to redirect that $150 a month to the Put It To Work category and have it build you a future. By redirecting that $150 a month, you can build great wealth for you and your family over time. That is changing a bad behavior into a good behavior by simply redirecting it.

EXAMPLE 3

What if during this program, you realize that your habit for the last five years of buying a $5 lotto ticket every morning at the convenience store has cost you $1,064,521. The $5 a day earning a 10 percent compounded return would be worth $1,064,521 at the end of 42 years. You realize that you could greatly increase your odds of becoming a millionaire by redirecting this daily behavior to the right behavior of putting the $5 a day into your 401(k) account or your IRA. In this example you have taken a very strong established habit and redirected it to make you a millionaire.

REDEFINE IT

Redefining a behavior is like putting a fence around the behavior. You still have the behavior, but you have given it boundaries. You have it under control, and it cannot wander off and get you into trouble. It has to stay in the yard. You determine where to put the fence and how high it will be.

How do you redefine a behavior? Once again, the best way to explain this is to give you a few examples.

EXAMPLE 1

Let's say you are the type of person who keeps eating until your plate is empty. If you eat at a fast food restaurant, you eat until all of the food is gone, and then you stop. If you eat at home, you eat until your plate is clean, and then you stop. If you have done this all of your life, then it is going to be a very strong habit. You may even still hear your mother's voice whispering, "Clean your plate, dear." Let's say you decide that you want to eat healthier or maybe lose a little weight. Instead of trying to change a lifelong, very strong habit of eating everything on your plate, you reach your goal by redefining "everything on your plate." Instead of putting the usual amount of food on your plate next time, you put a smaller portion on your plate. You eat until it is gone, and then you stop. Over a period of several weeks, you continue to redefine the notion of "everything on your plate" gradually until you have reduced the amount you are eating by 25 percent. The key is that you have redefined the boundaries that your behavior will operate within. I guarantee you that it will be easier to redefine the boundaries of a behavior than it will be to stop a behavior. Another way to attack the same problem is to simply use a smaller plate. When you fill up the plate, it will automatically be a smaller portion of food but will appear to be a full plate. There are different methods that will work for different personality types.

EXAMPLE 2

If you have the habit of eating a piece of pie every night for dessert, you may decide that you want to change that behavior to be healthier. You could redefine it by having a piece that is half the size of the piece you usually have or have a piece every other night.

If you redefine, you eat pie, but you have reduced the negative impact of the behavior by 50 percent.

EXAMPLE 3

If you are the type that spends all the money you have then,
If you have $500, you spend it all.
If you have $700, you spend it all.
If you have $75, you spend it all.

At first glance, this looks like a very destructive, maybe even irresponsible, behavior. What would you say if I told you that you could reach all of your financial goals even with this type of behavior? You do not have to eliminate this behavior. You simply need to redefine it. If you redefine "all you have," you can still reach your financial goals.

If every month you have around $500 left after paying your bills, and every month you spend all of the $500, you spend all you have.

If you decide that next month, you will have $300 automatically deposited into your 401(k) or IRA, then you will only have $200 left. You have redefined "all you have." Starting next month, you will still spend all you have, but by redefining the boundaries from $500 to $200, the behavior operates within newly redefined boundaries. You can move toward your financial goals without going cold turkey and trying to give up a very strong behavior.

BASIC #4
MAKE IT A HABIT

> *A habit is something you can do without thinking –*
> *which is why most of us have so many of them.*
> *Frank A. Clark*

HABITS ARE HARD TO BREAK

The good news is that good habits are also hard to break. You have to do something 20 to 30 times before it really becomes a habit. The longer you can do the right behavior, the more it becomes a strong unaware right habit. Protecting, encouraging, and celebrating a right behavior will allow you to do it long enough for it to become a permanent habit.

Once you are doing the right behaviors that will take you to your goal of a great financial success, you want to make sure you turn them into permanent habits.

Here are three ways to turn a right behavior into a long-term right habit:

- **Protect it.**
- **Automate it.**
- **Delegate it.**

PROTECT IT

Once you have a good behavior, protect it.

EXAMPLE 1

If you are having $500 a month automatically deposited into your 401(k) account, you want to make sure you never stop that behavior and you never take money out of the 401(k) account. One great way to protect this habit is to have a $1,000 emergency fund - Step 6 and a Survival fund – Step 8. If you have an emergency fund and a survival fund, you will not be tempted to reduce your monthly contributions or make withdrawals from the 401(k) account if you experience a financial emergency.

Your good habit will be protected.

EXAMPLE 2

If you have developed the right behavior of bringing snacks to work instead of using the expensive vending machines, then you need to protect that right behavior. One way to protect this behavior is to keep an extra supply of snacks in your desk or in the break room refrigerator, so that if you forget your snacks you will not be tempted to go back to the vending machine and restart a wrong behavior.

> *The best way to break a bad habit is to drop it.*
> *Leo Aikman*

AUTOMATE IT

How do I automate a behavior? One of the most effective and quickest ways to make sure a right behavior continues is to automate it. If you know that something needs to be done on a regular basis, but you are afraid you will forget to do it or not have the dedication or discipline to do it, then automate it.

> *It is easier to prevent bad habits than to break them.*
> *Benjamin Franklin*

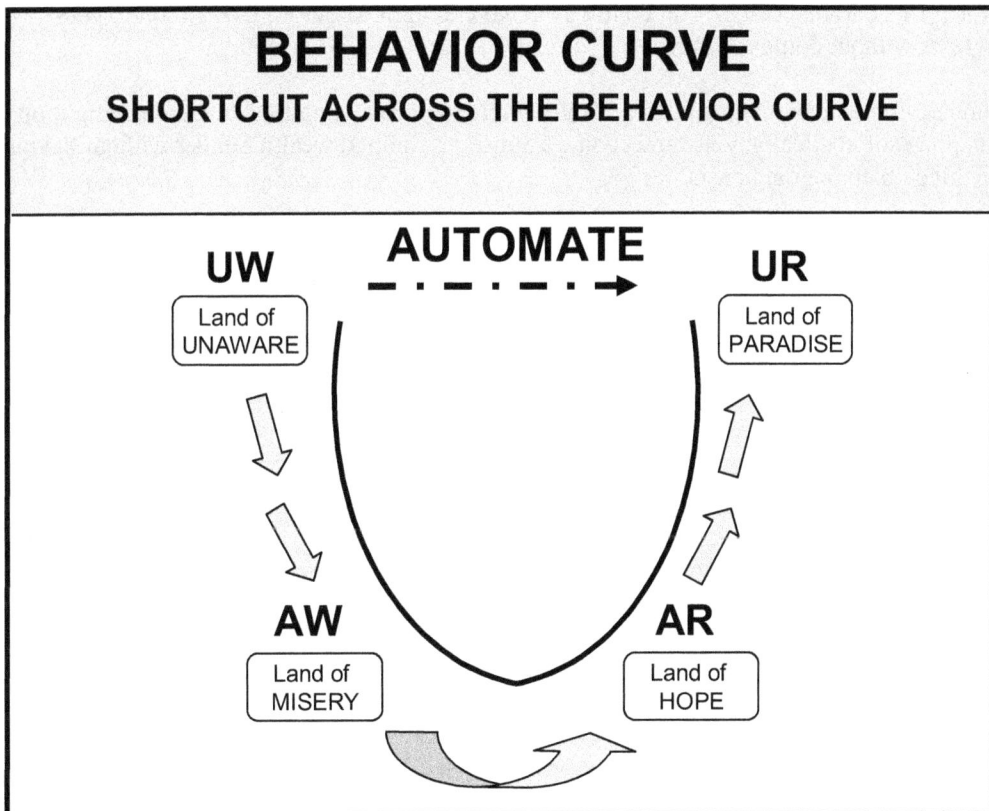

BEHAVIOR CURVE
SHORTCUT ACROSS THE BEHAVIOR CURVE

AUTOMATE

UW
Land of
UNAWARE

UR
Land of
PARADISE

AW
Land of
MISERY

AR
Land of
HOPE

Automating a behavior can provide a shortcut across the behavior curve. If you simply automate the behavior, you do not have to make the sometimes long and difficult journey around the behavior curve. Automating right behaviors is the secret to being financially successful without having to become a totally different person. With automation you do not have to be a super-disciplined person to reach high levels of financial success.

EXAMPLE 1
I really like having a nice green lawn. I know that one of the things that must happen to ensure a green lawn is for it to be watered three times a week for 30 minutes. In today's world, with all of the different demands on my schedule, the best way for me to make sure this happens is to make it happen automatically. I put a timer on the sprinkler system, set it once, and then three times a week it comes on for 30 minutes. I do not have to remember to do it or be disciplined enough to stick with it. I set it once and forget about it, and the lawn looks great.

EXAMPLE 2
If you know that the best way to build wealth is to make regular deposits into your 401(k), IRA, or other investment, then why run the risk of forgetting to do it or not being disciplined enough to do it? Simply automate it with automatic deposits and never worry about it again.

Just like the time settings on the sprinkler system, the auto deposit is set up once and then every month it happens automatically. You do not even have to think about it. Every month, your fortune grows without doing anything.

Do not underestimate the extreme power of this simple tool. By using this tool and setting it up once to happen automatically, you can become a super-disciplined wealth builder without having to do anything on an ongoing basis.

DELEGATE IT
How do I delegate a behavior? Delegation is a great way to turn a right behavior into a right habit. Delegation is when you turn the responsibility of performing a task over to another. You do not perform the task yourself. If you do not have the willpower or the time to continue doing a right behavior, you should consider delegating it.

EXAMPLE
If you have redirected the wrong behavior of spending $8 every day buying your lunch to the right behavior of bringing your lunch, but you do not have the time every night to make a good lunch, you might want to consider delegating this task to another member of your family. The first time you are not able to make your lunch, you will be right back in line paying $8 for your lunch. This is one way that your spouse or one of your children could contribute to the cause of reaching Financial Success. This is one of the reasons you went through Step 2 – Work Together. Every member of your team will have ways they can contribute to the success of the team.

Delegate—do not dump! You should not use delegation just to make someone else do the task that you either do not want to do or do not have time to do. When you delegate a task, you should use the task to develop the other person and their skills. Do not just hand the task over without teaching the other person how to do it properly.

Here is a tool that I use when I conduct leadership training and want the leaders to delegate the right tasks in an effective and responsible way.

THE DO-DO TOOL

> *I Do – You Watch*
> *I Do – You Help*
> *You Do – I Help*
> *You Do – I Watch*
> *You Do – Call Me If Needed*

The Do-Do Tool is a very simple, yet powerful, five-step way to successfully delegate a task.

Step 1 - *I do* the task and *you watch* me do it. This step allows you to see how the task is performed and to get familiar with my expectations. Since you are only watching in this step, you do not feel the stress to make sure everything goes perfectly.

Step 2 – *I do* the task and *you help* me do it. In this step you will be responsible for helping me complete the task. This step allows you to get involved and actually perform part of the duties. You will become more familiar with the task, and we can identify and clarify anything you do not understand. Repeat this step until you have been able to perform all the different parts of the task and you are very familiar with the entire task. In this step you are helping, but you are not responsible for the task.

Step 3 – *You do* the task and *I help*. The responsibility of successfully completing the task is shifting to you, but you are not completely on your own. I am helping you with the task, and together we will make sure it is successful. We can stay in this step for as long as needed and repeat the task as many times as necessary to ensure that you are ready to take the task over completely.

Step 4 – In this step, *you do* the task and *I watch*. You are in control of the task, and you are performing it by yourself. You are responsible for successfully completing the task, but I am still there watching just in case you need help. You are responsible for the task, but not alone. We can stay in this step until you are comfortable and confident that you can own the task going forward.

Step 5 – In this step, *you do* the entire task. The task has been fully delegated to you, and you are responsible for its successful completion. You fully own the task, but I will be available if you need to call me.

This tool is great because it is simple, and it allows you to delegate a task in a step-by-step responsible way and prepare the other person to be successful and learn new skills. It also helps you turn a right behavior into a right habit.

BEHAVIOR FORM

GOAL: _____

1. BEHAVIOR: _____

2. RIGHT Takes you TOWARD your goal	**WRONG** Takes you AWAY from your goal
3. How Could You Start Doing It _____ _____ _____	How Could You Stop Doing It _____ _____ _____
If you are doing it, how could you: **Protect it** _____ _____ **Automate It** _____ _____ **Delegate It** _____ _____ _____	If you cannot Stop it, how could you: **Redirect it** _____ _____ **Redefine It** _____ _____

THE BEHAVIOR FORM

This very simple form helps you keep right behaviors and change wrong behaviors into right behaviors. You can use this form for any behavior. The form has 3 simple steps.

STEP 1

List the behavior. (It could be a behavior you are doing now or one you are considering.)

EXAMPLE

Spending $7 every morning at the coffee shop on the way to work

STEP 2

Decide if the behavior is right (takes you toward your goal of a great financial life) or wrong (takes you away from your goal). Put a check mark by either right or wrong.

STEP 3

If it is a right behavior list ways you could:
Start it.
Protect it.
Automate it.
Delegate it.
This will help make it a long-term right habit.

If it is a wrong behavior list ways you could:
Stop it.
Redirect it.
Redefine it.
This will help you turn a wrong behavior into a right behavior.

Note: You can use this form with the Plus Delta and Start/Stop/Continue forms in Step 2 - Working Together. The items you listed on the plus side of the Plus/Delta form (things that are working well) and the items you listed in the start or continue section of the Start/Stop/Continue form can be listed on this form as right behaviors. You can identify ways to protect, automate, or delegate these behaviors to make them permanent right habits.

This behavior form is a great tool to help you identify behaviors and maintain or change them to make sure you are doing the things that will bring you to a great financial life.

ADDITIONAL BEHAVIOR TIPS

Here are some additional tips to help you develop and keep the right behaviors that will take you to your goal of a great financial life.

PROGRESS NOT PERFECTION

Your goal is not to be perfect. Your goal is to develop and maintain the right behaviors that will build your financial success. If you stumble or even fall as you develop right behaviors and eliminate wrong behaviors, that is okay. The secret is to never give up. It may take several tries to start a right behavior or to stop a wrong behavior. The key is to make sure you are making progress, not reaching perfection. Keep going. You can do it!

> *Repetition of the same thought or physical action develops into a habit which, repeated frequently enough, becomes an automatic reflex.*
> *Norman Vincent Peale*

REMEMBER YOUR GOAL

Remind yourself of your goal—the reason you are doing this program. Remind yourself how great it will be when you have a great financial life. Think about what that goal really means—a lifestyle of financial peace, free of stress and panic over finances. You will be financially strong and looking forward to a bright future where you can pursue your dreams.

TRY IT FOR 30 DAYS

Remember that it takes 20 to 30 days to form a new habit or to break an old habit. If you want to start a right behavior or stop a wrong behavior, commit to it for 30 days. Determine that you will stick to it for 30 days no matter what. At the beginning it may be difficult, but as you continue forward day after day it should get easier. During the 30-day trial you can build enough momentum to keep it going as a new permanent right behavior.

> *I've missed more than 9,000 shots in my career. I've lost almost 300 games. Twenty-six times, I've been trusted to take the game-winning shot and missed. I've failed over and over and over again in my life. And that is why I succeed.*
> *Michael Jordan*

GET A BUDDY

Sometimes it is easier to start a new right behavior or stop a wrong behavior with the help of a buddy. Team up with your spouse or a friend and commit to help each other until the goal is reached. It can also make the process more enjoyable when you share it with another person.

DO IT FOR ANOTHER

Think of the good your new right behavior will do for others. Think of the benefit to others when you are no longer doing the wrong behaviors.

ENCOURAGE IT

Another way to make sure a right behavior becomes a right habit is to encourage the behavior.

EXAMPLE

If your spouse has developed the right behavior of getting movies from the library instead of renting or buying them, you should encourage that behavior. You should thank her and praise her when she brings home free movies from the library instead of spending $3 to $5 for each rental or $13 to $18 for each purchased movie. You could even tell your spouse that she can have a portion of the money she is saving to spend as she pleases.

If you encourage right behaviors, they will continue and they will become right habits.

CELEBRATE IT
This is a fun way to turn a right behavior into a right habit.

EXAMPLE
If you have developed the right behavior of putting a certain amount of money in an account each month to build a 6-month cash survival fund of $24,000, then you should celebrate once you reach that goal. It is not a lot of fun to just move on to the next goal and the next and the next without ever taking a little time to celebrate and be thankful that you have been blessed with reaching a goal.

Take a little time and think about how nice life is getting as you complete each of the 10 steps of this program and you move closer to the wonderful goal of a great financial life.

REWARD YOURSELF
I had a friend who decided she wanted to pay off her house (Step 10 – Pay Off House). The right behavior that she decided to start was paying $500 extra on her house payment every month. A way to stick with the new behavior was to reward herself when she reached her goal of paying her house off completely. When she reached her goal, she planned to buy a mink coat. When times got tough or she was tempted to spend the $500 on something else, she would think about the mink coat and how nice it would feel to wear it, and that would motivate her to stick with the right behavior and reach her goal. She did pay her house off early, and she did buy her mink coat. Think about how nice it must be for her to not have a house payment—to have all of that extra money every month. You can be in that same situation with the right behaviors.

Consider using a reward to establish and keep your right behaviors. Choose a reward that is appropriate for you and the behavior you are starting. It could be dinner at your favorite restaurant, a vacation, a new outfit, etc.

You can have a big reward at the end when you reach your goal, you can have smaller rewards along the way, or you can do both. The reward of the mink coat was at the end when she reached the main goal. She could also have put smaller rewards along the way. For example, at the end of each year she could have treated herself to dinner at her favorite restaurant.

I recommend that you have a big reward at the accomplishment of your goal, but also have rewards along the way to keep you motivated and moving forward. One large reward in the future can seem too far away. The rewards along the way will seem more attainable. Working toward each reward along the way will eventually bring you to the big reward at the end.

WATCH COMBINATIONS

Combining two behaviors together can create a very powerful force.

I have noticed that sometimes people combine two things together so often that they start to believe that they cannot have one without the other. For example, if a person takes a break at work and smokes a cigarette, they have combined the break with the cigarette. If they take another break and smoke another cigarette two times a day for the next two weeks, they are continuing to combine these two items together. After awhile, they will begin to combine these two items without even thinking about it. In a sense, these two items have joined together. This person could easily find themselves on break smoking a cigarette and not even realize they were doing it. This combination can become very powerful. Every time you do one behavior (take a break), you automatically do the other behavior (Smoke a cigarette). If you combine these two items for a long enough time, they can become almost inseparable. The one behavior becomes a trigger for the other behavior, and it becomes a very strong habit. If you decide that you want to stop the smoking behavior, then every time you take a break it will trigger a temptation to do the smoking behavior.

The combination of behaviors can also work for you. If you decided to redirect the smoking behavior you could go for a walk when you take a break instead of smoking a cigarette. If you combine the behavior of taking a break with taking a walk instead of smoking a cigarette for a long enough time, you can make the combination of taking a break and taking a walk stronger than the combination of taking a break and smoking a cigarette.

Be aware of the power of combining two behaviors together and make sure you are using that power to start and keep right behaviors not wrong behaviors.

It is important to remember these basics of behavior as we move forward in this program. They will be key factors as we build your financial future. You have learned the basics of money and behavior; now it is time to learn the basics of marketing self-defense.

ACTION ITEMS

Basics of
Money

Basics of
Behavior

ACTION 3 →

Marketing
Self-Defense

We are what we repeatedly do. Excellence, then, is not an act, but a habit.

Aristotle

IMAGINE:

- Having full knowledge of the key principles of marketing self-defense
- Having total control when you are shopping
- Being able to control your impulse buying
- Your children not asking for things in the store
- Driving home from the store feeling good that you only bought what you planned
- Buying the same things you have always bought, but spending much less
- Never regretting your purchases
- Having powerful weapons that will beat any marketing campaign
- Being able to tell instantly if a deal is good
- Having extra money to build wealth and pursue your dreams

When it comes to spending your money, *you are in a war.* This battle is between an enemy who would have you spend all of your money and you and your commitment to put your money to work to build a strong financial future. The enemy's goal is to get you to spend as much money as possible. Your goal is to buy what you need for as little as possible so you can put the extra dollars (employees) to work for you.

It is important that you win the war for your dollars. Knowing and applying the basics of marketing self-defense will allow you to have the extra dollars (employees) you need to reach a great financial life. You are not fighting this war simply to win, but for the wonderful lifestyle of peace, stability, and financial strength.

In this section, I will teach you how to be a warrior and create an effective battle plan. I will also give you powerful weapons and teach you how to use them.

MARKETING BASICS

Basic #1	You are in a war.
Basic #2	Know your enemy.
Basic #3	Know yourself.
Basic #4	Know the terrain.
Basic #5	Weapons & tactics

BASIC #1
YOU ARE IN A WAR

While you are in this program, I want you to consider yourself in a war. You are in a war for your dollars. The enemy is any person, store, company, or government institution that wants your dollars. You are in this war 24 hours every day. Your enemies are bombarding you with messages about their products and services all day and all night. You are being ambushed with temptations constantly. They have master warriors setting traps for you everywhere you go. They are constantly collecting information on your moves and behaviors. They are paying to obtain information about you from others. They have cameras everywhere to learn your habits and preferences.

I am not saying that these enemies are doing anything wrong or illegal. They are in business to make money, and that is great, but if you want to reach your goal of a great financial life, you need to act as though you are in a war and take the battle seriously. I guarantee you, they are taking it seriously.

Winning the war means having a high score on all 10 of the steps on the scoreboard.
Winning the war means reaching a great financial life and the wonderful lifestyle it brings.

Your enemies in the war for your dollars want you to have as much money as possible flow into the Spend It bucket. That is how they make money. *You win the war by winning the battles.* The battles are fought on the outgo part of the diagram below.

THE BATTLEFIELD

INCOME

OUTGO

SPEND IT

KEEP IT

PUT IT TO WORK

The war is won by gaining control of your outgo and winning the monthly battles between spending and putting money to work. Your objective is to spend your money wisely so you can live your life fully and still move as much money as possible from the Spend It bucket to the Put It To Work bucket. Remember, moving dollars from the Spend It bucket to the Put It To Work bucket is how you engage the Big 3 of money and start building your fortune.

If you want to reach a great financial life, it is critical that you win the war for your dollars.

3 FASTEST WAYS TO LOSE A WAR

1. **Do not realize you are in a war.**
2. **Let the enemy create the rules.**
3. Obey the enemy's rules.

DO NOT REALIZE YOU ARE IN A WAR
The fastest way to lose a war is to not realize you are in a war. Most people do not realize they are in a war for their dollars. They wander around the battlefield with no objective, no battle plan, no weapons, and no basic training in the strategies or tactics of war. Their enemies, who do have an objective, a battle plan, a vast array of weapons, and very expensive and sophisticated training in the art of war easily win the war for their dollars every day, month after month. The enemy ends up with more of their money than they do. I am going to help you change that!

EXAMPLE
When you go to a grocery store hungry and without a list, you are not acting as though you are in a war.

LET THE ENEMY CREATE THE RULES
Another fast way to lose a war is to let your enemies create the rules of engagement. If you let the enemy set the rules of engagement, then you are at a disadvantage. They will surely set rules that work in their favor.

EXAMPLE
When the credit card companies send you your monthly bill, they list a minimum payment amount. That is their attempt to create the rules. They want you to pay as little as possible each month so you will end up paying a lot more over time. Remember the Big 3 and their powerful friend compound interest. Remember the demonstrations of increasing each of the Big 3 elements (amount, interest rate, and time). When you increase any one of these elements, the total amount you earned increased greatly. (Review those examples.) When you *owe* money, the Big 3 work against you. Remember that the most powerful of the Big 3 was Time. If you increase time, you increase the total amount dramatically. When the credit card company lists a small minimum payment amount, they are increasing the time it takes you to pay the money back. The extra time allows the powerful effects of compounding to work against you longer, and you end up paying a lot more. They are also charging you a high interest rate. Remember, the interest rate was the second most powerful element of the Big 3. When they encourage you to pay the minimum payment each month they are using the two most powerful elements of the Big 3, plus the devastating power of compounding interest against you. They know the power of the Big 3 very well and they will use its power to beat you in the war for your dollars.

This is an example of letting the enemy create the rules. If you let the enemy set the rules, they will set them to their advantage. You need to set the rules of engagement to your advantage. You, not they, need to decide how much you will pay each month. *You* can decide how quickly you will be free from debt and win the war. In Step 7 – Pay Off Debt, I will teach you how to get completely free of the devastating effects of credit card debt once and for all. I will teach you how to take control and set your own rules of engagement.

Here are other examples of the enemy setting the rules:
- Taking 30 years to pay off your house
  (In Step 10 – Pay Off Your House, I will show you how to pay it off years early and save thousands and thousands of dollars.)
- Waiting until you are 65 to retire
  (Retirement has nothing to do with age. It has everything to do with the amount of money you have. You can retire when you are 39 if you have enough money. In Step 9 – Plan Retirement, I will show you how to set up a simple retirement plan, and you can determine when you will retire.)
- Making you pay a $3 fee to get your own money out of an ATM machine
- Buying Christmas presents in November and December when the stores say you should. Make your Christmas list in January. Buy extremely discounted items throughout the year, store them in a closet until Christmas, and save hundreds of dollars every year. You can

even buy for *next* Christmas at *this* year's after-Christmas sales. You decide when you buy Christmas presents, not the retailers.

OBEY THE ENEMY'S RULES

Another fast way to lose a war is to obey the enemy's rules. If you obey the rules of the credit card company and pay only the minimum monthly amount, you will lose the war for your dollars. You could end up paying twice as much for each purchase and take many years to pay it off. The credit card company used the Big 3 as a weapon against you, and they have been winning the battle. If you decide to make your own rules of engagement and pay the full amount every month, or better yet not even use your credit cards, you will be able to redirect the money that would have gone out the Spending bucket paying for interest into the Put It To Work bucket. That amount will work, earning more and more each year. If you decide to obey your own rules of engagement, then you can win the war for your dollars.

Note: I am not saying that you should not honor due dates, contract terms, or other legal obligations. You should pay your bills on time and honor all legal agreements. I am talking about rules of engagement on the marketing front.

HOW TO WIN THE WAR

I have shown you the three fastest ways to lose a war and how to avoid them. Now I will teach you how to win the war.

One of the oldest writings on military strategy, *The Art of War*, was written around 500 B.C. Its author is widely believed to be Sun Tzu. For 2,500 years it has proven to be a great guide in the conduct of war. It covers the basic principles of war and how to increase the chances for victory. It has also become a popular business book.

THE PREMISE OF THE ART OF WAR IS:
1. **Know your enemy.**
2. **Know yourself.**
3. **Know the terrain.**

BASIC #2
KNOW YOUR ENEMY

You have to know your enemy in order to be victorious in war. It is difficult to fight an enemy if you know nothing about them. I know your enemy. My undergraduate degree was in marketing. I also have an MBA with an emphasis in marketing, and I have taught marketing classes in universities at the undergraduate and MBA level. At one time, I was your enemy.

WHO IS YOUR ENEMY?

Your enemy is any entity that wants you to give them your money. Retail stores, utility companies, insurance companies, governmental agencies, banks, and any establishment that gets your money from the Spend It bucket can be your enemy. The enemy spends billions of dollars a year and hires millions of sales people and support staff to try to get you to spend your money on their products and services.

The main thing you need to know is that everything your enemy does is designed to meet their main objective of getting you to give your money to them.

You are greatly outnumbered, but with the weapons I will give you in this section you will be able to defeat this massive army and win battle after battle in this war.

BASIC #3
KNOW YOURSELF

I shared earlier the great advice: "Expect people to be themselves and you will rarely be wrong." In this section I want you to alter that advice a little to "Expect yourself to be yourself." If you will make your marketing battle plans and engage in the marketing war expecting that you will be yourself, you will do well. If you go forward into battle hoping that you will all of a sudden develop strengths you did not have before or will acquire new skills out of thin air, you will not do well.

As you move forward on your journey to your ultimate goal of a great financial life, be honest with and about yourself. God made every person unique. He gave every person a certain mix of strengths (gifts) and weaknesses. Know your individual strengths and weaknesses. Use your strengths and manage your weaknesses. If you have a particular strength, then use it as you fight the marketing battles for your dollars. If you have a particular weakness, then protect yourself in that area or get help from another source.

This is also a time to make sure that you are combining your strengths with the other members of your financial success team (spouse, children, etc.). Remember, the team strength charts in Step 2 – Working Together section. As individuals on the battlefield you can be defeated, but as a team working together with combined strengths, you can win.

BASIC #4
KNOW THE TERRAIN

QUESTION:
Who wins in a fight between an alligator and a bear?

ANSWER:
It depends on *where* they fight.

If they fight in the water, the alligator will win. If they fight on the land, the bear will win. Both are powerful animals, great hunters, and vicious fighters, but either one can be defeated if it is not fighting on the terrain that best suits its strengths. If the bear wants to win, he should fight on the land. If the alligator wants to win, he should fight in the water.

This is a strategy you can use when you engage in the marketing battle. Your battle plans and decisions should happen on *your* terrain, not on *theirs*. You should be making battle decisions on your turf, in the comfort of your home, not in the middle of their turf, the store.

The main thing you need to know about the terrain is that in most cases the enemy will own it. The places you will go to wage battle will be designed, owned and operated by your enemy. So the best thing you can do is make your battle decisions on your own terrain before you go to battle and spend as little time on their terrain as possible when you engage in battle.

When you walk into a store every aisle, every shelf, and every product has been designed and placed in a way that will get you to buy as much as possible. The lighting, the temperature, even the music has been especially chosen to create an atmosphere that will entice you to buy as much as possible. The items you need on a regular basis, milk, bread, eggs, etc., are typically placed at the back of the store to lure you deeper into enemy territory, hoping you will buy more as you walk past the many products on your way. All the candy and other items that are placed at the checkout counter are there to tempt you and your children while you wait in line. Nothing is accidental about the design of stores. Every aspect is planned, designed and constructed to get you to buy more, and if you do not have the right weapons and tactics, you will lose the battle for your dollars.

Do not make your critical battle decisions on their terrain. Do not wait until you are in the store to decide what you will buy. Make a list in the comfort of your home on your own terrain before you go to the store.

ONLY FOR A TIME
I do not want you to do this forever, but until you reach a great financial life, I want you to view shopping like a military Special Forces mission. This is your objective:

- Get in.
- Acquire what you need—only what you need.
- Get it for the lowest possible cost.
- Get out.

In order to make your mission successful you need to identify exactly what you are going to get before you go in. As soon as you get what is needed, get out of the store.

Special Forces teams make their battle plans and set their objectives on their own turf before they enter the enemy's territory.

Note: After each shopping trip, do a Plus/Delta debrief. The Plus/Delta form will help you identify what is working in your battle plan and what can be improved.

WHAT IF YOU REALLY ENJOY SHOPPING?
If you really enjoy shopping, I do not want to take that enjoyment away from you. I do not want you to totally give up the pleasure you get from shopping, but I do want to limit the negative impacts of using shopping as a form of entertainment and enjoyment.

If you are desperate for the process of buying, you can pacify yourself with a "shopping trip" to the library. You can bring home a pile of movies, magazines, books, CDs, and sometimes even artwork without spending a dime!

REWARD & REDEFINE

We are now going to use two tools from the behavior basics section to allow you to still get your shopping fix without jeopardizing your goal of a great financial life:

On a regular basis, give yourself a reward for your battle victories and treat yourself to a shopping trip. You can go without a list, and you can look at everything you want, but here is the key: Redefine your shopping behavior. Take a certain amount of money, and put it in an envelope. This envelope will redefine (put a fence around) your shopping behavior. This is the amount you determine appropriate on your own turf. As a reward to yourself, you can buy anything you want, but you cannot under any circumstances spend more than the amount of money in the envelope.

For example, you set aside $100 each month in an envelope that you can spend on a shopping spree and buy whatever you want. At the end of the month, reward yourself by going to the mall and walking around for however long you want and buying whatever you want. You can get your shopping fix without harming your progress to reach a great financial life. Just remember, do not spend more than you have in the envelope.

The amount and frequency of your redefined reward is up to you. Try to strike a healthy balance between enjoying your reward while maintaining progress toward your goal.

NOW WHAT?

So you are at war with an enemy who is well-funded, well-equipped, well-trained, experienced, who knows themselves, knows you, knows the terrain, and has a well-designed battle plan. Big deal!

Victory does not automatically go to the side with the most money, and it does not automatically go to the side with the largest army. Victory goes to the side that is the most committed to reaching their goal and best uses their knowledge of the enemy, themselves, and the terrain. Victory also goes to the side that has the most effective weapons and tactics and uses them effectively. In the remainder of this section I will give you several weapons and tactics that are very simple and extremely powerful. They will help you win battles no matter what the enemy throws at you.

You can win this war! Remember, you are the one with the power. You have what the enemy wants—your money. All you have to do is keep it.

You know the first four basics:

Basic #1   **You are in a war.**
Basic #2   **You know your enemy.**
Basic #3   **You know yourself.**
Basic #4   **You know the terrain.**

Now you will learn how to use the most powerful tools and tactics available to help you win the battle for your dollars. These tools are simple and extremely powerful. Most importantly, you can begin to use them immediately. Any one of these tools used properly can pay for this program a hundred times over.

BASIC #5
WEAPONS AND TACTICS

TACTICS
The weapons and tactics presented in this section are simple to use and very powerful.

TACTIC #1 - GUERILLA WARFARE
Guerilla warfare is a tactic that is used when a relatively small number of soldiers fight a war against a much larger, more powerful army. It is also used in situations where the small army fights on a terrain owned or occupied by the larger army. The guerilla warriors do not engage the enemy in the open with sheer force. They would lose that type of battle. The guerilla forces spend most of their time planning and then they choose their own battles on their own terms. They choose the time and terrain that will give them an advantage and increase their chance of victory in each battle. This is a very effective way to win a battle against a much larger enemy.

There are several key elements of guerilla warfare that will help you win each battle.

MOBILITY
A small number of troops are much more mobile than a large army. They can move from place to place very quickly to avoid the enemy or to engage the enemy when and where they want.

You are much more mobile than your enemy. You can shop at any store you want, and you can change locations from week to week depending on which store has the best deals and gives you the best chance of winning the battle. You are mobile, and you can choose where and when you will fight.

USE THE ENEMY'S WEAPONS AGAINST THEM
Another very powerful tactic of guerilla warfare is for the small army of soldiers to capture the weapons of the larger army and use them against them.
In a war setting, the small army has limited weapons and resources. So one of their main tactics is to capture weapons and resources from the larger army and use them to win battles. In this situation, the smaller army is actually being supplied by the larger enemy. The smaller army can make raids on the supply centers of the larger army or they can take weapons left behind by the larger army after each battle. Once the smaller army obtains these weapons, they can use them against the larger army. This is a very efficient way to obtain weapons and resources. The guerilla forces do not have to design, produce, or pay for the weapons. They only have to know how to get them from the enemy and how to use them.

You can use this technique in your battles. There are several weapons that the enemy has that you can use against them. This includes: P.U.P. (Per Unit Price), coupons, loss leaders, and special sales. These are powerful weapons that the enemy produces, but you can use them to win battles and eventually the war for your dollars.

The P.U.P. is a powerful weapon that you can use to win a battle no matter what the enemy throws at you. It is powerful, simple, and it is provided by your enemy. I will show you how to use the P.U.P. weapon in the upcoming weapons section.

TACTIC #2 – A.I.D.S.
Marketers use a very powerful tool called A.I.D.S.

MARKETING PROCESS OF A.I.D.S.

A ttention

I nterest

D esire

S ale

This is the process people go through when they buy things. It is a process that you must understand to win the marketing battle for your dollars.

HOW IT WORKS

ATTENTION
The first thing a marketer must do is get your attention. If they do not get your attention, they will never get your interest, desire or the ultimate goal the sale. The thousands of signs you see on the way to work and the thousands you see on the way home are an attempt to get your attention. The TV commercials you see and the radio ads you hear are trying to get your attention. The window displays you see in the mall and the covers of magazines are trying to get your attention. The crazy clown on stilts at the local car dealer is simply trying to get your attention.

If they get your attention, then they can take you to the next step: interest.

INTEREST
If the marketer is successful at getting your attention, then the next step is to get you interested in whatever they are selling. The sign that tells the marketer that you have entered into the interest phase is if you begin to gather information such as reading a brochure or asking about financing, colors, sizes, or delivery dates. Any activity to get more information indicates that you have entered into the interest phase. Once they get you to the interest phase, their next step will be to get you to the desire phase.

DESIRE

After they have gotten your attention and you have moved into the interest phase, their goal will be for you to move into the desire phase. The desire phase is where you begin to fall in love with the product or service. You picture your family in that new house; you picture your hair blowing in the wind as you drive that new convertible. You stand in front of that window display as you picture yourself in that new red dress, walking along the beach holding those new shoes in your hand. The desire phase is where you say things like, "Honey, I think that Hummer will fit in the garage," or "Think of all the family time we can have in that new boat," or "Honey, picture just the two of us standing on the deck of that cruise ship looking out over the beautiful waves."

The sign that tells the marketer you have entered the desire phase is anything you say, think, or do that indicates that you have already made the purchase mentally or emotionally.

SALE

Now that they have taken you through the attention phase, interest phase and desire phase, their next and final goal will be to get you to the sale phase. This phase is where they will actually close the deal. This is where you sign the contract. This is where you give them your money. This is where you very often lose the battle.

Here are a few examples of people going through the A.I.D.S. process.

EXAMPLE 1
CAR DEALERSHIP

If you pull up to the curb, park your car, get out, and start walking around the car lot, the car dealer can assume that they somehow got your attention. Maybe it was the clown on stilts, the flashing lights, the balloons and flags dancing in the wind, a TV or radio commercial, free hot dogs, or maybe a particular car. It really does not matter. If you are walking around the car lot, then it is clear that something got your attention.

The salesman comes out to greet you. You are standing next to a brand new beautiful red Dodge Ram pickup truck. The salesman asks, "Can I help you?" You answer, "How much is this truck?" You have just entered into the interest phase. You are now seeking information. Anything you do to get more information is a sign that you are in the interest phase. The salesman unlocks the door of the truck, and you climb in. You can smell the leather. He asks you if you want to start it up. You say, "Yes." The engine makes a beautiful noise, even better than you imagined. The salesman asks you what kind of music you like. You answer, "Country." He tunes the satellite radio to your favorite channel, and your favorite song is just beginning. You sit there in that comfortable leather seat, listening to your favorite song, picturing in your mind what it would be like for all of your friends to see you pull up and get out of this fine truck. You have now entered the desire phase. You have mentally purchased the truck. You say things like, "This truck would carry the whole family, pull the boat, and I could use it to haul things. Besides, the truck I currently own will surely need repairs soon, and it is getting pretty banged up in appearance." You think, "Surely with the raise I am expecting at the end of the year, we could afford the payments." The salesman invites you into the manager's office, and together they show you (by playing the shell game with the Big 3: time, amount, interest) a monthly payment that you are excited about. They tell you that you will not have to make a payment for 3 months. You will have your big raise by then, and you decide "By George, I have worked hard. I have driven that old truck for years. I deserve a new truck, and besides, with monthly payments that low, I really would be dumb to walk away from this deal." So you say, "Let's do it!" You just entered the sale phase. The salesman and his manager start the paperwork, and the deal is closed.

EXAMPLE 2
LEATHER COAT

It is a Saturday afternoon, it is raining, and you do not have anything to do, so you go to the mall to walk around. Maybe you will run into a few of your friends, maybe get something to eat. As you are walking, looking at the people and all of the window displays, out of the corner of your eye you notice an attractive jacket on one of the mannequins in a window display (attention). You start to move toward the display. As you get closer, your heartbeat starts to pick up because you can see that it is a leather jacket the exact color you have always wanted, and the design of the jacket would fit you perfectly.

You go into the store to find out how much the jacket costs (interest—you are now seeking information). The salesperson walks with you out to the display, looks at the jacket, looks at you and says, "You were born to wear that jacket." It makes you feel better that someone else agrees with what you are thinking. Then the salesperson tells you that if you buy the jacket before Sunday when the sale ends, it is a mere $499. They can get you financing so good that you will not even feel like you are paying for it! Then the salesperson says, "Let's try it on!" The salesperson holds up the jacket as you slip your arms into the smooth, comfortable sleeves. You can smell the leather as you wrap the coat around you and look into the mirror. You smile. The salesperson says, "You look fabulous!" You stand there and picture getting complements. You picture people asking where you got that fabulous coat. You say, "This will go perfectly with 90 percent of my clothes." You have entered the desire phase. You have mentally purchased the coat. The salesperson says, "You can wear it out of the store if you like." You keep the jacket on, stuff your old jacket in the bag, whip out a credit card, and walk out of the store feeling like a new you! (Sale!)

EXAMPLE 3
GROCERY STORE

You walk into the grocery store, grab a cart, and head down the aisles. You do not have a shopping list. You do not know exactly what you need or how much you will spend. The only thing you do know is that you are hungry. You work your way up and down the aisles of thousands of products that are trying to get your attention. On the first aisle, you notice a big, attractive display for a new energy drink (attention). You pick up a can to read the label (interest). You picture yourself having more energy and how cool you will look holding an energy drink (desire). You put a six-pack of energy drinks into the cart (sale).

On the next aisle, you notice a beautiful magazine cover with illustrations on how to make your house more beautiful (attention). You pick up the magazine and thumb through it (interest). You picture your house looking like the pictures in the magazine (desire). You throw the $7.99 magazine into the cart (sale). Not only did you spend $7.99, the magazine may entice you to spend thousands updating your home.

As you pass through the bakery section, you catch the wonderful smell of cinnamon rolls cooking (attention). You go to the counter to get a better smell and see how much they cost (interest). The salesperson asks if you would like to taste a sample. You think, "I am hungry. Why not?" The cinnamon roll sample is fabulous. It tastes great and melts in your mouth. You picture how nice it would be to bring these wonderful creations to your family for breakfast tomorrow morning (desire). You say, "Give me a dozen," spending $12 and buying tons of calories (sale).

You repeat this process all throughout the store. Something gets your attention, you become interested, then desire is created, then you throw it into the cart, sale. For an entire hour, it is attention, interest, desire, sale; attention, interest, desire, sale; attention, interest, desire, sale until you end up at the checkout counter with $249 worth of stuff that you did not plan to buy. You are not exactly sure what just happened. You get home, unpack everything, and realize that you do not have anything for dinner. You definitely lost that battle! You went onto the battlefield unprepared and unarmed. You fought a well-prepared enemy on their own terrain and you lost.

There are several keys the enemy will use to make sure the A.I.D.S. process works:

- No time lags between phases
- Smooth transition from one phase to the next
- Each phase must work together. If a person bails out of a phase, they have to start all over by getting your attention again.

PROTECT YOURSELF FROM THE A.I.D.S. PROCESS
The best way to protect yourself is to be aware that the A.I.D.S. process is at work and to know how to avoid entering it. You also need to know how to escape if you find yourself in one of the phases of the process.

THERE ARE SEVERAL OTHER WAYS TO PROTECT YOURSELF
- Do not look at catalogs for entertainment.
- Do not use shopping as a form of entertainment.
- Shop with a list. (See the weapons section.)
- Use the 1 for 10 Rule. (See the weapons section.)
- Use the P.U.P. (See the weapons section.)
- Use the T.A.P. (See the weapons section.)

DO NOT LOOK AT CATALOGS FOR ENTERTAINMENT
If you look through catalogs for entertainment, you are allowing yourself to be exposed to a lot of items that can get your attention. The next thing you know you have proceeded through the interest phase, through the desire phase, and you find yourself on the phone or online ordering things. Stop looking through magazines and you will greatly reduce the number of items that are able to get your attention. If they do not get your attention, they cannot get your money!

DO NOT USE SHOPPING AS A FORM OF ENTERTAINMENT!
If you use shopping as a way to entertain yourself, you are taking a big risk that you will end up exposed to the A.I.D.S. process. When you spend your time walking around the mall, you are just asking for something to get your attention. You are putting yourself right in the middle of a sea of marketing, slogans, graphics, and displays. If you stop using shopping as a form of entertainment, you will greatly reduce the chances of something getting your attention and entering the A.I.D.S.

process. When you go shopping, have a list and only buy what is on the list, and when you get what is on your list, leave!

If you use these powerful tips, you will go a long way to protecting yourself from the often disastrous results of the A.I.D.S. process.

I am not saying that you should not buy things. I am not saying that you should not enjoy life. I am saying that if you want to reach your goal of a great financial life and reach it faster, you do need to understand the A.I.D.S. process and protect yourself and your great financial future from its negative impact. You are the one who should decide how you spend. You should protect yourself from the manipulation of the marketing process. Let these tools help you.

WEAPONS
In the movie *Braveheart*, William Wallace is adopted by his uncle after his dad and brother are killed in a battle when he is about 7 years old. In one scene he is drawn to his uncle's sword. His uncle tells him that he must first learn how to use his brain, and then he will teach him how to use the sword. You now know how to think like a warrior, now it is time to introduce you to your weapons and teach you how to use them well.

WEAPON #1 - SHOPPING LIST
A shopping list is a powerful tool that can protect you from the marketer's A.I.D.S. process. If you decide what you need to buy in the calm comfort of your home (your terrain) instead of deciding what you will buy in the middle of the store with thousands of products screaming to get your attention, you will protect yourself from the crazy overspending results of going through the A.I.D.S. process on every single item you buy.

When you fill out a shopping list before you go shopping, you are deciding what you will buy (creating your battle plan). You are not leaving it up to the products that get your attention and take you through the A.I.D.S. process. When you use a shopping list you are using your mind to make decisions instead of your senses and emotions. You now enter the store on a specific mission to obtain specific items and then get out.

I view shopping as a sort of Special Forces mission. There are very specific items I need to get that are located on enemy territory, and I must go in, obtain those items, and escape unharmed.

When you use a list, you can hit the grocery store, get your basket, and head down the aisle with a purpose. You will get each item on the list at the lowest possible price and you will not purchase anything not on the list. Once you have obtained all of the items on the list, you will leave.

Every time you enter a store and get only what is on your list for as little as possible, you have won the battle. Every month that you move dollars from the Spend bucket to the Put It To Work bucket, you have won the battle.

You will spend much less using a list because you will no longer wander around the store giving your (attention) to every different product that calls out to you.

DO NOT SAY "NO"—SAY "NOT YET"

There will still be situations when a product that is not on your list will get your attention. This is the moment of truth—the showdown. Since you cannot always count on yourself to be strong, I have developed something to help you win these showdowns. It is called "not yet." It can be difficult for people to say no, so I am asking you to say, "Not yet." One section of the shopping list I have designed for this program is called the "not yet" section. When you desire an item that is not on your list, you simply write it down in the "not yet" section of the list. When you create your next shopping list, you look at the "not yet" section of your previous list in the calm comfort of your terrain. If you decide that you still want to purchase those items, then go ahead and write them on your new list. This way you are making a logical decision to buy the item instead of buying it on impulse because of the power of desire in the A.I.D.S. process.

If you decide to use a shopping list, then stick to your guns. Commit that you will not buy anything that is not written on the list. Do not add items to the list as you go. This discipline will cause you to become a very good list maker!

BUILD IN SOME WIGGLE ROOM

I understand that people are not perfect. As a matter of fact, this program was designed based on the principle of progress not perfection. So if the absolute rule of not adding any items to the list once you are in the store is too rigid for you, then at least establish a wiggle room amount (a dollar amount that you are allowed to add to the list each time you shop). For example, if your wiggle room amount is $10, then you can add $10 worth of additional items to the list each time you shop. Anything above the $10 wiggle room amount will have to go on the "not yet" section of the shopping list. This will give you a little bit of a cushion for those items you truly do need but forgot to write on the list.

Using a shopping list is also great when you are shopping with children. They can have input on the list while you are making it at home. When you get into the store and all of those really cool, exciting products start calling out to get their attention, all you have to say is, "Let me check. Nope, it is not on the list. We are only buying things on our list today." After you say that a few times and stick to it, they will realize that no matter what they ask for the answer will be the same: "It is not on the list." It reduces your workload of trying to protect them from the A.I.D.S. process, and it will teach them firsthand how to have discipline and self-control when they shop. After a while, they will start to answer their own questions: –"This is not on the list, so we are not going to buy it." Remember, if something is not on the list but has merit, you can tell them, "We can add it to the 'not yet' list."

Using a shopping list is a very powerful weapon. It will protect you from the A.I.D.S. process and allow you to get what you need while spending less so you can put the dollars you previously wasted to work for you and reach a great financial life.

WHAT ABOUT GIFTS?

When you use a shopping list and you list "Gift for Colton," you may not know exactly what you want to buy Colton. You may want to look around to get ideas. That is fine, but I recommend that when you first list "Gift for Colton," you also put a dollar limit next to it. Example: "Gift for Colton, $20." That means that you will not spend more than $20 for his gift. If you do not do this, you can easily be tempted by $50 to$70 items. Only items costing $20 or less are allowed to get your attention.

DOES MAKING A SHOPPING LIST TAKE TOO LONG?
USE THE TRASH TRIGGER

One reason people do not use a shopping list is because they do not want to take the time to fill out the list when they are ready to go to the store. It takes too long to look in the refrigerator, in the cabinets, and on the shelves to see what items need to be bought and then write them on a list. This can take time and is typically not much fun. When you are ready to go to the store you want to just go.

I have a solution for you. It is called the trash trigger. Here is how it works:
Place your shopping list in the kitchen somewhere near the trash can. Every time you throw an item in the trash can, you simply write it on the shopping list to replace it.

EXAMPLE

If you use a can of tuna and you throw the can into the trash, you simply put a mark on the shopping list next to tuna. If you use the last slice of bread and you throw the bread wrapper in the trash, you simply put a mark on your shopping list next to bread.

Every time you use something up and you throw the package in the trash, you mark the item on the shopping list so you can buy it on the next trip to the store. Every time you throw something in the trash, it is triggering you to write it on the shopping list.

This is the same system stores use to automatically reorder items that have been purchased. When you buy an item at the store and the cashier scans it as an item sold, the computer automatically adds it to the list of items to be ordered to restock the shelves.
With the trash trigger, you build the list as you go. No more taking 30 minutes to fill out the shopping list when you are ready to go to the store. You build the list each time you throw something in the trash. When you are ready to go shopping, you simply grab the list and go.

Note: The Financial Success in a Box Kit contains a supply of shopping lists created and customized for this program. It makes the process of using a list simple and effective.

WEAPON #2 - 1 FOR 10 RULE
Wait 1 hour for every $10 of cost.

This is one of the most powerful tools of all to protect you from the A.I.D.S. process. If something gets your attention that is not written on your shopping list, you become interested. Desire builds and you are about to move to the sale phase, but then this tool can save you. This tool says that you cannot move to the sale phase until you have waited 1 hour for every $10 the product costs.

EXAMPLE

You are walking through a department store when you notice a great-looking leather wallet in the display case (attention). You walk over to the case to get a better look and to see how much it costs (interest). You ask the salesperson behind the counter if you can see the wallet. They take the wallet from the display case and hand it to you. The leather feels great; you can even smell the leather. As you open the wallet, it has the weight and feel of a finely made product. You can picture all of the people you will impress every time you open this wallet (desire). You are about to say, "I'll take it!" when you remember the 1 for $10 rule. The wallet costs $40. According to the 1 for $10 rule, you need to wait one hour for every $10 of cost. You need to wait 4 hours before you can buy this wallet. You look at your watch and see that it is three o'clock. You cannot buy this wallet until seven o'clock this evening. You hand the wallet back to the salesperson and decide to come back at seven o'clock and buy it then.

Here is why the 1 for $10 Rule works. In order for the A.I.D.S. process to work, you must go smoothly from one phase to the next without a big time gap between the phases. The 1 for $10 Rule puts a huge time gap between the desire phase and the sale phase, exactly where you need it the most. The 1 for $10 Rule allows you to get away and let the desire dissipate and allows you to escape from the A.I.D.S. process. Remember when you bail out of the A.I.D.S. process, the marketing will have to start all over again. They will have to get your attention again. When you hand the $40 wallet back to the salesperson and walk away, you are thinking that you plan to come back in 4 hours or maybe pick it up the next time you are at this store. The reality is that you will probably not come back because the desire will have a chance to fade away. You will also have time to remember the bills you need to pay, the financial goals you are trying to reach, and the fact that you can buy that wallet after you reach Financial Success and enjoy it a lot more. With the 1 for $10 Rule, you are not saying no, you are just saying not yet.

> *No temptation has seized you except what is common to man. And God is faithful; he will not let you be tempted beyond what you can bear. But when you are tempted, he will also provide a way out so that you can stand up under it.*
>
> *1 Corinthians 10:13*

EXAMPLE 1
If you see a $50 video game that you absolutely have to have, you have to wait 5 hours before you can buy it.

EXAMPLE 2
If you see a $340 outfit in a catalog, you will have to wait 34 hours before you can buy it.

EXAMPLE 3
If you see a $687 flat-panel TV, you have to wait 69 hours before you can buy it— almost 3 days.

The 1 for $10 rule inserts a time gap between desire and sale and allows you to escape the power of the A.I.D.S. process. It protects you from the negative effects of impulse buying.

Do not underestimate the power of the 1 for $10 Rule. Participants of my past classes that have used it say they rarely if ever go back and purchase the product. If they do, it usually was because the product was a need instead of a want.

WEAPON #3 - ALWAYS GET THE SMALLEST P.U.P.

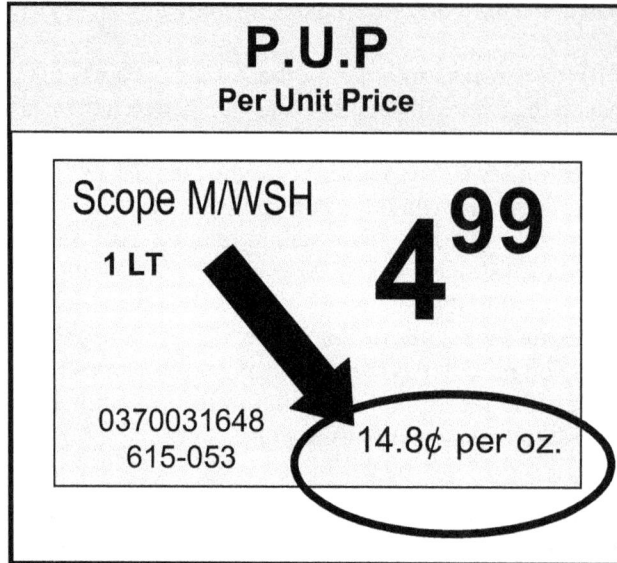

What if I told you I had a weapon that would instantly defeat anything that the marketers throw at you? Would you be interested in it? This tool cuts right through any type of marketing campaign, whether they use a coupon or package design, etc. It does not matter what they throw at you; this cuts right to the bottom line. You can use it in every buying situation to instantly identify the best value. When in doubt, look at the P.U.P.

The P.U.P. (Per Unit Price) is one of the most powerful weapons you can have in the marketing battle for your dollars. It is powerful and simple. It cuts through every marketing tactic that comes your way. It cuts through the fancy images, the eloquent words, and the emotional appeals. It quickly and simply tells you which product to choose.

WHAT IS IT
P.U.P. (**Per Unit Price**) or (price ÷ number of units)
The P.U.P. (Per Unit Price) is a way to tell how much something costs per basic unit; i.e., per ounce, per pound, per gallon, per item, per use.

EXAMPLE
An 8-ounce can of corn that costs 80 cents has a P.U.P. of 10 cents per ounce.
(80 ÷ 8 = 10¢) **P.U.P. = 10¢**

A 10-ounce box of wheat crackers that costs $1.20 has a P.U.P. of 12 cents per ounce.
(120 ÷ 10 = 12¢) **P.U.P. = 12¢**

A 16-ounce box of noodles that costs $4.00 has a P.U.P. of 25 cents per ounce.
(400 ÷ 16 = 25¢) **P.U.P. = 25¢**

The P.U.P. can even be used to calculate the Per Use Price for items such as boats, jet skis, RVs, and vacation condos. This can give you the information you need to determine how much something is costing per use.

HOW IT WORKS
In most stores, the P.U.P. is posted on the price label on the shelf (see example) for each product. Not only is the price listed, but the P.U.P. is listed also. You do not even have to calculate the P.U.P. This makes it very easy to scan each label to see which product has the lowest P.U.P. That is your best value. The posted price marked on the product does not tell you if it is a good deal compared to other products; the P.U.P. does. Using the P.U.P. is a great guerilla tactic. It is a weapon produced and supplied by the enemy that you can use to win the war for your dollars.

EXAMPLE
On the grocery shelf, there are 16 different types of canned corn. They come in different brands, labels, and prices and are offered in four sizes. It would take a rocket scientist to figure out which was the best deal. There are so many different options. With P.U.P., you do not have to do calculations. Simply look at the price per ounce on each of the price labels mounted on the shelf and buy the one with the lowest P.U.P.

I have taught my children to totally disregard all of the marketing efforts in the packaging and labeling and even disregard the price of a product. They look directly at the P.U.P. on the price label. That number tells the best value. Beautiful packaging can cause you to pay more for something than you should. Look at the P.U.P!

ALWAYS PICK THE SMALLEST P.U.P

EXAMPLE 1
The shelf at the grocery store has 10 different types and sizes of ketchup.

Product 1	P.U.P. = 2¢
Product 2	P.U.P. = 4¢
Product 3	P.U.P. = 22¢
Product 4	P.U.P. = 8¢
Product 5	P.U.P. = 16¢
Product 6	P.U.P. = 21¢
Product 7	P.U.P. = 13¢
Product 8	P.U.P. = 4¢
Product 9	P.U.P. = 17¢
Product 10	P.U.P. = 27¢

The range is two cents to 27 cents P.U.P. on virtually the same product. In this example the lowest P.U.P. is two cents. That is the best deal!

RULE: ALWAYS PICK THE SMALLEST PUP

EXAMPLE 2
The shelf at the grocery store has 9 different types and sizes of flour.

Product 1	P.U.P. = 2¢
Product 2	P.U.P. = 4¢
Product 3	P.U.P. = 22¢
Product 4	P.U.P. = 8¢
Product 5	P.U.P. = 16¢
Product 6	P.U.P. = 21¢
Product 7	P.U.P. = 13¢
Product 8	P.U.P. = 4¢
Product 9	P.U.P. = 17¢

The range is two cents to 22 cents P.U.P. on a product as basic as flour. In this example, the lowest P.U.P. is two cents. That is the best deal!

RULE: ALWAYS PICK THE SMALLEST P.U.P
The P.U.P. not only allows you to compare items next to each other on the shelf, it allows you to compare items between stores. You can compare the P.U.P. of ketchup at three different stores and find the best deal.

You cannot always trust that you are getting a good deal. Just because the product looks cheap does not mean it is. Just because you are buying it in bulk does not mean you are getting a good deal. Just because you are using a coupon does not mean you are getting a good deal. The single best indicator that you are getting a good deal is the P.U.P. (Per Unit Price).

Note: Using the P.U.P. to make your purchasing decision also protects you from the A.I.D.S. process. If you are only looking at P.U.P. price labels, it is unlikely that a fancy product or label will get your attention, interest, desire, and sale and tempt you to buy something that is not a good value.

THE INCREDIBLE SHRINKING PACKAGE
P.U.P. also protects you from the incredible shrinking package. Many companies will leave the price of their product the same and reduce the size of the product in the package. This tactic is not necessarily noticed by the customer so they do not realize they are not getting as good a deal as they used to. They are paying the same price, but getting less product.

A popular cereal company chose to shrink cereal boxes, not prices. A newspaper article pointed out that the company reduced the size of its cereal packages by an average of 2.4 ounces on five of its brands while charging the same prices. The move was made to offset increasing production costs. A year earlier, a competitor also reduced its cereal package sizes while continuing to charge similar prices.

When a company reduces the size of its product and charges the same price, it is actually raising the price. When you get less for the same price, then the price has gone up. Companies know when you are looking at products on the store shelf you will notice if the posted price has gone up, but you will probably not notice that the size of the package has been reduced. You keep buying the same product week after week paying the same price, while the amount you get gets smaller and smaller. It is all about behavior. They can reduce the size of the package while charging the same price, and they make more profit. Most of the time the public will not even be aware that these changes are happening unless a recipe no longer works because it called for "a can" of condensed milk and it has decreased by two ounces.

The P.U.P. weapon will protect you from the incredible shrinking package tactic of the enemy. When you look at the P.U.P. on each product instead of the posted price, you will be aware when the package size is reduced. If they reduce the size of the package and the price stays the same, then the P.U.P. will go up. Remember, the P.U.P. is the price divided by the number of units. If the number of units is reduced, then the P.U.P. will go up.

EXAMPLE

A 20-ounce box of cereal that costs $2.40 has a P.U.P. of 12 cents per ounce.

(240 ÷ 20 = 12¢) **P.U.P. = 12¢**

If the size of the box is reduced from 20 ounces to 15 ounces and the price stays at $2.40, then the P.U.P. will go up:

The new 15-ounce box of cereal that costs $2.40 has a P.U.P. of 16 cents per ounce.
(240 ÷ 15 = 16¢) **P.U.P. = 16¢**

The price has remained the same, $2.40, but the P.U.P. has increased from 12 cents to 16 cents.

Even though the posted price of the box of cereal did not increase, the price you paid increased 25 percent (12¢ P.U.P. to 16¢. P.U.P.).

You paid 25 percent more for the same product and you where probably not even aware of it. When they shrink the package and keep the price the same, you pay more!

Make sure you use the P.U.P. weapon, and you will not be fooled by the incredible shrinking package. If they shrink the package and keep the price the same, the P.U.P. has to go up, and you will notice it. The P.U.P. will protect you!

THE INCREDIBLE SHRINKING DIAPERS
When my wife and I had our first baby, I went to the store quite often to buy diapers. The diaper companies make it very easy to buy diapers. When your baby is a newborn you buy the pack of diapers that has a size 1 on it. As the baby gets bigger you start buying the package with the size 2 and then 3 and 4 until you get up to the package with the size 5 on it. The process is very simple. When we realized that the size 1 diapers were getting a little small for our baby, I went to the store to get the size 2 package. I anticipated that I would have to pay more for the size 2 package of diapers, but when I got to the store I was pleasantly surprised that the price on the size 2 package of diapers was exactly the same price as the package of size 1 diapers. As I looked down the shelf

I noticed that all the different sizes of diapers had the same exact price. I thought it was nice that they would keep the price the same even though the diapers were bigger. We worked our way through several sizes of diapers, I realized that we were running out of diapers faster and faster as we moved up in sizes. On one trip to the store I discovered what was really going on. The price was the exact same on every size but the number of diapers in the package for each size was different. Each larger size contained fewer and fewer diapers. I had discovered the incredible shrinking package. The marketers knew that I had grown used to paying a certain price when we were using the size 1. When I moved up to the size 2 they had a choice: either increase the price or decrease the size of the package. If I were faced with paying a higher price for the next size, I would probably check other diaper brands to see if I could get a better deal. They knew that I was less likely to notice a shrinking package than an increasing price.

I recently went to a large discount store to see if the diaper companies were still using the incredible shrinking package tactic. Here is what I found:

DIAPERS

SIZE	PRICE	# OF DIAPERS	P.U.P.
1	$10.24	56	18¢
2	$10.24	48	21¢
3	$10.24	40	25¢
4	$10.24	34	30¢
5	$10.24	30	34¢

In the example above you can see that the diaper companies are still using the incredible shrinking package tactic. All of the examples are of the same brand. As you can see, in all different sizes you are paying the same posted price, $10.24, but each larger size contains fewer and fewer diapers. The P.U.P. goes up as the size goes down because you are getting fewer diapers. The P.U.P. on the size 5 diapers is almost 100 percent higher than the size 1 diaper. If you are looking at the posted price you may not notice that you are actually paying more, but if you use the P.U.P. you will notice when something becomes less of a deal.

BULK DOES NOT ALWAYS MEAN CHEAPER
Some products are sold in bulk packages, but that does not necessarily mean it is a good deal. Some companies know that people have grown used to the idea that a bigger package means a better deal, and they rely on the fact that you will not look at the P.U.P. A fast food Mexican restaurant had a special. Buy a single taco at the regular price of 79 cents, or you could buy a package of 10 tacos for $7.90. How dumb do they think we are? If you buy the 10-pack, you are not getting a better deal and you are simply spending more. P.U.P. will protect you from things that look like a good deal but are not.

YOU CANNOT FOOL THE P.U.P.
P.U.P. will allow you to stand in the grocery store aisle, looking at 25 different deals on salsa and instantly tell which one is the best deal. Do not underestimate the power of this tool just because it is simple. If you want to cut through all of the marketing and ensure that you get the best value every time, use the P.U.P. (Per Unit Price) weapon and you will greatly reduce the amount you spend and free up money that can go to work building your future of a great financial life.

It is your choice to prefer a more expensive bottle of ketchup or can of corn, but can you really taste the difference? Do a family taste test. Is the extra money worth it or would you rather spend it elsewhere?

BRAND LOYALTY
If you are brand loyal to a particular product, you can still use the P.U.P. weapon. The variation in P.U.P. for the same brand of product will amaze you. The range for peanut chocolate candy goes from 16 cents per ounce to 75 cents per ounce depending on where you buy them and the size and type of package. Every package contains the exact same peanut chocolate candy, but the range of P.U.P. is 59 cents. Depending on where and how you buy them, you could pay more than 400 percent higher than the best value. Even if you want to stick to a specific brand, P.U.P. will still allow you to get the best deal within that brand.

P.U.P. TRAINING
I took my children on a shopping trip to a major discount superstore to teach them how to use the P.U.P. weapon. We had our list (made in the comfort of our home, not on enemy territory) and we proceeded to get each item on the list. For each item on the list, I showed the children how to scan the P.U.P. for each different option and choose the smallest P.U.P.

EXAMPLE
I asked my nine-year-old daughter to get a bottle of Ranch salad dressing. She walked over to the shelf, scanned all the different P.U.P.s for Ranch salad dressing, and discovered that the lowest P.U.P. was 8.3 cents per ounce and the highest P.U.P. was 17.1 cents per ounce. She grabbed the bottle with the lowest P.U.P. and threw it in the cart. By simply scanning for the lowest P.U.P., we paid $2.99 instead of $6.16 for the 36-ounce bottle of dressing, a savings of $3.17. We bought the dressing for less than half of what it would cost at the high P.U.P. cost. That amount does not sound like a lot, but when you multiply it by the thousands of things you buy week after week, month after month, year after year, it can really add up. Imagine if you could cut your grocery bill by 50 percent or more by simply using the P.U.P. weapon and scanning for the lowest P.U.P. when you buy.

I told my six-year-old son that applesauce was the next thing on the list (prepared in the comfort of our home with careful consideration, not on enemy territory). He went to the applesauce shelf and began to scan the P.U.P.s for each applesauce product. He was on a mission. He was going to find the lowest P.U.P. no matter what it took. In a few seconds he said, "Here it is: 3.4 cents per ounce." I scanned the 10 to 15 choices of applesauce to check his answer and he was right. The lowest P.U.P. for applesauce was 3.4 cents per ounce. He was so proud. He grabbed that 50-ounce jar of applesauce and put it in the cart. He was very proud that he had been successful finding the least expensive option. The high P.U.P. for applesauce on the shelf was 7 cents per ounce, more than twice as high as the lowest P.U.P. price. Because my six-year-old son took a few seconds to scan for the lowest P.U.P., we only paid $1.70 for the 50-ounce jar of applesauce instead of $3.50 for the applesauce with the highest P.U.P. We saved $1.80. He cut our cost on that one item by more than 50 percent compared to the high P.U.P. product.

This weapon is so simple my six-year-old son can use it to find the best deal in less than 60 seconds. With this simple weapon a six-year-old can defeat an enemy who spends $280 billion a year against him in the battle for his dollars.

He will win the war because he has learned how to use the simple weapons that will help him win the battles.

HOW MUCH CAN P.U.P. SAVE YOU?

We continued through the store getting the items with the lowest P.U.P. until we completed our list. I was very curious to see what kind of an impact using P.U.P. would have on our total bill for that trip. I was amazed!

THE GRAPH BELOW SHOWS THE RESULTS

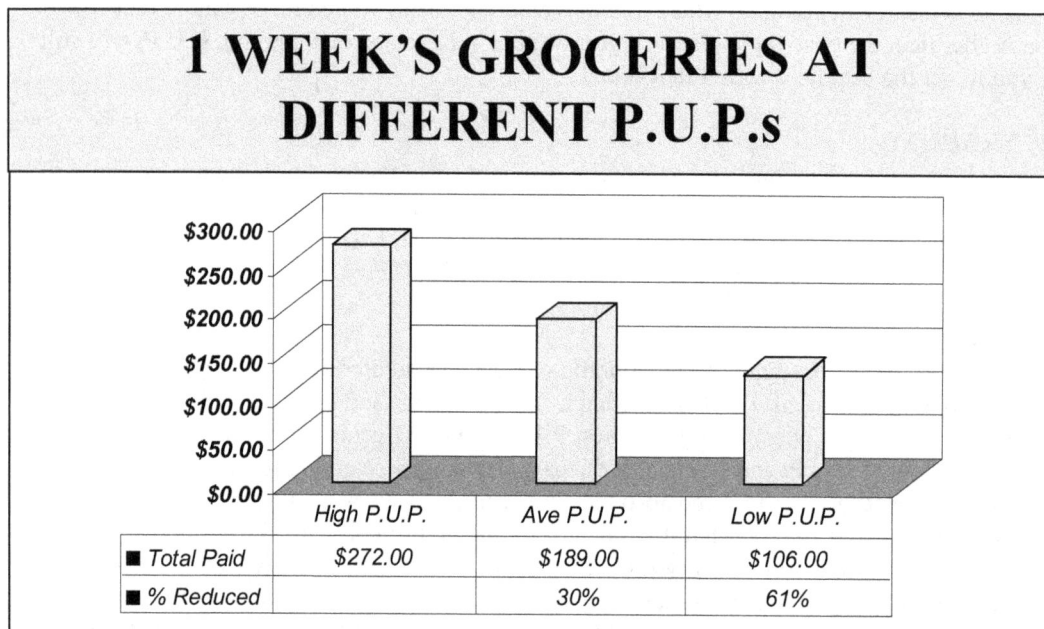

1 WEEK'S GROCERIES AT DIFFERENT P.U.P.s

	High P.U.P.	Ave P.U.P.	Low P.U.P.
■ Total Paid	$272.00	$189.00	$106.00
■ % Reduced		30%	61%

We saved a lot by purchasing products at the low P.U.P. level. On this particular shopping trip we purchased more than 30 different products, and we recorded the lowest P.U.P. and the highest P.U.P. for each product. We only compared similar products. We actually purchased the products at the lowest P.U.P. level, and we spent a total of $106. If we had purchased the same products at the highest P.U.P. level, we would have spent a total of $272. We would have spent more than twice as much money and ended up with the same amount of stuff. I also calculated what the total price would be if we had purchased the products at the average P.U.P. level. The total would have been $189. The amount that you will save by using P.U.P. will depend on where you have been in the past in the P.U.P. range. The higher in the range you have been, the more you will save by using the lowest P.U.P. By purchasing the products at the low P.U.P. level, we spent $106 instead of $272. We saved $166 in one trip by simply scanning for the lowest P.U.P. We reduced our bill by 61 percent. Imagine how much we will save in a year. Imagine how much you could save in a year if you used the P.U.P. weapon and reduced your grocery bill by 30 to 60 percent.

HOW DIFFERENT CAN P.U.P.s BE?

P.U.P.
LOW & HIGH

As you can see in the graph above, there is a big difference between P.U.P.s for basically the same products. On this trip to the store, there where more than 20 different options for a basic bottle of ketchup with a P.U.P. range from 3.7 cents per ounce to 15.5 cents per ounce. That is a more than 400 percent difference. There were more than 60 different options to buy a bottle of barbecue sauce with a P.U.P. that ranged from 4.4 cents per ounce to 10.9 cents per ounce. That is a more than 100 percent difference. In the product category of shampoos and conditioners, the high P.U.P. was as much as 700 percent higher than the low P.U.P.

Another interesting effect of using the P.U.P. weapon is that you will no longer care about fancy packaging and slick advertising on the shelves. You are focused on the P.U.P. and nothing else. This weapon protects you from the effects of the A.I.D.S. process. If you are only looking at the P.U.P., then all of the other fancy tactics the marketers are using will not get your attention, interest, desire, or sale. When my six-year-old son was scanning the P.U.P.s for applesauce, he did not care about the cute little pictures and individual packets that had been designed to get his attention as a youngster. He was focused on finding the lowest P.U.P.

SIMPLE TO USE
P.U.P. is very simple to use. Look at your shopping list for the next item to purchase (such as mustard). Go to the area of the store where mustard is located.

Once you are in the mustard section, use the 3 simple P.U.P. steps:

- **Scan** the P.U.P.s of all the mustard options.
- **Grab** the bottle of mustard with the lowest P.U.P.
- **Move on** to the next item.

In three simple steps, scan, grab, and move on, you just got the best deal possible on mustard, and it only took you a few seconds. As you move through the store you can get the best possible deal on each item you buy by doing the scan, grab, and move on process and reduce your total bill by as much as 60 percent.

You are already using P.U.P. in other areas of your life. When you purchase gas for your car you are looking at the P.U.P. The price per gallon is the P.U.P. That is how you decide which location has the best deal on gas.

When you use the P.U.P. weapon you will be able to get the best deal on each item you purchase, which will allow you to spend less and move money from the Spend It bucket to the Put It To Work bucket and reach your goal of a great financial life.

Note: The custom Financial Success in a Box shopping list included in the kit provides a place to record the P.U.P. of each product so you can compare the P.U.P.s between different stores. After you have used it awhile, you will just know whether a P.U.P. is a good deal or not.

If the P.U.P. is not posted, you can easily calculate it. (Price ÷ Units = P.U.P.)

I recommend that you make a commitment to use the P.U.P. weapon for at least three months (90 days) to solidify it as a new right habit.

COMBINE WEAPONS
When you combine the shopping list and P.U.P., shopping becomes effective.
- You make your list on your own terrain before the battle.
- You use P.U.P. to get the best deal possible on every item on the list.
    Scan.
    Grab.
    Move on.
These weapons allow you to walk into the store at any time and get the best possible deal in a few seconds. You win the battle every time!

WEAPON #4

T.A.P.
T otal **A** mount **P** aid

WHAT IS IT

Another powerful weapon you can use is called T.A.P. (Total Amount Paid). This is a weapon you use when you are purchasing larger items that are not sold on a per unit basis, for example a refrigerator, car, computer, house, etc. T.A.P. is the weapon you would use if you were making payments on an item. T.A.P. is just as powerful and simple to use as P.U.P.

T.A.P. = (Payment amount x number of payments) it is the total amount paid.

EXAMPLE
Buy a house.
Sale price: $200,000

Method of Payment	T.A.P.
Cash	$200,000

Method of Payment	T.A.P.
15-year loan at 6% interest	**$303,788**

$1,687.71 monthly payment x 180 months
You paid $103,788 in interest.

Method of Payment	T.A.P.
30-year loan at 6% interest	**$431,676**

$1,199.10 monthly payment x 360 months
You paid $231,676 in interest.

EXAMPLE
Buy a Car
Sale price: $25,000

Method Of Payment	T.A.P.
Cash	**$25,000**

Method Of Payment	T.A.P.
3-year loan at 7% interest	**$27,789**

$771.93 monthly payment x 36 months
You paid $2,789 in interest.

Method of Payment	T.A.P.
6-year loan @ 7% Interest	**$30,688**

$426.23 monthly payment x 72 months
You paid $5,688 in interest

The enemy uses a weapon called M.A.P. (Monthly Amount Paid). Here is how it works. You walk into a car dealership and see a car you want to buy for $25,000. You tell the salesperson that you like the car, but the price is too high. He responds by asking, "How much do you want to pay per month?" He is moving you away from the T.A.P. or total price of the car, and he wants you to think in terms of M.A.P. (Monthly Amount Paid). If you respond by saying, "I would be comfortable with a monthly payment of around $400," he knows that by manipulating the Big 3 of time, amount, and interest he can get you a monthly payment of $400. He can leave the interest amount the same and move the time element out far enough to give you the $400 monthly payment. If he moves the time element, duration of the loan, out to 6 years he can get you a monthly payment of exactly $426.23. That sounds great to you. You buy the car and commit to make the $426.23 payment for the next 72 months.

You tell your friends you got this fabulous car for $25,000. But did you really? Calculate the T.A.P. on your new car. By moving the time element out to 6 years, the T.A.P. (Total Amount Paid) goes up to $30,688 ($426.23 x 72 months). You paid $30,688 for a $25,000 car just so you can get the monthly payment you want.

The salesperson wants you to concentrate on the M.A.P. not the T.A.P. because he knows that he can sell you on a $426 a month payment. They also know that they would not be able to sell you on the idea of paying more than $30,000 for a $25,000 car, even though that is what is actually happening. They focus your attention on the M.A.P. and hope you will not think about the T.A.P. The credit card companies also want you to think in terms of M.A.P. instead of T.A.P. That is why they print your minimum payment amount on the bill each month. They absolutely want you to pay the minimum amount and no more. If you pay only the minimum monthly amount, then you are thinking in M.A.P. terms and you will end up paying a T.A.P. of 2 to 3 times more for every item than its original price.

If you paid the store $1,000 for that new TV, but you paid the credit card company another $1,000 in interest by making only the minimum payments each month, you paid $2,000 or more for a $1,000 TV because you were thinking in M.A.P. terms instead of T.A.P. terms.

When you pay only the minimum payment each month, you are dramatically increasing the T.A.P. (Total Amount Paid) because the time element of the Big 3 is being increased dramatically. If you owe money, the Big 3 work against you. The higher the interest rate and the longer the amount of time you take to pay, the higher the T.A.P.

THE BIG 3

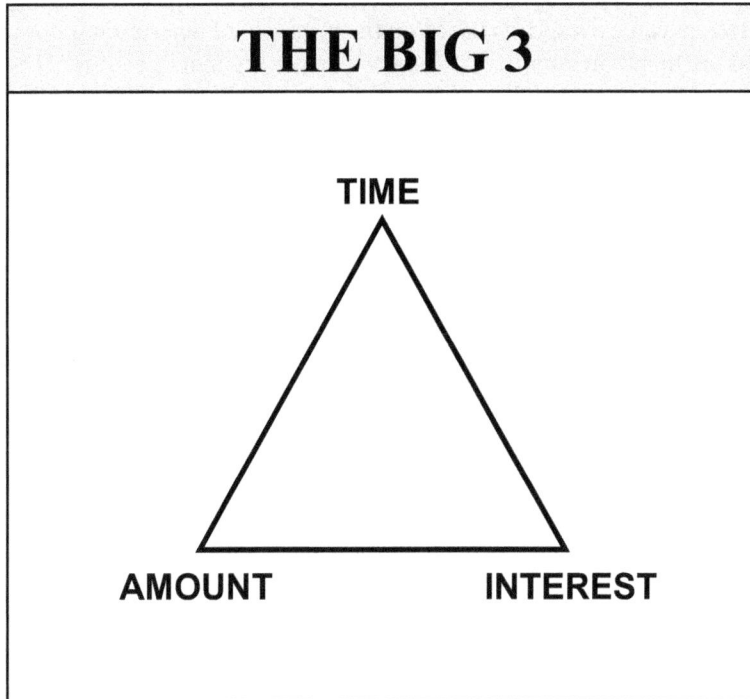

THE BIG 3

TIME

AMOUNT   INTEREST

Salespeople and bankers will use the Big 3 to play a shell game. In the shell game, a pea is put under one of three shells, and they quickly switch them around until you have lost track and do not know where to find the pea. They know about the Big 3, and they are going to move the shells around however they need to make the sale. They know how people think, and they know that you will be attracted to a low monthly payment. They are able to make the monthly amount smaller and raise the time and/or interest. They can move the shells so that you think you are getting a great deal because you only have to pay a small monthly amount, but they have actually increased the overall size of the triangle so that you pay a much higher total for the purchase.

The T.A.P. tool is exactly like the P.U.P. in that it cuts right through all of the marketing and promotional smoke and lets you instantly compare different scenarios by calculating the T.A.P. of each. You no longer need to try to figure out what the salesman is up to. You simply calculate amount of payment times the total number of payments to get T.A.P. The T.A.P. is the amount that you will pay out of your pocket for that item.

The Big 3 are always at work. The only question is this: Are they working for or against you?

These great tools are not designed to keep you from buying things and keep you from having a fun, full life. They are designed to help you live your life fully while building a strong, stable financial future. They are designed to put you in control. There is a powerful, wonderful reason to use these tools. It is called your Financial Success.

WEAPON #5 - ENVELOPE SYSTEM

WHAT IS IT
The envelope system is a very useful tool that has been around for a long time. It is a simple system consisting of a set of envelopes that are used to control the amount of money you spend each month in different categories. It is based on the principle of determining how much money you want to spend per month in a particular category before the month begins. It is a great way to control your behavior by putting a dollar limit on the amount you can spend in a particular category.

HOW IT WORKS
If you wanted to limit the amount of money your family spends eating at restaurants to $100 per month, you would simply take an envelope out of the envelope system and label it "Eating Out." On the first day of each month you would put $100 cash in the envelope. You would use the money in that envelope to pay for any restaurant meals. If you find yourself on the 15th of the month with only $25 left in the eating out envelope, then you would slow down because you would only have $25 left for the rest of the month.

If you decide that you want to limit the amount of money you spend on entertainment to $150 per month, then you would take one of the envelopes from the envelope system and label it "Entertainment." On the first day of each month you would put $150 cash in that envelope, and you would use the money in that envelope to pay for anything that fell into the entertainment category. Decide in advance what is and is not included in the category. You would use the envelope to modify your behavior throughout the month to make sure you stay within the $150 limit for that category.

The envelope system is a fabulous way to control your behavior so you can reach your financial goals. The envelope system puts a fence around your behavior so you will stay within the limits. The fence allows you to spend, but protects you from spending too much.

The envelope system works great on spending categories that are not necessarily concrete or defined. For instance, groceries, entertainment, and clothing are categories that are not specifically defined and can get out of control if not regulated. You probably will not use the envelope system for spending categories that are concrete and well-defined such as house payments, utility bills, etc. If you refer to the dashboard form in Step 1, you will see envelope icons next to the categories that work well with the envelope system. I have included an envelope system in the complete Financial Success in a Box Kit.

I have an envelope labeled "Snack Money." Every week I put $10 in the envelope and that is the money I use to buy sodas, candy bars, etc. throughout the week. Ten dollars is the amount I have identified as the maximum I am willing to spend for snacks per week. If it is Tuesday and I have already spent $7 on snacks, then I will pace my behavior so I do not run out of money too soon. When the $10 is gone, I can buy no more snacks until the next week when I replenish the envelope.

The purpose of the envelope is to help you control your behavior and to modify your behavior before you spend too much money. The purpose is not to depress you or take all of the fun out of life. Be careful when you are choosing the amount to put in the envelope each month. The goal is to choose the amount that will get the job done in the best economical way. If you choose an amount that proves to be too low even after several attempts to stay within that amount, then increase the amount until you reach the appropriate amount. If you choose a monthly amount that is too high and you have money left in the envelope at the end of each month, then adjust the amount down until you reach the appropriate amount. It will probably take a few months to get the amounts in each envelope to the appropriate level. You will have to determine for yourself the appropriate monthly amount in each category. The goal is to create a balance between spending in a particular category and self-control.

Caution: Only carry the cash you will need for that particular shopping trip. Do not take an entire month's grocery money to the store to buy one week's groceries.

WHAT IF I HAVE MONEY LEFT AT THE END OF THE MONTH?
If you have money left in any of the envelopes at the end of the month, you basically have four choices:
- Add the leftover amount to the next month as a reward, and let it accumulate.
- Put the leftover amount in savings.
- Put the leftover amount toward debt repayment.
- Use the leftover amount however you want as a reward.

If you continue to have money left in the envelope at the end of each month, then you should probably reduce the monthly amount permanently and redirect the extra money.

Use the envelope system to help you keep your monthly spending within each category at the appropriate level. The envelope system can help you reduce the number of arguments with your spouse about how much he or she is spending on certain categories, and it can help you reach your financial goals sooner.

> *Strategy without tactics is the slowest route to victory.*
> *Tactics without strategy is the noise before defeat.*
> *Sun Tzu*

From now on when you enter a battle, you will play by your own rules. You will have your list (your battle plan), you will know the two tactics for success, you will have your five powerful weapons, and you will know how to use them.

Every time you go shopping, buy only what is on your list and pay as little as possible. Then you have won the battle. Every time you win a battle, you are closer to winning the war for your dollars.

> *If you know neither the enemy nor yourself, you will lose every battle*
> *If you know yourself, but not your enemy,*
> *for every victory gained you will also suffer a defeat*
> *If you know the enemy and know yourself,*
> *you need not fear the result of a hundred battles.*
> *Sun Tzu – The Art of War*

Now you are ready! You need not fear the result of 100 battles. No longer will you wander onto the battlefield unprepared and unarmed. Here is how you win the marketing war for your dollars:

HOW TO WIN
- Realize you are in a war.
- Do not let the enemy set the rules.
- Do not play by the enemy's rules.
- Know your enemy.
- Know yourself.
- Know the terrain.

USE THESE TACTICS
- Guerilla warfare
- A.I.D.S. process

USE THESE WEAPONS
- Shopping list
- 1 for 10 Rule
- P.U.P.
- T.A.P.
- Envelope system

Get very familiar with your weapons. In military basic training, the leaders make sure that the new recruits are so familiar with their weapons that they are able to totally disassemble and reassemble their rifle with a blindfold over their eyes. This is to make sure that the soldier can use it successfully under any conditions.

SUMMARY

MONEY BASICS

#1   Everything is either **input** or **outgo.**

#2   Put as much of the **outgo to work** as possible.

#3   Use the **Big 3** to build wealth.

#4   **Compound interest** is a powerful ingredient.

#5   **Do not touch it -** let it grow.

BEHAVIOR BASICS

#1   Have a powerful goal.

#2   It is right or wrong.

#3   Keep the right; stop the wrong.

#4   Make it a habit.

MARKETING BASICS

#1   You are in a war.

#2   Know your enemy.

#3   Know yourself.

#4   Know the terrain.

#5   Weapons & Tactics

You are now fully prepared to move forward and reach your dream of a great financial life.

CONGRATULATIONS!

You now know the basics of money, behavior and marketing self-defense. You have come a long way!

- You have completed Step 1 – 10 Step Plan. You are following the simple 10-step plan.
- You have completed Step 2 – Work Together. You are working together toward the same financial goals and using each other's strengths.
- You have completed Step 3 – The Basics. You are familiar with the basics of how money works, how behavior works, and how to win the marketing battle for your dollars.

You can now move your dot on Step 3 of the scoreboard form to a score of 10.

SCOREBOARD

Now it is time for Step 4 – Giving. What does "giving" mean? It means to get plugged into the awesome power of giving.

Move forward and conquer Step 4 - Giving.

BEHAVIOR FORM

GOAL: _____

1. BEHAVIOR: _____

2. RIGHT Takes you TOWARD your goal	**WRONG** Takes you AWAY from your goal
3. How Could You Start Doing It _____ _____ _____	How Could You Stop Doing It _____ _____ _____
If you are doing it, how could you: **Protect it** _____ _____ **Automate It** _____ _____ **Delegate It** _____ _____ _____	If you cannot Stop it, how could you: **Redirect it** _____ _____ **Redefine It** _____ _____

THE BASICS
To Do List

ITEM	COMPLETED
Use Behavior Form	
Use Shopping List	
Use "1 for 10 Rule"	
Use P.U.P. Weapon	
Use T.A.P Weapon	
Use the Envelope System	
Do Plus/Delta Form	
Do Start/Stop/Continue	
Celebrate Completion of Step 3	

_____   _____
               Signature   *Date*

_____   _____
               Signature   *Date*

STEP 4

GIVING

Give and it will be given to you; good measure, pressed down, shaken together, running over, they will pour into your lap. For by your standard of measure it will be measured to you in return.

Luke 6:38

IMAGINE

Imagine how great the world would be if every person gave a percent of their income to help others.

Imagine:
- Being able to help others on a regular basis.
- Helping others around the world with your generosity.
- Giving 10 percent of your income to your church and having more Financial Success than ever before.
- Being blessed even more because of your giving.

PURPOSE

INTRODUCE YOU TO GIVING

The purpose of this step is to show you how to plug in to the power of giving. I will also show you a simple five-step process that will help you start giving and help you make your life and the world much better.

I want to introduce the topic of giving early in the 10-step process because I want you to make giving a high priority. Remember, we are going to put the big rocks in first! If you wait until you have everything else under control and only give if you have money left over, you will probably not become much of a giver. One of the foundational principles of this program is to put your money to work for you. When you give, you are putting your money to work for others. That is powerful.

ACTION ITEMS

ACTION 1 ➤ | Decide Give or Not Give

ACTION 2 ➤ | Decide How Much

ACTION 3 ➤ | Decide To Whom

ACTION 4 ➤ | Do It

ACTION 5 ➤ | Automate It (Optional)

ACTION 1
DECIDE GIVE VERSUS DO NOT GIVE

The first thing you need to do before you get the other areas of your finances in great shape (the remaining six steps) is decide whether you will be a giver or not. If you are going to be a powerful giver, you need to design it into your plan early. It will not work to wait until the end of each month and give only if there is money left over. If you want to get plugged into the awesome power of giving and make the world a better place, you need to make it a priority.

To me this step is a no-brainer. If you have been blessed, why would you not help others who need help?

GOD GAVE YOU EVERYTHING YOU HAVE

The earth is the Lord's, and all it contains, the world, and those who dwell in it.
Psalm 24:1

Yours, O Lord, is the greatness and the power and the glory and the majesty and the splendor, for everything in heaven and earth is yours. Yours, O Lord, is the kingdom; you are exalted as head over all. Wealth and honor come from you; you are the ruler of all things. In your hands are strength and power to exalt and give strength to all.
1 Chronicles 29:11, 12

Every good thing bestowed and every perfect gift is from above, coming down from the Father of lights.
James 1:17

Imagine you had two children. One is a 12-year-old boy and the other is a 10-year-old girl. You tell both of them that you are going to give each of them $10 a week, and you want them to use $1 of the $10 to help some of the less fortunate families in the neighborhood. There are children in the neighborhood who do not have winter clothing and never have enough food to eat. You make it very clear that it is your will that a small portion ($1 of the $10) of what you give them be used to do your work of helping others in the neighborhood. You want to bless them by making them a distributor of your good works. You could easily give the $1 directly to the needy neighbors yourself, but you want your children to receive the joy and blessings that come with doing your good works. You want them to understand that there is nothing quite like the feeling of helping others.

One month later as you sit at the dinner table with your family, you ask your son and daughter how they have used the now $40 you have given them. Your 12-year-old son tells stories of the great toys and games he bought at the thrift store for only $30. He is proud that he got them at a great discount. He also states that he has been very disciplined and managed to save $10 of the $40 (a 25 percent savings rate), but there is no talk about the $4 that was to be used to help the less fortunate families in the neighborhood. You are proud of him for being thrifty in his spending, and you are proud of him for learning the discipline of saving, but you are disappointed that he did not use the $4 to help others as you had instructed him. You are disappointed not only because the neighbors did not receive the help, but also because your son did not receive the blessings and joy he would have received by helping others. You gave him $40 and told him that $4 of the $40 was to be used to do your will and help others, but for whatever reason, he chose not to obey. You love your son and you always will love him, but you are disappointed that he chose not to give.

Your daughter gives her report. She also got great deals on toys and games at the thrift store for $20. She also managed to save $10 (25 percent) of the $40. She admits that she has no idea where $6 of it went. Then she tells stories of how she used the $4 to help people in the neighborhood. While she was at the thrift store, she spent $2 to buy a pair of snow boots for a little boy two houses down who did not have boots for the winter. She also bought a can of corn, a can of cranberry sauce, and two cans of green beans for a family across the street who did not have food for Thanksgiving dinner. She shares how happy and thankful the little boy and the family across the street were when she delivered the boots and the food. She also tells of the wonderful way she felt as she walked back home knowing that she had helped others. She was not sure who had been blessed more, the people she helped or herself.

You are proud of your daughter the same way you were proud of your son. She was thrifty in her purchases and a disciplined saver just like her brother. You are also proud of her because she has carried out your will and been generous by using $4 to help the neighbors. Your daughter has learned something very profound that your son has not yet learned. She has learned that if she obeys her father and puts a percentage of the money he gave her to do what he asked, then several great things happen. The receiver is blessed, the giver is blessed, and the father is pleased. You are likely to tell your daughter, "Well done, good and faithful servant! You have been faithful with a few things; I will put you in charge of many things. Come and share your master's happiness!" There is a very good chance that you will be willing to give even more to someone who manages it properly.

I believe this example illustrates the way God sees us. We are His children. He has given us everything we have. He owns everything. He has told us to use a certain percentage of what He has given us to do His work and will. He has also given us free will, and we make the choice whether we will be obedient or not. Trust me, if we make the choice to be obedient and give, we will receive the blessings God promises. If we make the choice not to give, God will still accomplish His will, we will simply be missing out on the wonderful blessings of being a part of His work.

God gave us everything we have. He even gave us His only Son. "For God so loved the world that he gave his one and only Son, that whoever believes in him shall not perish but have eternal life" (John 3:16).

I pray that you will be like the daughter in the previous example and do God's will by being a generous giver.

When you give:
- The receiver is blessed.
- You are blessed.
- God is pleased.

Everybody wins. What could be better?

> *90% with God > 100% without God.*

YOU CAN'T TAKE IT WITH YOU!
You will *ultimately* become a giver! You have no choice. When you die, everything you "own" will be given to someone else. You will never see a hearse with a moving trailer attached. While you are alive, why not give to do good instead of giving it to credit card companies and the mortgage company?

WHY GIVE?
REASON # 1 - THE NEED IS GREAT.
The need for help around the world is great. In the world, more than:

- One billion people live in absolute poverty.
- Three billion people live on less than 2 dollars a day.
- Eight hundred million people go to bed hungry.
- Five hundred million children are orphans.
- One and a half billion people have no access to medical care.
- One hundred twenty million children are outside of an educational system.
- Religious freedom is denied to 2.2 billion people.
- Twenty-five million people are enslaved.
- Seven hundred million live in urban slums.

The fact is that it takes money to help people in poverty, and it takes money to spread the gospel. The only way a lot of the help will be received is if people give!

REASON #2 - GIVING BLESSES YOU.
Think of how you feel when you see your children sharing with each other. It makes your heart glow. I believe God feels the same way when we share with each other.

> *"... remember the words of the Lord Jesus, that He Himself said, "It is more blessed to give than to receive."*
>
> *Acts 20:35*
>
> *"Give, and it will be given to you. A good measure, pressed down, shaken together and running over, will be poured into your lap. For with the measure you use, it will be measured to you."*
>
> *Luke 6:38*
>
> *Honor the Lord from your wealth, and from the first of all your produce; so your barns will be filled with plenty, and your vats will overflow with new wine.*
>
> *Proverbs 3: 9, 10*
>
> *There is one who scatters, yet increases all the more, and there is one who withholds what is justly due, but it results only in want. The generous man will be prosperous, and he who waters will himself be watered.*
>
> *Proverbs 11:24, 25*

These Scriptures point out the fact that *we* are actually blessed when we give to others. These Scriptures excite me. What a great deal to be able to help others and receive blessings yourself.

REASON #3: GIVING PLEASES GOD.

> *God loves a cheerful giver.*
>
> *2 Corinthians 9:7*
>
> *Do not neglect doing good and sharing; for with such sacrifices God is pleased.*
>
> *Hebrews 13:16*

These Scriptures are pretty straightforward. When we give, it pleases God.

REASON #4 - WE ARE CALLED TO GIVE.

If you are a Christian, then I believe you are called to give. It is called the tithe.

Honor the Lord from your wealth, and from the first of all your produce; so your barns will be filled with plenty, and your vats will overflow with new wine.

Proverbs 3:9, 10

In the New Testament, in the Books of Matthew and Luke, Jesus told the scribes and Pharisees that they should tithe and at the same time not neglect justice, mercy, faithfulness, and the love of God.

Woe to you Pharisees! For you pay tithe of mint and rue and every kind of garden herb, and yet disregard justice and the love of God; but these are the things you should have done without neglecting the others.

Luke 11:42

Woe to you, scribes and Pharisees, hypocrites! For you tithe mint and dill and cumin, and have neglected the weightier provisions of the law: justice and mercy and faithfulness; but these are the things you should have done without neglecting the others.

Matthew 23:23

ALSO CONSIDER THE FOLLOWING:
- People all over the world have needs, not wants, that they are unable to meet on their own.
- The only way some of those needs will be met is if someone gives.
- If we do not give, who will?

ACTION 2
DECIDE HOW MUCH TO GIVE
You now need to decide how much you will give on a regular basis. I recommend choosing a percentage, not a fixed amount. Then it will grow and contract with your income.

GIVING

If you are a Christian, I believe you are called to tithe. The word *tithe* means 10 percent.

> *Thus all the tithe of the land, of the seed of the land or of the fruit of the tree, is the Lord's; it is holy to the Lord... every tenth part of herd or flock, whatever passes under the rod, the tenth one shall be holy to the Lord.*
> *Leviticus 27: 30-32*
>
> *"Bring the whole tithe into the storehouse, so that there may be food in My house, and test Me now in this" says the Lord of hosts, "if I will not open for you the windows of heaven, and pour out for you a blessing until it overflows".*
> *Malachi 3:10*
>
> *Will a man rob God? Yet you are robbing me! But you say, "How have we robbed you?" In tithes and offerings. You are cursed with a curse, for you are robbing Me, the whole nation of you!*
> *Malachi 3:8 & 9*

Invariably, the question comes up: "Do I tithe on gross income or net income?" I will use the answer my former pastor used: "It depends on whether you want a gross or net blessing." I am sure this question could be debated for centuries, but I personally believe we are called to tithe on our gross income, not the net income.

EASY TO CALCULATE
God made it easy to calculate the tithe:
Simply move the decimal point one position to the left.

EXAMPLES

INCOME	TITHE
$100	$10
$250	$25
$500	$50
$1,000	$100

FINANCIAL SUCCESS IN A BOX

If your gross income is $100, you simply move the decimal point one position to the left and your tithe is $10. If your gross income is $250, moving the decimal point to the left one position would make your tithe $25, etc.

God also made the tithe a percentage so everyone gives the same proportion of their income. It is not a fixed amount.

If giving 10 percent of your gross income sounds like a lot, maybe even impossible right now, let me ask you a question. If you were able to free up 10 percent of your gross income through being less wasteful, increasing your income, or redirecting funds, would you give?

When I coach people and organizations to help them reach a higher level of potential, we really need to answer two questions: Are they *able* and are they *willing* to move to a higher level of potential? These are two very different questions. *Able* means you have the skill set, knowledge, and resources. *Willing* is attitude, passion, and motivation. Willing means you want it! This program can make you able. The question is, "Are you willing?"

ACTION 3
DECIDE WHERE TO GIVE.

"Bring the whole tithe into the storehouse, so that there may be food in My house, and test Me now in this," says the Lord of hosts, "if I will not open for you the windows of heaven, and pour out for you a blessing until it overflows."
Malachi 3:10

The Levites shall bring up the tenth of the tithes to the house of our God, to the storehouse.
Nehemiah 10:38

All Judah then brought the tithe of the grain, wine, and oil into the storehouse.
Nehemiah 13:12

You shall bring the very first fruits of your soil into the house of the Lord your God.
Exodus: 34:26

These verses tell us that the tithe should be brought into the house of the Lord. I personally give the tithe to the local church I attend. I trust the church to use the tithe to do God's work. I also give directly to other organizations and charities, but that is considered an offering above and beyond the tithe (of 10 percent).

We are also encouraged to give to the poor.

"He who gives to the poor will never want"
                                        Proverbs: 28:27

"For the poor will never cease to be in the land; therefore I command you, saying, "You shall freely open your hand to your brother, to your needy and poor in your land".
                                        Deuteronomy 15:11

"He who oppresses the poor reproaches his Maker, but he who is gracious to the needy honors Him "
                                        Proverbs 14:31

How blessed is he who considers the helpless... The Lord will sustain him upon his sickbed; in his illness, You restore him to health.

Psalm 41:1-3

He has given freely to the poor... his horn will be exalted in honor.

Psalm 112:9

You shall generously give to him [the poor], and your heart shall not be grieved when you give to him, because for this thing the Lord your God will bless you in all your work and in all your undertakings

Deuteronomy 15:10

Wealth and riches are in his house... He has given freely to the poor

Psalm: 112:3, 9

He who is gracious to a poor man lends to the Lord, and he will repay him for his good deed.

Proverbs 19:17

He who is gracious will be blessed for he gives some of his food to the poor

Proverbs 22:9

> *He who shuts his ear to the cry of the poor will also cry himself and not be answered.*
>
> *Proverbs 21:13*
>
> *He who oppresses the poor to make much for himself... will only come to poverty.*
>
> *Proverbs 22:16*

In the Old Testament, God even provided for the poor and needy through the way the harvest was performed.

> *Now when you reap the harvest of your land, you shall not reap to the very corners of your field, neither shall you gather the gleanings of your harvest. Nor shall you glean your vineyard, nor shall you gather the fallen fruit of your vineyard; you shall leave them for the needy.*
>
> *Leviticus 19:9-10*
>
> *You shall sow your land for six years and gather in its yield, but on the seventh year you shall let it rest and lie fallow, so that the needy of your people may eat... do the same with your vineyard and your olive grove.*
>
> *Exodus 23:10-11*

These verses make it very clear that we are to give to the poor. In Matthew 25:34-40 Jesus said that when we help the poor it is the same as helping Him directly. That is extremely powerful. Here are His words:

> *"Then the King will say to those on His right, Come, you who are blessed of My Father, inherit the kingdom prepared for you from the foundation of the world. 'For I was hungry, and you gave Me something to eat; I was thirsty, and you gave Me something to drink; I was a stranger, and you invited Me in; naked, and you clothed Me; I was sick, and you visited Me; I was in prison, and you came to Me.' Then the righteous will answer Him, 'Lord, when did we see You hungry, and feed You, or thirsty, and give You something to drink? And when did we see You a stranger, and invite You in, or naked, and clothe You? When did we see You sick, or in prison, and come to You?' The King will answer and say to them, 'Truly I say to you, to the extent that you did it to one of these brothers of Mine, even to the least of them, you did it to Me.'"*
>
> *Matthew 25:34-40*

Those words are amazing. Becoming a giver is truly powerful!

ACTION 4
DO IT

QUESTION

If there are three frogs sitting on a log and one decides to jump in the water, how many frogs are left on the log?

ANSWER

You probably answered, "There are two frogs left on the log," but the correct answer is three frogs. One of the frogs decided to jump in the water, but he did not actually jump in the water.

It is the same way when you decide to do something. It is the same way when you decide to give. The simple fact is deciding is not the same as doing! Deciding is mental and Doing is physical. You need to do both. Once you have decided to be a giver, decided how much to give, and decided where to give, you need to actually give.

FOUR WAYS TO GIVE 10 PERCENT OF YOUR INCOME

#1 JUST DO IT
Just decide that starting with your next paycheck; you are going to give 10 percent of your gross income. You are going to trust God that He will make the 90 percent go even further than the 100 percent did. I highly recommend this way of giving. It is a great way to fully trust the Lord.

God asks for the "first fruits." This is an act of trust and faith for us. If you give the first fruit, you have to trust God that there will be more to come. It is not the same to give the leftovers after you have depended on yourself. We are to depend on God for our provisions.

#2 90-DAY CHALLENGE
If jumping in head first, just doing it, and giving 10 percent from now on makes you nervous, then commit to a 90-day challenge. Commit to giving 10 percent for the next 90 days. Trust God to bless you! At the end of the 90 days, see how you are doing. I believe you will find that God will bless you and provide in ways you cannot even anticipate.

#3 REDIRECT THE FIRST 10 PERCENT of MONEY THAT IS FREED UP
Make a commitment that as you go through this program and start to save money, reduce expenses and pay off debt, that you will redirect the first 10 percent to giving.

EXAMPLE:
In this example, you make $5,000 per month and your current monthly expenses are also $5,000. In order to be able to give 10 percent ($500) you need to reduce your monthly expenses by 10 percent ($500). In the next month you reduce your monthly grocery bill by $100. You now redirect that $100 toward giving. Over the next year you pay off credit cards that were costing you $400 a month in payments. You would then redirect that $400 to giving. If you redirect the $100 that used to go to groceries and the $400 that used to go to the credit card companies, you would then be giving $500 per month. You would be giving 10 percent of your income by simply redirecting dollars that were being spent wastefully in other areas.

Most people are easily 10 percent to 20 percent or more inefficient or wasteful in their spending each month. By becoming a smarter consumer and eliminating debt payments you could become a great giver without reducing your standard of living or increasing your income.

#4 STAIR STEP
With this approach you would commit to giving a certain percent starting right now and then raise the percentage a certain amount at specific time periods until you reach the 10 percent level.

EXAMPLE
Decide to give 3 percent of your income starting right now and raise it 1 percent every 3 months until you reach the 10 percent giving level. In 3 months you would give 4 percent, in 6 months you would give 5 percent, in 9 months 6 percent, in 12 months 7 percent, in 15 months 8 percent, in 18 months 9 percent, and in 21 months you would be giving at the 10 percent level. Goal reached!

STAIR STEP

Step 3

Step 2

Step 1

JAN	APR	JUL	OCT	JAN	APR	JUL	OCT	JAN	APR
3%	4%	5%	6%	7%	8%	9%	10%	___%	___%

Step 1 - Fill in date of your next payday

Step 2 - Fill in the % you will begin to give on your next pay day

Step 3 - Fill in the rest of the dates and % for each step up to 10%

At the end of the chapter, find the stair step form.

> *We make a living by what we earn.*
> *We make a life by what we give.*
> Winston Churchill

NEW MONEY

No matter which of the four ways you use, commit right now that you will give 10 percent of any new money you receive. If you get a raise or a bonus, give 10 percent of it. This is new money that God has given you that you have not been relying on. Get off to a good start with any new money you receive by giving 10 percent.

GIVING

EXAMPLE

If you receive a raise of $300 a month, then you would begin to give 10 percent of that $300 or $30 a month going forward. If you receive a bonus of $5,000, you give 10 percent or $500. Any raises, bonuses, or inheritances are considered additional money. Raises and bonuses are money above and beyond what you have been making and living on. You can give 10 percent of the additional money from the start since you were not receiving it previously and it is money that is new to you. If you give 10 percent of all new money as you continue to raise your level of giving on current income, you will eventually reach your goal of giving 10 percent of your total income.

A GREAT IDEA
JOIN THE 9-1-1 GROCERY GIVERS' CLUB

Use your grocery cart to be a giver. Use the child seat in the shopping cart as a way to give to the less fortunate. For every 9 items you put into the larger basket, put 1 item in the smaller basket to give to your church or local food bank. It is a very easy and affordable way to give food and supplies to help others. It is also a great lesson to teach your children so they can be givers starting at an early age. As you go through the store you simply say, "**9** for us, **1** for others for **1** great world." This technique also models the tithe (10 percent) that God calls us to follow. Can you even imagine how much food would be given to worthy causes if every person in our country did this when they shopped? The amount would be staggering. The positive impact would be enormous.

ACTION 5
AUTOMATE IT

Normally I would recommend that you automate as many right behaviors as possible, but in the case of tithing, I believe there are benefits and possible drawbacks to automating this behavior. I will discuss the benefits and drawbacks, but ultimately the decision to automate has to be yours.

BENEFITS

One benefit of automating giving is that you will ensure it happens on a regular basis without having to be disciplined.

BEHAVIOR CURVE
SHORTCUT ACROSS THE BEHAVIOR CURVE

AUTOMATE - - - - →

UW
Land of UNAWARE

UR
Land of PARADISE

AW
Land of MISERY

AR
Land of HOPE

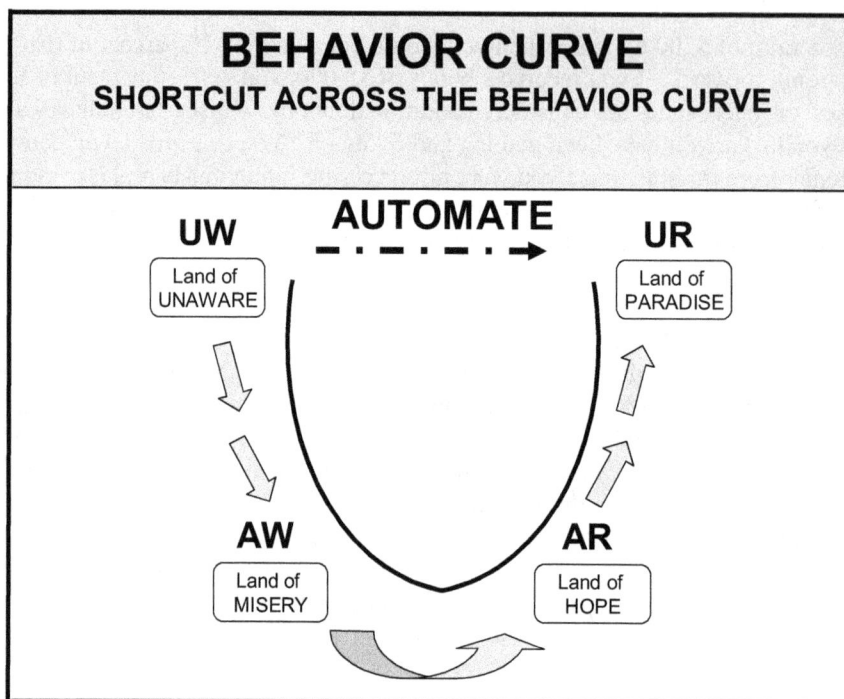

Remember the wonderful benefits of automating a behavior in Step 3. If you automate a behavior, then you instantly go to the UR (Unaware/Right) behavior point. You are doing the right behavior every paycheck without even having to be aware of it. It simply happens automatically, and you do not have to have any discipline or even think about it. Automation can save you from the sometimes arduous journey around the behavior curve.

POSSIBLE DRAWBACK
If you automate your giving, you separate yourself physically from the act of giving. I have chosen not to automate our giving because I feel it is important to physically give to the church, charities, etc. There is something that keeps me in tune with the power of giving when I physically participate in the act of giving on a regular basis. It is also important for our children to see us physically giving. It reinforces the behavior to them.

You need to decide if automating your giving is the right choice for you. If you struggle with having the discipline to give, then I recommend that you automate the behavior. If you are totally dedicated to giving and you are disciplined enough to do it, then you do not need to automate it. The choice is yours.

GET STARTED
I encourage you to begin giving with your very next paycheck. You will be tempted to stop giving along the way, but I encourage you to stay strong and dedicated. The rest of this program will help you protect your ability and willingness to give. We will be building an emergency fund and a survival fund to protect you. So if this seems difficult at first, hang in there. It will get easier as we make progress in the next steps.

CONGRATULATIONS!

You now know how to be a powerful giver.

- You have completed STEP 1 – 10-Step Plan, and you are following the simple 10-step plan.
- You have completed STEP 2 – Work Together, and you are working together toward the same financial goals and using each other's strengths.
- You have completed STEP 3 – The Basics, and you are familiar with the basics of how money works, how behavior works, and you know how to win the marketing battle for your dollars.
- You have completed STEP 4 – Giving, and you know how to be a powerful giver.

You can now move your dot on Step 4 of the scoreboard form to a score of 10.

SCOREBOARD

Now it is time for Step 5 – Put Money to Work.
What does Put Money to Work mean? It means putting your dollars to work for you. It means you will learn a simple way to put your money to work to build amazing amounts of wealth over your lifetime. This step is where your financial life begins to build great power.

Move forward and conquer Step 5 – Put Money to Work.

GIVING ACTION ITEMS

ACTION 1

ACTION 2

ACTION 3

ACTION 4

ACTION 5

Decide Give or Not Give	Yes	No	Done
Decide How Much	_____%	_____%	Done
Decide to Whom	_____	_____	Done
Do It			Done
Automate It (Optional)	Yes	No	Done

STAIR STEP

Step 1 - Fill in date of your next payday

Step 2 - Fill in the % you will begin to give on your next pay day

Step 3 - Fill in the rest of the dates and % for each step up to 10%

GIVING
To Do List

ITEM	COMPLETED
Fill Out Giving Form	
Start Giving (Next Paycheck)	
Celebrate	

_____   _____
Signature   *Date*

_____   _____
Signature   *Date*

STEP 5

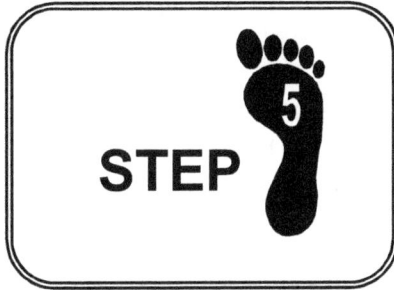

PUT MONEY TO WORK

FINANCIAL SUCCESS IN A BOX

FINANCIAL SCOREBOARD

NAME: _____   DATE: _____

STEP 1	I have a step-by-step plan to follow to reach financial success
10 STEP PLAN	1 No 2 3 4 5 Maybe 6 7 8 9 10 Yes
STEP 2	I work together with my spouse in all areas of our finances toward common goals (if you are single, mark the 10)
WORK TOGETHER	1 Never 2 3 4 5 Sometimes 6 7 8 9 10 Always
STEP 3	I know key success factors of money, behavior change and marketing self-defense
THE BASICS	1 No 2 3 4 5 Maybe 6 7 8 9 10 Yes
STEP 4	I currently give to my church, charities, etc. on a regular basis
GIVING	1 Never 2 3 4 5 Regularly 6 7 8 9 10 10% Gross
STEP 5	I currently save the following % of gross income every paycheck (includes savings, 401K, IRAs, etc)
PUT MONEY TO WORK	1 1% or less 2 3 4 5 2% 6 7 8 9 10 3% Gross
STEP 6	I currently have the following amount in a dedicated cash emergency fund
EMERGENCY FUND	1 $0 2 $200 3 $300 4 $400 5 $500 6 $600 7 $700 8 $800 9 $900 10 $1000
STEP 7	I currently owe the following total amount in consumer debt (includes credit cards, student loans, etc. – everything except your house)
PAY OFF DEBT	1 $20,000+ 2 3 $16,000 4 5 $12,000 6 7 $8,000 8 9 $4,000 10 $0
STEP 8	I currently have a cash survival fund that will cover my total expenses for
SURVIVAL FUND	1 1 Month 2 3 2 Months 4 5 3 Months 6 7 4 Months 8 9 10 6 Months
STEP 9	I contribute to my retirement fund every month and I know I will have enough (If you are currently retired, mark 10)
PLAN RETIREMENT	1 No 2 3 4 5 Maybe 6 7 8 9 10 Yes
STEP 10	I pay extra on my mortgage (If you do not have a mortgage, mark 10)
PAY OFF HOUSE	1 Never 2 3 4 5 Regularly 6 7 8 9 10 Paid Off

Fill in the circles that best describe your current situation

Connect the Dots

Total the Points

If your score is less than 90, you need this program

Work for a dollar once then make it work for you.

You can become a millionaire by doing 15 minutes of work.

IN THIS STEP YOU WILL:
- Start BUILDING YOUR FORTUNE
- Create your own MONEY MACHINE
- Push your FINANCIAL SNOWBALL down the hill
- Get YOUR MONEY working for you
- Get your EMPLOYER'S MONEY working for you
- Get the GOVERNMENT'S MONEY working for you
- Get the POWER OF COMPOUNDING working for you
- CHANGE YOUR FINANCIAL LIFE FOREVER!

IMAGINE

Imagine paying yourself before you paid the government or any of the other bills that eat away at your income. Imagine instead of paying dollars to the government putting those dollars to work for you for 10, 20, 30, or even 40 years building Financial Success 24 hours a day, 7 days a week, 365 days a year.

IMAGINE:
- Giving yourself a 3 percent raise by simply filling out a form
- Putting your employer's money to work for you building your Financial Success for 10, 20, 30, or 40 years
- Putting the government's money to work for you 24 hours a day, 365 days a year, year after year after year
- Putting $200 a month in your 401(k) each month, but only reducing your spending cash by $75
- Building a fortune using other people's money

PURPOSE

PUT YOUR MONEY TO WORK
In this step, I will show you a simple step-by-step process that will help you put your money, the government's money, and your employer's money to work building your fortune.

If I told you that you could become a millionaire by doing 15 minutes of work you would probably not believe me, but it can be true! It will take about 15 minutes and the only other thing I want you to do after that is nothing. Do nothing and let it grow. If you will do the 15 minutes of work followed by years of doing nothing, you could build a fortune of more than $1 million, $2 million or even $3 million dollars.

If I made that proposal, would you be interested? That proposal is exactly what I am making in this section. When you take the 15 minutes and complete the five steps, you will trigger the release of an amazing financial machine that will use not only your money, but your employer's money and the government's money to build a great fortune for you. It will happen automatically without you having to be super diligent and disciplined. The only thing you will have to do is leave the money machine alone so it can grow.

It only takes about 15 minutes to fill out the paperwork to join your company's 401(k) plan. Let me show you how simple and how powerful these 5 steps can be.

EXAMPLE
Bryan and Stacy are married and have a household income of $50,000. They are both 25 years old. They decide that they want to accept my proposal and spend the 15 minutes it takes to fill out the paperwork to join the 401(k) plan where they work. The company they work for has a 3 percent match, which means that the company will contribute a dollar to their 401(k) account for every dollar Bryan and Stacy contribute, up to 3 percent of their annual gross income. If Bryan and Stacy contribute 3 percent of their $50,000 annual income or $1,500 a year ($50,000 x .03 = $1,500) then the company will also contribute the company match of $1,500 to their account. Bryan and Stacy will be contributing $1,500, and the company will contribute $1,500 for a total of $3,000 per year. They just gave themselves a 3 percent ($1,500) raise. They are also putting the government's money to work for them because the dollars they will contribute to the 401(k) are pre-tax dollars. This means they get to contribute the $1,500 to the account before they pay taxes on it. So they take the 15 minutes to fill out the paperwork, and they activate their personal money machine.

This is how the money will grow:
Every month they will automatically contribute $125 ($1,500 ÷ 12 months = $125).
The company will automatically contribute $125. (The company matches up to 3 percent.)
Every month $250 will automatically deposit into their 401(k) account.

Contribution: $250 deposited every month at a 10 percent return
Return: $1,460,555 when they are age 65
          $1,774,202 when they are age 67
          $2,372,386 when they are age 70

They took 15 minutes to do the paperwork. They left it alone. It grew automatically to $2,372,386.

THAT IS POWERFUL!

ACTION ITEMS

PUT IT TO WORK

 **ACTION 1** → Enroll in 401 K

 **ACTION 2** → Choose Amount

 **ACTION 3** → Choose Investment

 **ACTION 4** → Automate It

 **ACTION 5** → Do Not Touch It

You can become a millionaire by doing
15 minutes
of work.

> *Your money should be busier than you are.*

It is important to understand the extreme power of this simple step. The example is a couple who took 15 minutes to put 3 percent of their income to work and they became multi-millionaires. Three percent of their income is not a large amount. Imagine the Financial Success they would have if they put 10 or 15 percent of their income to work.

This can work for you.
You just have to pull the trigger and do it!

In the previous example, I used a couple who were 25 years old. If you are older than 25, do not worry. I will show you in Step 9 – Plan Retirement how to save enough money to have a great retirement.

> *It's not what you make, it is what you put to work that counts.*

KEEP IT SIMPLE!
The world of money can seem vast and complicated. In this section I am going to keep it simple. There are only a few key things you need to know to put your money to work. I will take you step-by-step through this section. Do not get mired down by trying to know everything about every financial tool. The goal of this section is for you to learn the basics so you can get started. You can take time to expand your knowledge of additional financial tools and concepts later after you have the basics working for you.

ACTION 1
JOIN YOUR COMPANY 401(k)
Enroll in your company's 401(k) plan up to the company match amount.
(If you work for a non-profit or the government you will enroll in the 403(b) or 457 plan. If you do not have a 401(k), 403(b), or 457 then you will open an IRA.)

WHAT IS IT?
A 401(k) is a pre-tax retirement account. Pre-tax retirement accounts allow you to make contributions with pre-tax dollars. You can make contributions with dollars before you pay taxes on them. The pre-tax account is not an investment. It is like a container into which you put your investments.

HOW PRE-TAX ACCOUNTS WORK:

If your gross income on your monthly paycheck is $4,000, and you want to contribute $100 to your pretax retirement account, you would contribute the $100 before you pay taxes on it. So you would contribute the $100 and that would make your gross income $3,900. You would then pay taxes on the $3,900, not the $4,000. You would not be required to pay taxes on the $100 you earned or any money it generates until you withdraw it many years from now when you retire. As you will see later in this chapter, this is a very powerful tool for building financial success. The money you would have paid in taxes can now grow by generating interest and compounding it for years and years.

In a pre-tax account, you are allowed to put the government's money (money you would have paid in taxes) to work for you to build Financial Success.

A 401(k) is a pre-tax account that is sponsored by an employer for employees to build a retirement account. 401(k) plans allow employees to make pre-tax contributions and their money grows tax-deferred until they start making withdrawals. Withdrawals are typically made after the participant reaches the age of 59½. When money is withdrawn at retirement, the participant pays taxes on it as regular income.

There are also 403(b) plans for employees of non-profit organizations and 457 plans for government employees.

The benefits of the 401(k), 403(b) and 457 plans are enormous. Making pre-tax contributions and having your money grow tax-deferred until you retire can give you Financial Success.

CRAZY MATH
Yours, Mine, and Theirs

When you pull the trigger and start contributing to a pre-tax account like a 401(k) or an IRA you will encounter a wonderful thing that I call crazy math.

WHAT IS IT?

Crazy math is when you start contributing $200 a month to your 401(k), but your take-home pay (spending money) only goes down by $75 per month. Crazy math occurs when you put the government's money (money you would have paid to the government in taxes) and your employer's money (the company's matching contribution) to work for you. The only way to make this happen is to join your company's 401(k) plan and start contributing a percentage of your income to it.

HOW IT WORKS

How can you contribute $200 a month to your 401(k) plan and your take-home pay only goes down $75 a month?

To keep the math simple, let's say you decide that this month you will start contributing $100 a month to your 401(k) plan at work. This $100 will come out of your gross income (income before taxes), not your net income (income after taxes have been taken out). The $100 will be a pre-tax contribution. You are not paying taxes on this $100. This means that if you are in a 25 percent tax bracket, you are contributing $75 of the $100, and the government is contributing the other $25. The $25 you would have paid in taxes to the government is now being contributed to your account, and it will work for you year after year after year earning interest and compounding more and more interest. One hundred dollars is being contributed to your account each month, but your spending money is not reduced by $100; it is only reduced by $75. This is powerful; you put in $75 and the government "puts in" $25.

If you are in a 25 percent tax bracket, then your spending money will only go down $75 for every $100 you decide to contribute.

EXAMPLE:

Monthly Contribution	**Your Spending Money Only Goes Down**
$100	$75
$200	$150
$300	$225
$400	$300
$500	$375

IT GETS EVEN BETTER.

If your company has a matching contribution, things get even better.
- You contribute $100 (your $75 + the government's $25)
- Your company contributes $100 (your company's matching contribution)
- TOTAL MONTHLY CONTRIBUTION = $200

You have a total monthly contribution of $200 going into your account, but your spending money is only going down by $75 a month. That is a fabulous deal!

EXAMPLE: 25 percent tax bracket

Monthly Contribution (Including Company Match)	**Your Spending Money Only Goes Down**
$200	$75
$400	$150
$600	$225
$800	$300
$1,000	$375

As you can see in the example above, you can have large amounts contributed to your account without reducing your spending money by much at all. You are doing this by putting other people's money to work for you.

Yours, Mine, and Theirs

In the illustration on the next page, you can see how the $200 per month (your $75, the government's $25, and your employer's $100) with a 10 percent return compounded annually turns into $1,897,909.

$200 PER MONTH = $1,897,909

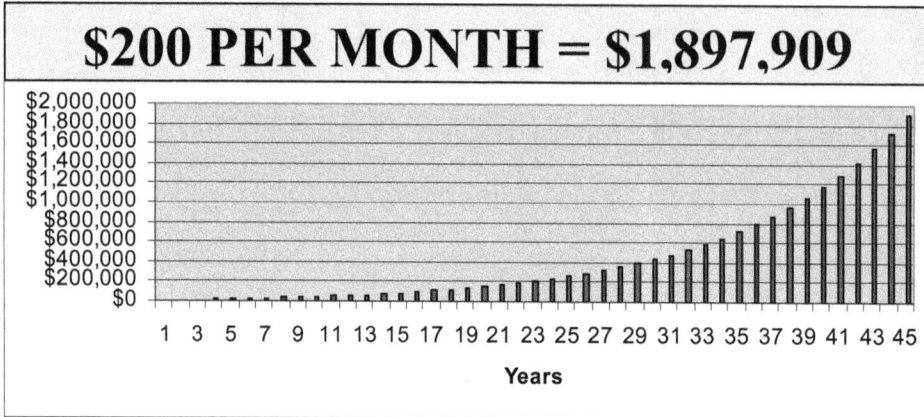

In the illustration below you can see how Yours, Mine and Theirs worked to build the $1,897,909 total:

Your $75 per month	38 percent	$ 711,716
The government's $25 per month	13 percent	237,239
Your employer's $100 per month	49 percent	948,954
Total		$ 1,897,909

This means that the government's contribution and your employer's contribution combined were responsible for 62 percent of the $1,897,909 total. Their contributions made more money for you than your own contributions made. This illustration alone should be enough to convince you to get started immediately.

$1,897,909
Yours, Mine & Theirs

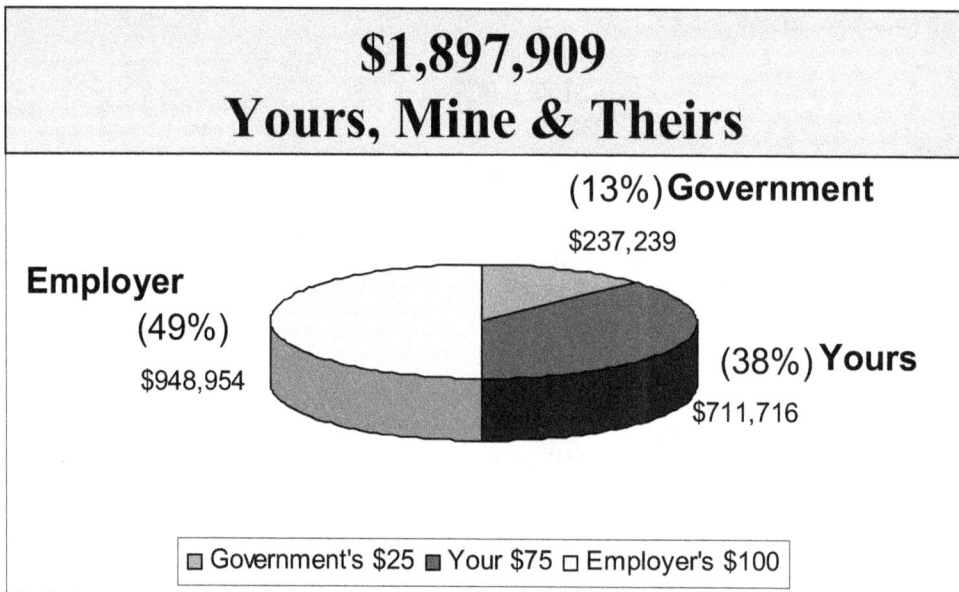

(13%) Government
$237,239

Employer
(49%)
$948,954

(38%) Yours
$711,716

☐ Government's $25 ■ Your $75 ☐ Employer's $100

If your company does not have a 401(k) or you are self-employed, you can use an IRA or SEP to get your money working for you.

IRAs

IRA stands for Individual Retirement Arrangement. People typically call them Individual Retirement Accounts. IRAs are similar to 401(k)s in that they provide tax advantages that help you save for retirement. There are several types of IRAs. In this section, I will cover the traditional IRA and the Roth IRA.

TRADITIONAL IRA

The traditional IRA is very similar to the 401(k) plan. You can make contributions with pre-tax dollars, and your money grows tax-deferred until you start making withdrawals at retirement. The withdrawals are taxed as regular income. So just like the 401(k), you get the great advantage of putting pre-tax dollars to work for years and years to build your Financial Success.

ROTH IRA

The Roth IRA is different from the Traditional IRA in that you do not contribute pre-tax dollars, but you do not pay taxes on withdrawals at retirement. You contribute using net dollars that you have already paid taxes on, but your money grows tax free, and as long as you meet the requirements, you will not pay taxes on the money when you begin withdrawing it.

TRADITIONAL OR ROTH?

The best way to decide if you should use a traditional IRA or a Roth IRA is to decide if you want your tax advantage now or when you retire. The traditional IRA gives you a tax advantage right now by letting you contribute pre-tax dollars now and not pay taxes until later when you retire. The Roth IRA gives you the tax advantage later. You contribute dollars that you had to pay taxes on, but later when you make withdrawals, you will not have to pay taxes on the money you withdraw.

So do you want your tax advantage now or do you want it later? You need to decide based on when it will benefit you most.

Get your company's 401(k) forms or go online and enroll in the plan!

Note: Your company's 401(k) plan will have specific guidelines on when you can enroll, contribution limits, etc. You can get familiar with the details when you enroll. If your 401(k) has specific times when you can enroll, then make sure you enroll on the first day you are eligible to join.

It can cost you a fortune if you wait.

ACTION 2
CHOOSE THE AMOUNT.

When you fill out the paperwork for the 401(k), you will be given the choice to contribute a fixed dollar amount each month or a percentage of your income. Choose a percentage. If you choose a fixed amount your contributions will never increase. If you choose a percentage, then your contributions will automatically increase as your salary increases, and you will build your fortune much faster.

What Percentage Should I Choose?

If your company offers a company match, then choose the percent up to the company match, but no higher.

EXAMPLE:
If your company matches your contributions up to 3 percent of your salary, then choose 3 percent as your monthly contribution amount. If your company matches your contributions up to 4 percent of your salary, then choose 4 percent as your monthly contribution. The idea in this section is to take full advantage of your company's matching contributions so you can put their money to work for you.

Right now, I do not want you to contribute any more than the amount the company will match. We will come back to this in Step 9 - Plan Retirement and raise the percentage to build your retirement plan. For now, we only want to choose the percentage that will take full advantage of your company's match.

If your company does not have a matching contribution or you decide to use an IRA, then choose 3 percent as your contribution. In this step, we are simply putting your money to work so you do not miss out on the powerful effects of compounding over time. We will increase your contribution amount later in Step 9 – Plan Retirement.

THE PERFECT EMPLOYEE
Money is the perfect employee. When you put it to work for you it:
- Works 24 hours a day, 365 days a year
- Never takes a vacation
- Never gets sick
- Never has jury duty
- Never complains

Its children (interest earned) and its grandchildren (compound interest) also work for you generation after generation.

ACTION 3
CHOOSE YOUR INVESTMENTS

401(k)s and IRAs are not actual investments. They are more like pre-tax containers for investments. If you use these containers to hold your investment, then you are allowed to contribute pre-tax dollars. Even though you have enrolled in your 401(k) or opened an IRA, you still need to choose the investments you want your pre-tax contributions to buy.

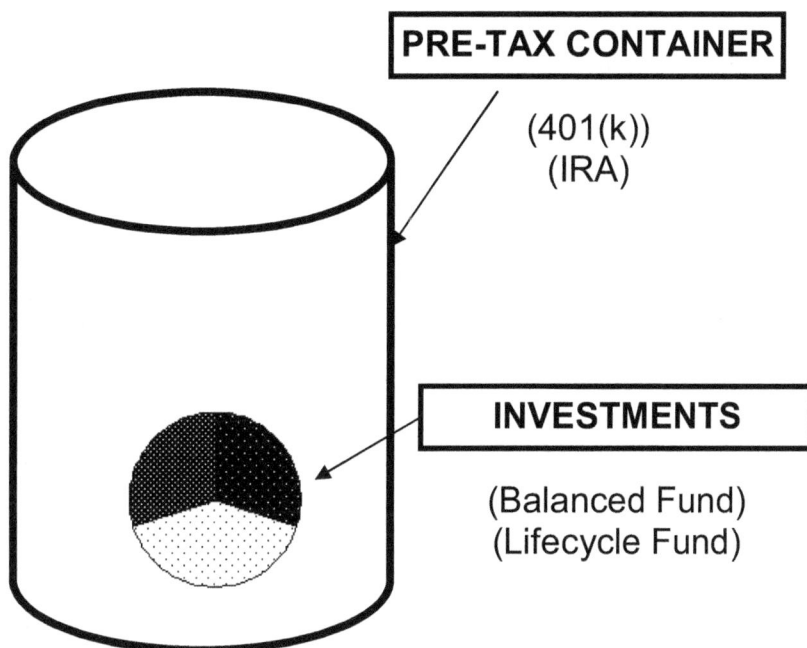

PRE-TAX CONTAINER

(401(k))
(IRA)

INVESTMENTS

(Balanced Fund)
(Lifecycle Fund)

There are many types of investments that have so many details that it would make your head spin. For our purposes in this step, I will introduce you to a couple of simple powerful investments that you can use to get started. Again, if you want to learn more about the world of investments, you can do that after we have taken care of the basics. Keep it simple!

MUTUAL FUNDS
Here is the definition that appears on the U.S. Securities and Exchange Commission's website: "A Mutual Fund is a company that pools money from many investors and invests the money in stocks, bonds, short-term money market instruments, other securities or assets, or some combination of these investments. The combined holdings the mutual fund owns are known as its portfolio. Each share represents an investor's proportionate ownership of the funds holdings and the income these holdings generate."

Mutual funds make investing very simple, and they provide great diversification. You can choose one mutual fund that contains stocks, bonds, and money market funds. Mutual funds make investing easy to understand.

THERE ARE BASICALLY THREE TYPES OF FUNDS IN WHICH TO INVEST:
MONEY MARKET FUNDS

Money market funds have one of the lowest levels of risk. They typically consist of treasury bills, commercial paper, and certificates of deposit. The main purpose of this type of fund is to try to protect and maintain the investor's principal. These funds typically have lower risk and lower returns.

BOND FUNDS

Bond funds consist of government and corporate bonds. A bond is a loan that entitles you to repayment with interest. Bond funds have a higher risk than money market funds, but they also typically have higher returns over time. One of the main purposes of bond funds is to provide steady growth and steady income.

STOCK FUNDS

Stock funds consist of the stocks of various companies. Stock funds have a higher risk level than money market funds and bond funds, but they also offer the possibility of higher returns. Stock funds contain different types of stocks, such as growth stocks, income stocks, different-sized companies, U.S. and international stocks.

THE SIMPLE SOLUTION IS A BALANCED FUND OR A LIFECYCLE FUND.

BALANCED FUNDS

A balanced fund is a mutual fund that combines a money market, bond, and stock component in one fund. Balanced funds are great for giving you diversification with a mix of safety, income, and growth. Balanced funds are also simple because you simply choose the balanced fund that has the right mix for you.

In the illustration below, balance funds A, B, and C all have a mix of money market, bond, and stock funds. Balanced fund A has a larger portion of stock and a smaller portion of bond and money market funds. Balanced fund A has a higher risk element, but it also has the potential for higher returns. Balanced fund B has a smaller portion of stocks and a larger portion of bonds and money market funds. Balanced fund B has less risk than fund A, but also has less potential for high returns. Balanced fund C has a very small portion of stock, a medium portion of bonds, and a large portion of money market funds. Fund C has very low risk, but may also have lower returns than fund A or fund B.

Fund A would be for a person who is a long way from retirement and can afford the higher level of risk in exchange for the possibility of high returns. Fund B would be for the person who is about halfway to retirement. It has less risk than fund A, but still has the potential for good returns. Fund C would be for the person who is close to retirement and does not want the higher level of risk of fund A or B.

BALANCED FUNDS

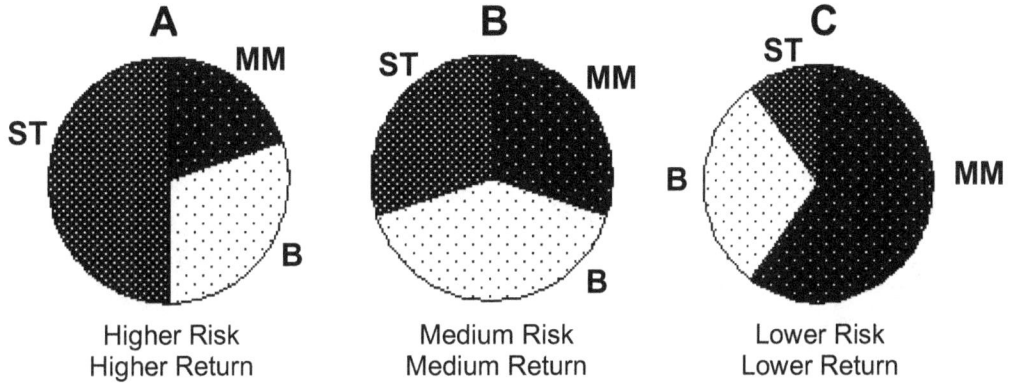

A

ST — MM — B

Higher Risk
Higher Return

B

ST — MM — B

Medium Risk
Medium Return

C

ST — MM — B

Lower Risk
Lower Return

LIFECYCLE FUNDS

A Lifecycle fund is a mutual fund that contains different proportions of money market, bond, and stock components based on the year you plan to retire. For example, if you will retire in the year 2030, you simply choose the 2030 fund. If you will retire in the year 2035, then you choose the 2035 fund. The mix of money market, bond, and stock amounts will be different depending on how long it will be until you retire. If you are 25 years old then, the proportion of stocks and bonds will be larger than the money market proportions because you can have a higher exposure to risk in exchange for more growth. As you move closer to retirement, the proportions of the lifecycle funds will be different. For example, if you are 45 years old, you may want a higher proportion of bonds and money market and a little less in stocks because you are not as willing to expose yourself to the higher levels of risk associated with stocks. So as you move closer to retirement, the lifecycle funds adjust the proportions of money market, bond, and stock proportions to adjust for your shifting emphasis from higher risk/higher returns to principal protection and stability.

LIFECYCLE FUNDS

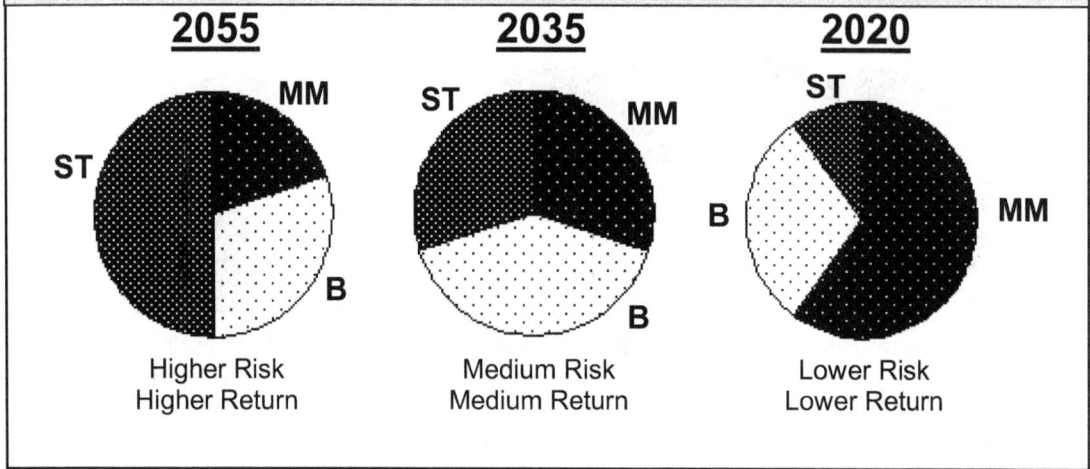

2055	2035	2020

MM · ST · B

ST · MM · B

ST · B · MM

Higher Risk
Higher Return

Medium Risk
Medium Return

Lower Risk
Lower Return

When you join your company's 401(k), 403(b), 457 plan or open an IRA, choose a balanced fund or a lifecycle fund that best fits where you are on your retirement path. Just make sure it has the proper mix of stock, bond, and money market funds. This is a simple way to make sure you do not have all of your eggs in one basket.

Note: To learn more about 401(k) plans, mutual funds, and other basic investment topics, search the Internet or go to www.investopedia.com and use the tutorials section of the website.

ACTION 4
MAKE IT AUTOMATIC.

Remember from Step 3 the importance of automating right behaviors. When you sign up for your 401(k), 403(b) or 457 plan, your deposits will be made automatically from your paycheck. If you open an IRA, then set up automatic deposits from your checking account or savings account. Do not rely on being disciplined enough to make the deposits yourself each month. Automate it to make sure it happens!

> *You may delay, but time will not.*
>
> *Unknown*

ACTION 5
NEVER, EVER TOUCH IT.

Make a commitment that no matter what, you will not touch the money that you have put to work in this Step 5 – Put It To Work. Make a commitment that you will be disciplined and strong and never touch your financial snowball.

I will help you keep your commitment to never touch this money and interrupt its phenomenal growth. In Step 6 – Emergency Fund, I will show you how to build an emergency fund to protect you from having to take money from the snowball every time your car or furnace breaks down. In Step 8 – Survival Fund, I will show you how to build a survival fund that will protect you and your family from major emergencies such as the loss of a job. The survival fund will pay your living expenses for extended periods of time (3 to 6 months) so you will not be tempted to take money from your financial snowball. It is a great feeling to get on the other side of a major financial crisis and be able to say, "I am so glad I did not have to touch the financial snowball to make it through. The snowball continued to grow at full speed and is continuing to grow."

Putting your money to work is a long term strategy to build Financial Success. You need to make a commitment that you will not touch your financial snowball—no matter what!

DO NOT WAIT!
Do not wait—put your money to work today. Waiting to start costs more than you think. Maybe you are thinking. "This all sounds good, but I will wait until next month or next year to get started. It will not cost me that much to wait." Waiting one year to start could cost you **$174,937**!

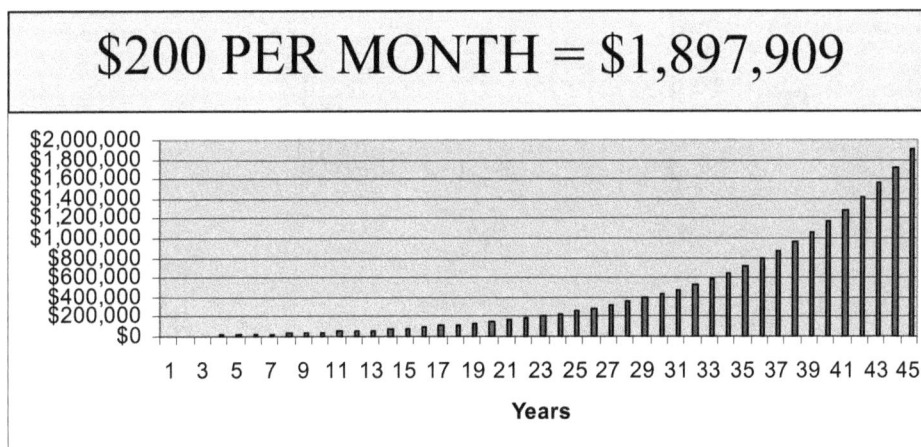

$200 PER MONTH = $1,897,909

In the example above, we have the same illustration we used earlier of a $200 monthly contribution at an annual interest rate of 10 percent compounding for 45 years. At the end of the 45 years it has grown to **$1,897,909.**

WHY DOES IT COST SO MUCH IF I WAIT?
Let's say you are 20 years old, you want to retire when you are age 65, and you are trying to decide if you should put your money to work now or wait until next year to get started.

As you can see in the illustration on the next page, by waiting one year to start the entire graph shifts to the right and your money only grows for 44 years instead of 45 years. The finish line does not move; it is the start line that moves. You still want to retire at age 65. When the graph shifts to the right you do not miss out on Year 1, you miss out on Year 45—the most productive year on the graph.

During Year 1, the account increases by $2,640 ($2,400 deposit + $240 interest). During Year 45, the account increases by $174,937 ($2,400 deposit + $172,537 interest).

If you think that waiting one year to get started will only cost you the $2,640 of Year 1, then you are seriously mistaken. It will actually cost you the $174,937 of year 45. Remember, the finish line does not move; it is your start line that moves. The whole graph shifts to the right and your money only grows for 44 years instead of 45 years.

A - Waiting 1 year to start costs you   **$174,937**   **(Year 45)**
B - Waiting 5 years to start costs you   **$729,464**   **(Years 41 through 45)**
C - Waiting 10 years to start costs you   **$1,182,404**   **(Years 36 through 45)**

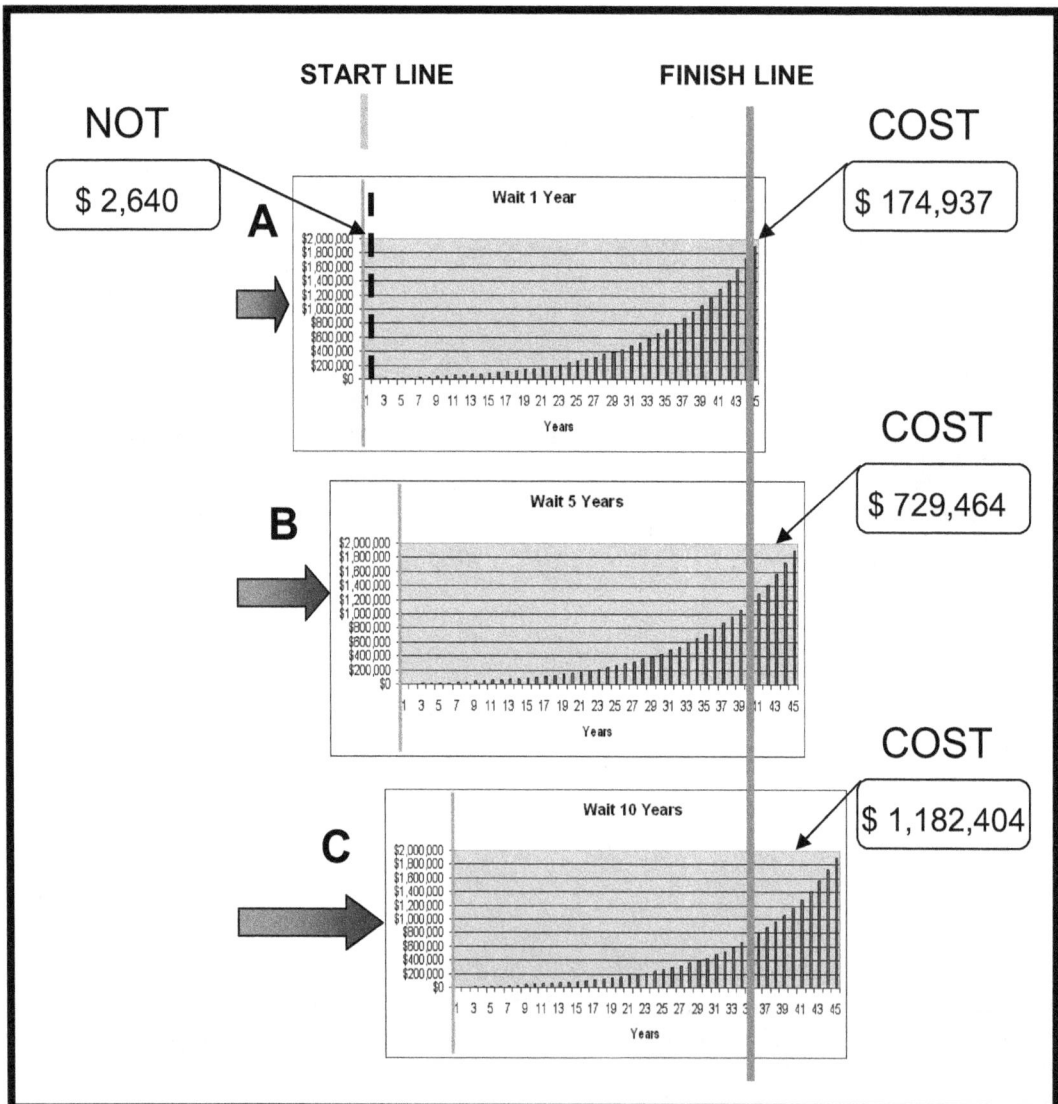

If you are in your 30s, 40s, 50s or 60s, do not let this example discourage you. Let it inspire you to get started and not miss out on any more productive years. Whether you are 40 years from retirement or 10 years from retirement, realize that those last years are the most productive. *Do not miss them by waiting to start.*

It is critical to your financial future that you put your money to work today!

CONGRATULATIONS!

YOU ARE HALFWAY THERE!

- You have completed Step 1 – 10-Step Plan, and you are following the simple 10-step plan.
- You have completed Step 2 – Work Together, and you are working together toward the same financial goals and using each other's strengths.
- You have completed Step 3 – The Basics, and you are familiar with the basics of how money works, how behavior works, and how to win the marketing battle for your dollars.
- You have completed Step 4 – Giving, and you know how to be a powerful giver.
- You have completed Step 5 – Put Money to Work, and you have the Big 3 working for you 24 hours a day, 365 days a year as your financial snowball grows bigger every time it rolls over.

You can now move your dot on Step 5 of the scoreboard form to a score of 10.

SCOREBOARD

Now it is time for Step 6 – Emergency Fund.

What does emergency fund mean?

It means creating a cash emergency fund that will protect you from emergencies such as car repairs, plumbing problems, and other unexpected financial surprises that inevitably happen to everyone. It means creating a cash emergency fund to protect the progress you have made so far in Step 1 through Step 5.

Move forward and conquer Step 6.

PUT IT TO WORK
ACTION ITEMS

ACTION 1 → Enroll in 401K — Done

ACTION 2 → Choose Amount — Equal to Company Match — or — 3% — Done

ACTION 3 → Choose Investment — Balanced Fund — or — Lifestyle Fund — Done

ACTION 4 → Automate It — Payroll Deposit — or — Checking Account — Done

ACTION 5 → Do Not Touch It

PUT IT TO WORK

ACTION 1 → Enroll in 401 K

ACTION 2 → Choose Amount

ACTION 3 → Choose Investment

ACTION 4 → Automate It

ACTION 5 → Do Not Touch It

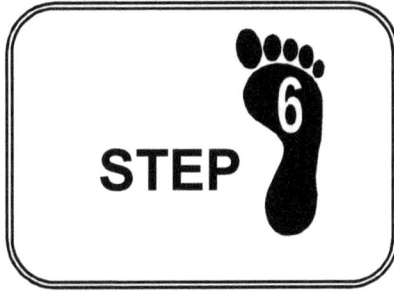

EMERGENCY FUND

SCOREBOARD

FINANCIAL SUCCESS IN A BOX

FINANCIAL SCOREBOARD

NAME: _____   DATE: _____

STEP 1 10 STEP PLAN — I have a step-by-step plan to follow to reach financial success
1 No 2 3 4 5 Maybe 6 7 8 9 10 Yes

STEP 2 WORK TOGETHER — I work together with my spouse in all areas of our finances toward common goals (If you are single, mark the 10)
1 Never 2 3 4 5 Sometimes 6 7 8 9 10 Always

STEP 3 THE BASICS — I know key success factors of money, behavior change and marketing self-defense
1 No 2 3 4 5 Maybe 6 7 8 9 10 Yes

STEP 4 GIVING — I currently give to my church, charities, etc. on a regular basis
1 Never 2 3 4 5 Regularly 6 7 8 9 10 10% Gross

STEP 5 PUT MONEY TO WORK — I currently save the following % of gross income every paycheck (Includes savings, 401K, IRAs, etc)
1 1% or less 2 3 4 5 2% 6 7 8 9 10 3% Gross

STEP 6 EMERGENCY FUND — I currently have the following amount in a dedicated cash emergency fund
1 $0 2 $200 3 $300 4 $400 5 $500 6 $600 7 $700 8 $800 9 $900 10 $1000

STEP 7 PAY OFF DEBT — I currently owe the following total amount in consumer debt (Includes credit cards, student loans, etc. – everything except your house)
1 $20,000+ 2 3 $16,000 4 5 $12,000 6 7 $8,000 8 9 $4,000 10 $0

STEP 8 SURVIVAL FUND — I currently have a cash survival fund that will cover my total expenses for
1 1 Month 2 3 2 Months 4 5 3 Months 6 7 4 Months 8 9 10 6 Months

STEP 9 PLAN RETIREMENT — I contribute to my retirement fund every month and I know I will have enough (If you are currently retired, mark 10)
1 No 2 3 4 5 Maybe 6 7 8 9 10 Yes

STEP 10 PAY OFF HOUSE — I pay extra on my mortgage (If you do not have a mortgage, mark 10)
1 Never 2 3 4 5 Regularly 6 7 8 9 10 Paid Off

① Fill in the circles that best describe your current situation

② Connect the Dots

③ Total the Points

If your score is less than 90, you need this program

Copyright © 2010

The wise man saves for the future, but the foolish man spends whatever he gets.

Proverbs 21:20

IMAGINE

Imagine having $1,000 cash or more in an emergency fund dedicated to protect you and your loved ones from unexpected emergencies.

Imagine:
- Not stressing out when your car needs repairs
- Not having to go deeper into credit card debt for every emergency
- Not having to rob your 401(k) or other investments to pay for emergencies
- Paying cash when emergencies happen
- Sleeping peacefully because you have prepared in advance for emergencies

Imagine the comfort you will experience knowing that you are protecting you and your loved ones from the negative impacts of emergencies.

PURPOSE

BUILD A $1000 CASH EMERGENCY FUND

The purpose of this step is to show you a simple step-by-step process that will help you build a cash emergency fund that will protect you and your family from the things that will threaten your Financial Success.

In this step, I introduce the subject of building an emergency fund. I will show you five simple action items that will help build a protective outer wall that will help protect you and your family from the emergencies that will happen on your journey to a great financial life.

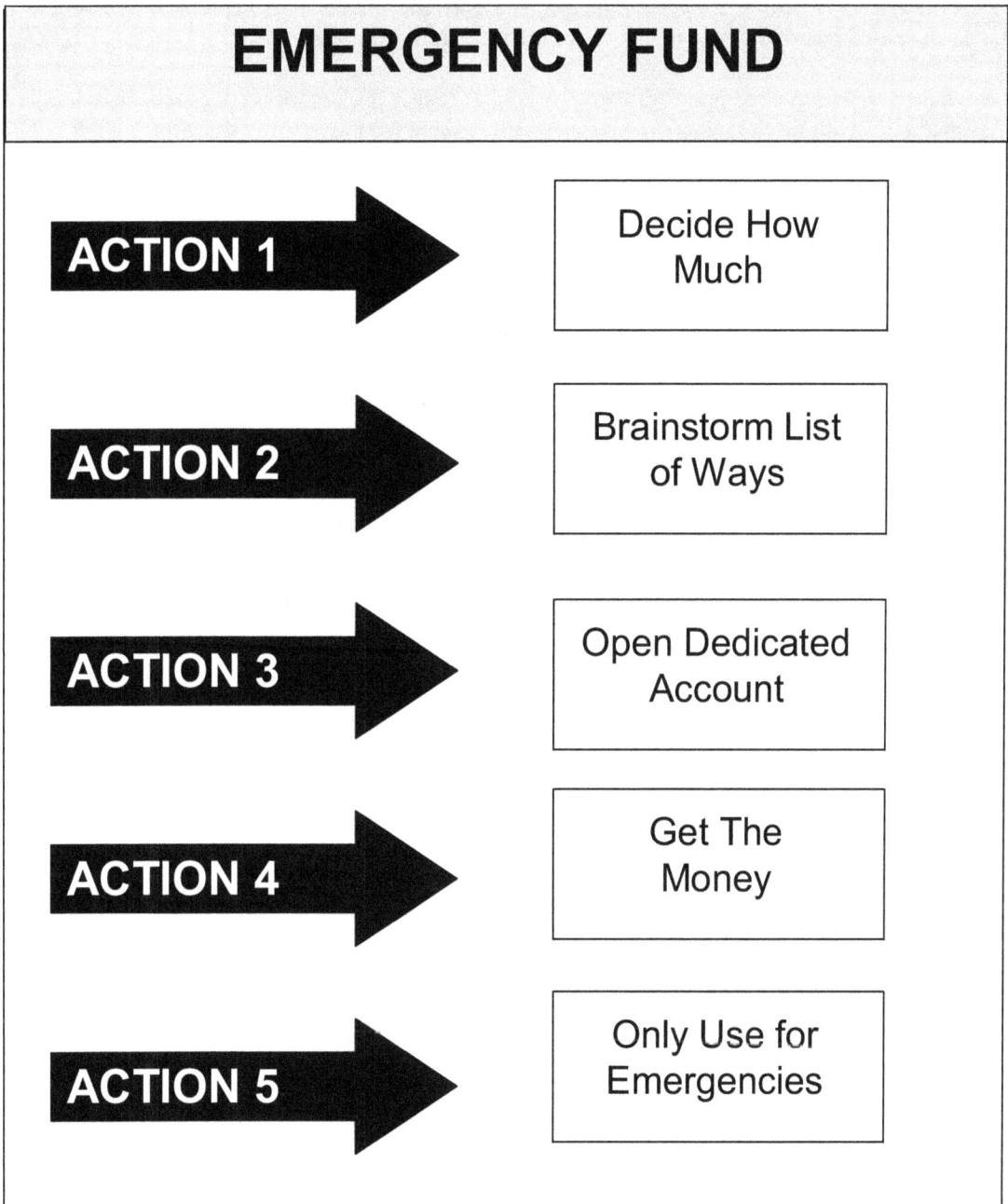

ACTION ITEMS

EMERGENCY FUND

ACTION 1 →	Decide How Much
ACTION 2 →	Brainstorm List of Ways
ACTION 3 →	Open Dedicated Account
ACTION 4 →	Get The Money
ACTION 5 →	Only Use for Emergencies

THE GREAT WALLS

Your cash emergency fund will be much like the great walls that were built to protect castles in medieval times. The castle walls were the primary barriers between the people who lived in the castle and any threat that would attack the castle from the surrounding area.

The walls were built to be impenetrable because if an enemy broke through the walls, it could have meant certain death for the inhabitants of the castle. There were two walls that protected the castle. There was an inner wall and an outer wall. The outer wall was the first line of defense against enemy attackers. The inner wall provided another line of protection in case the outer wall was breached.

In this section we will be building your financial outer wall. In Step 8 – Survival fund, we will build an inner wall that will provide an even greater level of protection to you and your financial future.

The castle's outer wall was a serious structure. It completely encircled the castle and its grounds. The outer wall was often 45feet high and 7 to 20 feet thick. The outer wall was often covered with steel plates to make it even tougher to penetrate. The outer wall also had 30- to 40-foot high towers allowing soldiers to look out over the countryside to spot attackers. The towers provided a high platform for the defending soldiers to wage war on their attacking enemy.

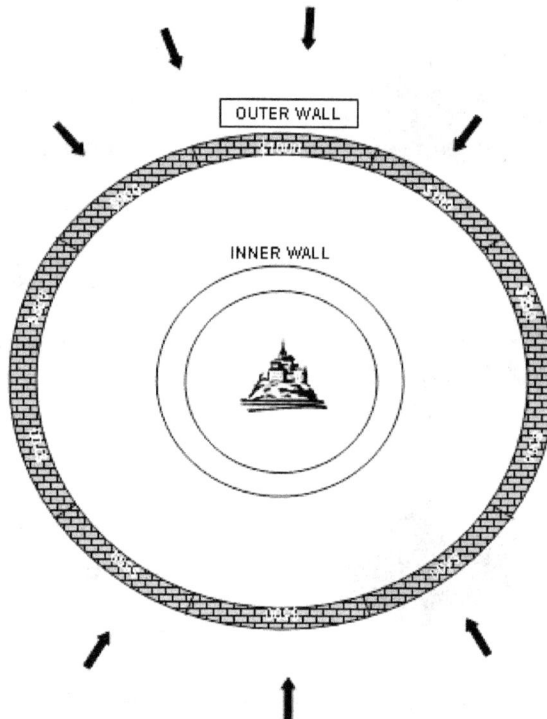

You need to build an emergency fund (outer wall) that will protect your financial castle from the attack of emergencies. You will be attacked—your car will break down, your refrigerator will eventually give out, and sooner or later your washer or dryer will suffer some type of problem. It is not a question of *if* you will have emergencies; it is a question of *when* your emergencies will happen. You need an emergency fund to protect from these emergencies so you can continue to make progress on your journey to Financial Success.

In this step, we are going to find $1,000 to work as soldiers to protect you while you complete the rest of your Financial Success Plan.

REASONS FOR A CASH EMERGENCY FUND

Reason #1: Having an emergency fund allows you to enjoy life much more because you do not have to worry about what emergency might come and how you would possibly take care of it. You can have a lot more peace in life if you know you have a cash emergency fund.

Imagine driving down the road and you hear a big bang under the hood of your car and steam starts pouring from under the hood. If you do not have an emergency fund, you probably think: "Oh no! How am I going to pay for this?" You panic. Your mind races as you pull to the side of the road: "Am I going to need a tow truck? This could cost hundreds and hundreds of dollars! Where am I going to get the money?" Your stomach feels sick, and you know the next few days are going to be horrible while you try to scrounge up the money to get the car repaired. Chances are you will end up paying for the repair with a credit card, and you will be in worse shape financially than you were before the emergency. You will spend years and years paying the minimum amount on the credit card, and you will end up paying two to three times more than the repair actually cost. This is no way to handle an emergency.

Now imagine the same scene, but this time you have a cash emergency fund. You are driving down the street, and you hear a big bang under the hood of your car, and steam pours out from under the hood. Your first thought is to get the car safely to the side of the road. Your second thought is: "I'm really glad I have a $1,000 emergency fund. It should take care of this even if I need a tow truck." You take a deep breath, call the tow truck, pay the repair shop in cash, and you are on your way. This is the way to handle an emergency.

EMERGENCIES ARE A LOT LESS TRAUMATIC IF YOU HAVE CASH TO PAY FOR THEM.

Reason #2: An emergency fund protects the progress you are making on building your great financial life. At this point you have your money growing in a 401(k) or IRA, and you do not want to have to touch your financial snowball every time you have an emergency. You also do not want to go further into debt every time you have an emergency by using a credit card or a home equity line of credit.

Having a cash emergency fund allows you to live with less worry and stress, and it protects the progress you are making toward building a strong, healthy financial life.

THE GNATS

An early explorer took an expedition party to Africa. They had many great adventures. When they returned home, the leader of the expedition was asked by a reporter, "Were you afraid of the lions, elephants, and the many other dangerous animals in the bush?" The leader of the expedition replied, "No, the lions, elephants, and even the rhinos were no problem; but the *gnats drove us crazy*!" That is often how it is in your financial life. It is not necessarily the *big* things that keep you from financial success, but it is the constant financial gnats or minor emergencies like appliances breaking down and car repairs that stop you from making progress. The emergency fund we will build in this section will protect you from those gnats.

ARE EMERGENCIES PREDICTABLE?
Most people would say that emergencies are not predictable. The very nature of an emergency is that it surprises and catches you off guard. I would agree that the specific emergencies may not be predictable. You may not be able to predict that your son will fall off his skateboard and need a trip to the emergency room, or that someone would hit your car and you would need to pay the deductible, but you can predict that some type of emergency is going to happen sooner or later. You may not be able to predict exactly what type or exactly when, but I guarantee that you can predict that something costly will happen. I am not being negative; I am being realistic. You are not going to live a life free of emergencies. They will happen. Believe me, they are much easier to handle if you have built a cash emergency fund in advance to handle them.

NO CREDIT CARDS
Using a credit card for an emergency fund is like using a lead life jacket; it only makes things worse.

LEAD LIFE JACKET
You may be tempted to use a credit card or a home equity line of credit for your emergency fund. Using debt as an emergency fund is very dangerous. Taking care of an emergency by going into debt is like falling off a boat and having someone throw you a lead life jacket. It might make you feel better to have the life jacket on, but you are now actually in a more dangerous situation. Incurring more debt during an emergency exposes you to more risk, not less. When you use debt for emergencies you are not actually paying for the emergency, you are simply spreading the negative financial effects of the emergency over a longer period of time. If you make minimum payments, you will end up paying a lot more for the emergency than if you had paid cash.

Do not use debt for emergencies. Have a cash emergency fund and be able to take care of emergencies without making your financial situation worse.

THE ACTION ITEMS
ACTION 1
DECIDE HOW MUCH MONEY
I recommend that you put $1,000 in your emergency fund ($500 if your annual income is less than $25,000). One thousand dollars is enough to protect you from many minor emergencies. I want you to choose an amount that is large enough to protect you from most emergencies but not so large that it ties up too much of your money. Remember, we will be building a larger survival fund in Step 8 that will protect you from major emergencies like the loss of a job or a major illness. The purpose of this emergency fund is to protect you from the financial gnats that try to stop or slow down your progress toward reaching your goal of a great financial life.

ACTION 2
MAKE A LIST
Make a list of the ways you could generate the $1,000 for your emergency fund.

Here are a few ideas:
- Have a garage sale.
- Sell things you never use.
- Sell the boat you rarely use.
- Reduce your monthly bills and put the extra toward the emergency fund.
- Cancel unused memberships.
- Work some overtime.
- Work a part-time job for awhile.

There are many ways to raise the money you need for your emergency fund.

You can't predict the future, but you can prepare for it.

ACTION 3
OPEN A SEPARATE, ACCESSIBLE, AND DEDICATED ACCOUNT.
Open a separate dedicated account for a cash emergency fund. Your emergency fund should be kept separate from all other money. If you try to keep your $1,000 emergency fund in your checking or savings account with your other money, I guarantee you will not be able to keep it separate. Even if you say, "I will always make sure that I keep at least $1,000 just for emergencies," if it is mixed in with other funds you will probably end up spending it on things that are not emergencies. Keep your emergency fund in a separate account dedicated only to emergency protection.

Keep your emergency fund in an account that is easily accessible. If you have an emergency you want to be able to get to the funds. Do not put your emergency funds in a CD (certificate of deposit) or other accounts that would be difficult to access or that charge penalties for early withdrawal. The emergency fund is not designed to generate large amounts of wealth like the money you are putting in your 401(k) or IRA. The emergency fund is designed to protect you and it needs to be accessible.

Go to your bank and open a money market savings account. Find one that has low or no fees and pays the highest interest rate you can get. This account is where you will keep your emergency fund, separate from your other money and accessible when needed.

ACTION 4
GET THE MONEY

You can use the emergency fund chart at the end of this section to track your progress. Make a copy of the chart and put it on your refrigerator so you can see your positive progress.

> *Don't just plan for what might happen.*
> *Plan for what can happen.*

LET'S GO HUNTING

Now it is time to actually find the money to put into your emergency fund. You may not know exactly where the $1,000 will come from to build your emergency fund. The money is there. You just need to find it.

I am reminded of a conference I attended on developing organizations and human potential. One of the sessions was about fun in the workplace and was conducted by a professional comedian. One of his demonstrations was very powerful and has stuck with me to this day. He had the challenge of presenting just after the lunch break. That is not an easy time for a presenter. People are full from lunch and typically a little tired. I will never forget what he did. He asked everybody if they were tired, and they said yes. He asked if anyone thought there was much energy in the room, and everyone said no. He then asked each member of the audience to look for the balloons that had been placed on their table and instructed them to inflate the balloons. Each table had four to five balloons. Then he asked each member of the audience to stand and hold the balloons in their hands. They were going to engage in a competition, and there would be prizes for the winners. The crowd started to show more energy at the possibility of competition and prizes. When he blew a whistle, each team was to throw their balloons in the air. The goal was to hit the balloons back and forth without holding the balloons. The team that still had a balloon in the air when all of the other teams had allowed their balloons to hit the floor would be the winning team. Everybody looked at each other and started to create strategies. The energy level was rising even more. The whistle sounded, and the whole auditorium erupted into activity and noise. People were jumping in the air, diving to keep balloons from hitting the ground, and yelling instructions to each other. They were shouting in victory when they saved a balloon and moaning in disappointment when a balloon bit the dust. The entire auditorium was full of high-level energy. The full-from-lunch, sleepy, no-energy crowd was now releasing enough energy to power a small town for a month.

What is the point? All that energy was present in the crowd even though they could not see it or sense it. It simply needed to be released. Once the audience was motivated and had instructions on how to do it, the energy was released.

It is probably the same way with your financial life. The dollars (energy) you need to build your emergency fund are probably already present. You simply need to identify them and be motivated to release them to do the work you want them to do. Let's get started!

Use the list of ways to raise $1,000 that you generated. Choose the best ideas from the list and get going. Have that garage sale, advertise the boat for sale, or work a little overtime this month.

Here are several additional ways to raise the money for your emergency fund:

CHANGE ROUND UP

A very simple task can get you started toward your $1,000 emergency fund. Round up all of the change in your house. Our family did this activity, and we rounded up $450 . That got us almost halfway to our goal of $1,000 in our emergency fund. We had jars of coins and a drawer that had tons of change in it. People get in the habit of stashing their spare change every night. Once in a while the pile will get big enough that they finally get around to depositing it into the bank. This change is doing no good if it is sitting around the house. Try this activity and see how much you are able to find. One note of caution: Do not include your children's piggy banks in this activity! If you require them to empty their piggy banks, then you may end up reducing their willingness to be part of the team that we started to develop in Step 2 – Work Together.

If you do the change round up and you do not find a lot of change, then there is another great thing you can do to help build your emergency fund going forward. Make the declaration that from this day going forward that you will put any change left at the end of the day into a jar dedicated to building the emergency fund or any other step on which you are working.

This may sound small, but it can actually have very large results. A guy decided the day his son was born that he would never spend another coin. Every piece of change that he received would go into a college fund for his son. When his son reached the age for college, there was more than $50,000 in his son's fund for college. Little things really add up over time.

Try the change roundup and get your emergency fund started.

MONKEY TRAPS

Another thing you can do to build your emergency fund is to identify the monkey traps in your life.

There is a story about how wild monkeys are caught in Africa. A trapper drills a hole in a coconut. Then he places several peanuts into the hole, ties the coconut to a tree, and waits for the monkey. The monkey will come to the coconut, reach his small hand through the hole, and grab the peanuts. When he grabs the peanuts, he makes a fist that is too large to allow his hand to come back out of the hole in the coconut. The trapper then runs over and captures the monkey. The monkey was not willing to let go of peanuts to save his life!

You are probably thinking the monkey is pretty foolish. All he has to do is release the peanuts and live a long, prosperous monkey life. He would be free to get all of the peanuts he would ever want the rest of his life, but he is placing so much value on those particular peanuts at this particular time that he is sacrificing his life trying to hold on to them. You may even be thinking that you would never be as foolish as the monkey, but the truth is that many of us are behaving just like him. We are holding on to something that is really worth peanuts, and it is causing us to sacrifice our financial life. We are unwilling to let go of that particular peanut in order to live a wonderful, prosperous financial future.

What is a monkey trap? A monkey trap is any item that is really worth peanuts in the long-term but is causing your financial future to suffer.

EXAMPLES:
A RECREATIONAL VEHICLE
It sits in the storage unit for 50 of the 52 weeks a year.
It has monthly payments, insurance payments, storage unit payments, and repair bills.
It is depreciating every year.

A BOAT
It is rarely used.
It has monthly payments, insurance payments, regular maintenance, and docking costs.
It is depreciating every year.

A MEMBERSHIP
It is not being used regularly, but the payments are being made every month.
It is on automatic deduction, so many months you do not even think about it.

A VACATION HOME/TIME SHARE
It is used four weeks a year, but is vacant the remaining weeks.
It has monthly payments, insurance payments, and repair bills.

I am not saying give up everything that is fun or gives you pleasure in life, but I am saying that you may want to let go of those things that are peanuts so that you are free to grab the things that will build a great financial life. It can be difficult, even extremely difficult, to let go of the peanuts. To actually sell the boat or cancel the membership, do not say no, say not yet. If you look at it as *doing* something positive to reach a very valuable goal, it is much easier than thinking of it as *letting go* of something. Once you reach financial success, you can have all of the peanuts you want. You should let go of anything that, in the big picture of your life, may be peanuts so that you can reach the magnificent financial future that God has made possible. I do not know about you, but I have decided that in my life I want to be smarter than the monkey! *I am not going to let peanuts cost me my financial life!*

Note: I recommend that every year you make it a habit to go through your life and identify any monkey traps that may be holding you back from reaching your full financial potential. They can materialize without your really noticing. Something that did add great value at one time may have become peanuts, and you are still holding on to it and paying for it. Any dollars tied up in monkey traps could be out working for you to build your great financial life.

TRACK SPENDING FOR A WEEK
Another way to raise $1,000 for your emergency fund is to track your spending. Get a checkbook register, and write down everything you spend for at least one week. Then take a look at the register to see where you could possibly reduce the amount you spend. When you do this you will start to see items that have slipped into your daily routine. For example, I tracked my spending for a week and discovered that I was spending $9 a day on sodas. I stopped at the convenience store on the way to work in the morning to buy a soda. I bought sodas out of the vending machine all

day. I also stopped at the convenience store on the way home to buy a soda. I was spending $9 a day ($63 a week, $3276 per year) on soda. If I started bringing my own soda to work, I could easily cut the cost by 70 percent or more. Better yet, I can dramatically cut the number of sodas I drink. Then I can put the money I save in my emergency fund. When you track your spending, you can spot the areas where you can reduce your spending and redirect the money you save into your emergency fund.

ACTIONS 5
USE ONLY FOR EMERGENCIES

> *Emergency: An unexpected and sudden event that must be dealt with urgently.*
>
> *Encarta Dictionary*

Spending $300 to buy a dress the night before a special event that you have known about for two months is not an emergency. Buying a brand new washer and dryer because the existing set makes irritating squeaking noises is not an emergency. Buying the matching dryer when only your washer really needs to be replaced is not an emergency.

Needing to replace the tires on your car after five years of use is not an emergency. Tires wear out and need to be replaced as a regular part of maintaining your car. There is nothing unexpected about your tires wearing.

Going to the emergency room because your child was seriously injured and then receiving a bill for $500 is an emergency. A water pipe unexpectedly rupturing in the bathroom is an emergency.

Use your emergency fund for true emergencies and not for things that could and should be planned for in advance.

Note: When you use some of the money in your emergency fund to pay for an emergency, replenish the funds as soon as possible. For example, if $400 is spent to pay for an emergency, put $400 back into the emergency fund as fast as possible. Maintain the $1,000 balance at all times.

> *The best time to build a protective wall is before you are under attack.*

CONGRATULATIONS!

YOU ARE MAKING GREAT PROGRESS!

- You have completed Step 1 – 10 Step Plan, and you are following the simple 10-step plan.
- You have completed Step 2 – Work Together and you are working together toward the same financial goals and using each other's strengths.
- You have completed Step 3 – The Basics, and you are familiar with the basics of how money works, how behavior works, and how to win the marketing battle for your dollars.
- You have completed Step 4 – Giving, and you know how to be a powerful giver.
- You have completed Step 5 – Put Money to Work, and you have the Big 3 working for you 24 hours a day/365 days a year as your financial snowball grows bigger every time it rolls over.
- You have completed Step 6 – Emergency Fund, and you have a strong emergency fund or outer wall to protect you from emergencies as you move toward your goal of a great financial life.

You can now move the dot on Step 6 of the scoreboard form to a score of 10.

SCOREBOARD

Now it is time for Step 7 – Pay Off Debt

What does pay off debt mean? It means getting rid of all of the debt that is keeping you from having a great financial life. It means getting free of the bondage of debt once and for all.

Move forward and conquer Step 7 – Pay Off Debt.

EMERGENCY FUND

1000 Soldiers

— $1000

— $800

— $600

— $400

— $200

EMERGENCY FUND
To Do List

ITEM	COMPLETED
Do Change Roundup	
Identify Monkey Traps	
Complete Ways To Make Money List	
Track Spending For a Week	
Celebrate	

_____   _____
Signature   *Date*

_____   _____
Signature   *Date*

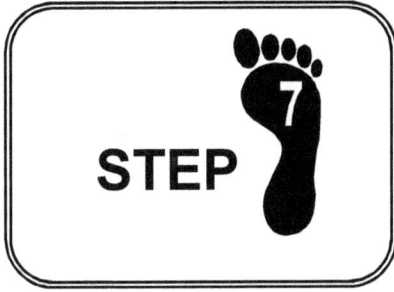

STEP 7

PAY OFF DEBT

FINANCIAL SUCCESS IN A BOX

FINANCIAL SCOREBOARD

NAME: _____   DATE: _____

STEP 1	I have a step-by-step plan to follow to reach financial success
10 STEP PLAN	1 No — 2 — 3 — 4 — 5 Maybe — 6 — 7 — 8 — 9 — 10 Yes
STEP 2	I work together with my spouse in all areas of our finances toward common goals (if you are single, mark the 10)
WORK TOGETHER	1 Never — 2 — 3 — 4 — 5 Sometimes — 6 — 7 — 8 — 9 — 10 Always
STEP 3	I know key success factors of money, behavior change and marketing self-defense
THE BASICS	1 No — 2 — 3 — 4 — 5 Maybe — 6 — 7 — 8 — 9 — 10 Yes
STEP 4	I currently give to my church, charities, etc. on a regular basis
GIVING	1 Never — 2 — 3 — 4 — 5 Regularly — 6 — 7 — 8 — 9 — 10 10% Gross
STEP 5	I currently save the following % of gross income every paycheck (includes savings, 401K, IRAs, etc)
PUT MONEY TO WORK	1 1% or less — 2 — 3 — 4 — 5 2% — 6 — 7 — 8 — 9 — 10 3% Gross
STEP 6	I currently have the following amount in a dedicated cash emergency fund
EMERGENCY FUND	1 $0 — 2 $200 — 3 $300 — 4 $400 — 5 $500 — 6 $600 — 7 $700 — 8 $800 — 9 $900 — 10 $1000
STEP 7	I currently owe the following total amount in consumer debt (Includes credit cards, student loans, etc. – everything except your house)
PAY OFF DEBT	1 $20,000+ — 2 — 3 $16,000 — 4 — 5 $12,000 — 6 — 7 $8,000 — 8 — 9 $4,000 — 10 $0
STEP 8	I currently have a cash survival fund that will cover my total expenses for
SURVIVAL FUND	1 1 Month — 2 — 3 2 Months — 4 — 5 3 Months — 6 — 7 4 Months — 8 — 9 — 10 6 Months
STEP 9	I contribute to my retirement fund every month and I know I will have enough (if you are currently retired, mark 10)
PLAN RETIREMENT	1 No — 2 — 3 — 4 — 5 Maybe — 6 — 7 — 8 — 9 — 10 Yes
STEP 10	I pay extra on my mortgage (if you do not have a mortgage, mark 10)
PAY OFF HOUSE	1 Never — 2 — 3 — 4 — 5 Regularly — 6 — 7 — 8 — 9 — 10 Paid Off

① Fill in the circles that best describe your current situation

② Connect the Dots

③ Total the Points

If your score is less than 90, you need this program

Copyright © 2010

The rich rule over the poor, and the borrower is slave to the lender
Proverbs 22:7

IMAGINE

Imagine what your life would be like if you had absolutely no debt other than your house.

Imagine:
- Not receiving another credit card bill the rest of your life
- No more monthly credit card payments
- Never again feeling stress because of high debt payments
- Being able to pay cash for all of the things you buy
- Never again being embarrassed when your credit card is rejected
- How free you will feel when you no longer have the burden of credit card debt

Imagine all of the great things you can do with the money you are currently wasting every month on debt payments.

PURPOSE

PAY OFF ALL CONSUMER DEBT

The purpose of this step is to show you a simple three-step process to pay off credit card debt and show how to protect yourself from ever getting into credit card bondage again. I will also show how to eliminate other debts such as student loans and even car payments. This is one of the most important steps of this program because it will free you from the burden of debt and make it much easier for you to complete the other steps and reach your goal of having a great financial life.

ACTION ITEMS

PAY OFF DEBT

ACTION 1 →	Drive the Stake
ACTION 2 →	Cut the Cards
ACTION 3 →	Use Credit Card Cascade

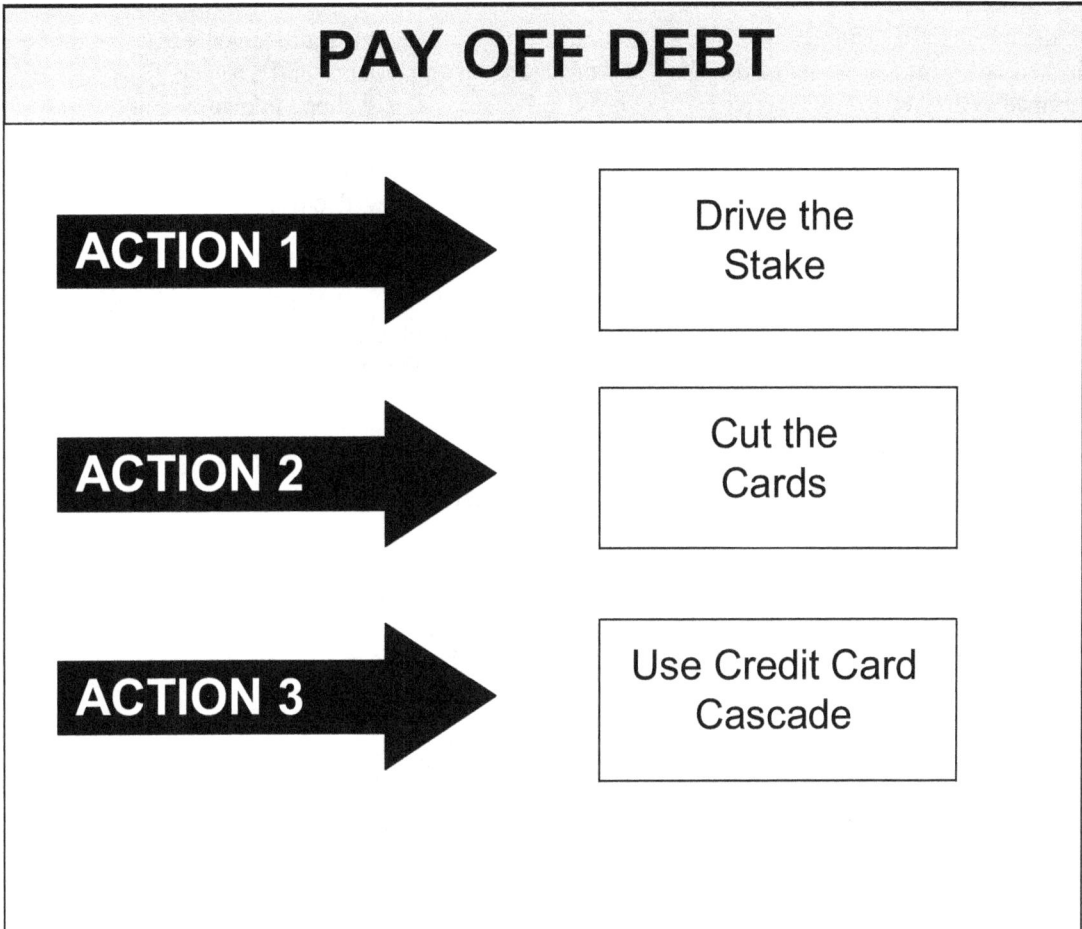

Note: In this section, I will talk specifically about credit card debt, but the steps and tools can be used to eliminate all forms of debt, including car and house payments.

Remember, we arc only going to concentrate on one step at a time. I want you to continue doing what you started in the previous steps, but your main focus will be on this step. I want to make sure that you do not get overwhelmed.

Remember: Progress, not Perfection!

BABY JESSICA STORY

When I think of how people feel when they are in debt, especially a lot of debt, I think of the "Baby Jessica" event that happened in 1987. You may remember the widely publicized story.

On the morning of October 14, 1987, a Midland, Texas, fire department received a call that a little girl had fallen into an abandoned well. They dispatched an ambulance and a rescue truck. Paramedics arrived to find that an 18-month-old baby, Jessica, had slipped down into an abandoned well that was only 8 5/8 inches in diameter (about the width of a piece of notebook paper). Jessica had slipped down into this tiny, dark pipe 20 feet below the surface. The paramedics used a flashlight to try to see Jessica in the pipe. They also used a garden hose as a temporary oxygen hose to make sure she had air to breath.

In situations like this, two rescues are actually happening. There is the psychological rescue and the actual physical rescue. They are both critical. The psychological rescue means that it is important to make contact with the person being rescued so they know that an attempt is being made. It gives them a reason to hang on. It gives them hope!

The rescuer shined a flashlight down the pipe, they yelled down the pipe to let her know that a rescuer was there and that she was not alone. An oxygen line was run down to help sustain her until the physical rescue could be completed.

That is what I am doing with this program. If you are down in the pipe of debt, I am shining a flashlight, yelling down the pipe, and letting down an oxygen hose to let you know—you are not alone! There is help! There is a way to rescue you from the pipe, and we are going to work on it together to get you out safely.

So the psychological rescue of Jessica had begun. Then it was time to start the physical rescue. They brought in a backhoe and started to dig. Less than two feet down, they hit solid rock and the backhoe could go no farther. Next, they called in a drilling team to get through the rock. While they were drilling, Jessica suddenly slipped another two to three feet down into the pipe. The vibrations of the drilling caused her to slide farther down. They lowered a camera into the pipe in an attempt to see her, but their view was obstructed by leaves that had piled in the pipe on top of her.

She was wedged in this small, dark pipe 22 feet under the ground with her left leg dangling and her right leg pulled up with her right thigh pressed against her chest. She was wedged in! Pressure was causing the pain, but it was also keeping her from falling farther into the pipe.

This scene may describe how you feel in your own hole of debt. It may seem dark, cold, and scary. You may feel trapped 22 feet below the ground. You may feel pressure and pain. You may feel stuck, but you do not have to be stuck forever. There is *hope*! The three simple steps I provide in this section can help get you out of the hole.

They resumed drilling. After about 8 hours, they had drilled a rescue shaft down to about 23 feet deep. Their plan was to dig across to the well pipe and put a pin through it to prevent Jessica from slipping any further down into the pipe. This was a critical step.

This is why we are going to have you cut up your credit cards in this section. When you cut up your credit cards, it is like putting a steel pin in that well pipe to make sure you do not slip any further into the well shaft of debt.

The next step for the rescuers was to tunnel across to the well shaft to Jessica. It was approaching dusk, but they would be drilling through the night. The first night, the temperature in the well shaft pipe got down to 60 degrees Fahrenheit. A utility company hosed warm air down to baby Jessica. The diggers worked in 45 minute shifts all through the night. The rescue shaft was only big enough for one digger at a time. The digging continued through the second day and night. On the third day at 4:40 a.m., the diggers broke through to the well shaft that held Jessica. Just after noon, paramedics were sent into the rescue shaft to try to free Jessica from the well shaft prison. It took them several hours and several different attempts. Finally at 7:55 on the third night, after 58 hours in the well, they lifted baby Jessica safely from the depths of the well. The world cheered!

This was a very frightening, heroic story with a positive ending. That is how I want your credit card story to end—*VERY POSITIVELY!*

If you feel like you are trapped in a well of debt, take heart; there is hope. You can get out of that well and stay out forever! I am shining the light down to you. I am yelling down to you to let you know that I am here to help. The psychological rescue has begun. Now it is time to start the physical rescue (the three simple steps). Look forward to that great day when you are lifted out of that hole, never to go back again. That is a day that you also will cheer!

Jessica learned her lesson and never fell in a well again. Her parents capped the well to keep her safe. There was another reason she did not ever fall into a well again. She changed—she grew. Because of the publicity of her story, many other children may have been saved by parents who checked their property for uncapped wells.

THE RULES OF HOLES
The story of baby Jessica reminds me of the Rules of Holes. There are several versions of the Rules of Holes. Here is my version:

RULE #1
DO NOT FALL IN A HOLE
The best way to get out of a hole is never to fall into one in the first place. If you currently have no credit card debt, then make a vow to never, ever have any credit card debt in the future. If you vow to avoid consumer debt completely, then you can avoid the difficult climb out of the debt hole.

Tips to help you avoid falling into the hole of debt:

- Have a cash emergency fund.
- Do not apply for any credit cards (while in stores, airports, etc.).
- Avoid the credit card display table on your college campus.
- Do not do "90 day same as cash" offers.
- Just say no—do not charge anything.

- If you struggle to say no, say not yet. (Buy items later with cash when you are totally out of debt.)
- Pay cash for purchases.
- Save up for items *before* you buy them.

RULE #2
STOP DIGGING

If you find yourself in a hole, then you were not successful applying Rule #1. If you find yourself in a hole owing $1,000, $3,000, $10,000, or any amount in credit card debt, then Rule #2 is stop digging *immediately!* If you are in a hole and you want to get out of it, you simply must stop digging. You must stop using your credit cards. The deeper you get into a hole, the longer it will take and the more effort it will require to get out. That is why I will encourage you to cut up your credit cards in this section.

RULE #3
CLIMB OUT

Once you stop digging, the next step is to climb out of the hole as fast as possible. Being in a hole of debt is a serious issue, and you need to treat it as such. You do not want to spend time in this hole. The rescuers worked nonstop around the clock to rescue Jessica because they knew that every minute she stayed in the hole increased the likelihood that things would get worse. You may be thinking, "How could things get worse for me?" How about the loss of overtime you have grown used to at work, your spouse losing their job, and your income being cut in half or your job is eliminated? Then the debt hole that did not seem so deep or scary a few days ago now seems much deeper and much more of a threat to your financial well-being. Climb out of the debt hole as if your financial life depended on it. Take this step seriously and free you and your loved ones from the bondage of this debt.

The good news is that you are not in this alone. You do not have to climb out all by yourself. I have a rescue ladder and I am throwing it down to you. The rescue ladder has three simple steps. If you will take each step one at a time, you can climb out of the hole of debt and never fall in again.

TWO CATEGORIES

Every person fits into one of two categories when it comes to credit card debt.

Do have credit card debt.
Do not have credit card debt.

If you do not have credit card debt:
- Apply rule #1. (Do not fall into a hole.)
- Avoid debt like the plague.

If you do have credit card debt:
- Apply rule #2. (Stop digging.)
- Apply rule #3. (Climb out as fast as you can.)

I KNOW HOW YOU FEEL

I know what it feels like to be in a debt hole. I know what it feels like to get collection calls from creditors. I know what it feels like to write a big check every month to the credit card company. I know what it feels like every month to think about all of the great things you could do with the money you are giving to the bank. I know how you feel. That is why I am so passionate about helping you become free of debt.

WHY DOES IT HAPPEN?

When I began teaching financial classes, I wondered why so many intelligent, hard-working people who should know better were so far into credit card debt. There are many reasons people get into credit card debt, but I have discovered three main reasons.

REASON #1: IT IS NOT TANGIBLE.

The first reason is that the debt is not tangible. It cannot be seen or touched. I think people get into big trouble with credit card debt because they do not see how big it is getting. They have one card with a $2,000 balance, a card over here with a $1,500 balance, a hardware store card with $950 for the riding mower, and another card with a balance of $850 from last Christmas. They are juggling all of these cards in their minds and paying the minimum on each, and they just do not see how big the problem is getting.

There is a reason that gambling casinos have people exchange their cash for plastic chips. It seems like play money; it does not seem real. I believe there would be a huge decline in the gambling industries if people had to use paper money: real $20, $50, and $100 bills. This is the same with credit cards. They are plastic. Studies show that people spend much more with credit cards than if they used real money.

If you have a leak in your roof, it is tangible. You can see the few drips of water coming down from the ceiling every time it rains. You can see the little stain marks on the ceiling. You can see it, and you know you have a problem. As time goes by, if the few drops leaking from the ceiling turn into a steady stream of water and the water stain gets as big as a dinner plate, you can see it. It is tangible. You are aware that the problem is getting bigger, and you need to take action before the whole ceiling falls in and there is a major catastrophe on your hands.

With credit card debt, it is easy not to see that the problem is getting bigger and bigger, and before you know it your financial ceiling is caving in and you have a huge mess to clean up.

I consider credit card debt a major enemy to you and your goal of reaching a great financial life. So if you are fighting an invisible enemy, what should you do? You make the enemy visible so you can combat it. Have you seen the movie *The Invisible Man*? They had to make him visible by throwing powder or paint on him in order to see him. I have discovered two great ways to make the enemy credit card debt visible so you can defeat it. The first method is called debt chains. In one of the early classes I taught, I gave each participant a stack of paper strips and asked them to make a paper chain for each of their debts.

They made a chain like the ones children make in school. They took a strip of paper, bent it into a circle, and stapled the ends together to form a link in the chain. The next strip of paper was inserted through the first link, formed into a circle, and its two ends were stapled together to form the second link in the debt chain. Then came a third link, then the fourth link, etc. The students were to make one chain for each debt.

If you have seven credit cards, one student loan and one car loan, you will have 9 chains. Each link represents one payment you still have to make.

EXAMPLE
$1,000 balance consumer charge card = $50 minimum payment = 20 links

EXAMPLE
$27,000 car balance = $400 minimum payment = 68 links

I was not sure what the results would be when I first gave this assignment. The next week when the students returned, I was shocked! There were debt chains everywhere! One young student brought in four big grocery sacks filled with her debt chains. She constructed them while she watched a football game with friends. Her friends thought she was a nut, but she was determined to complete the assignment. This was the first time she could actually see her debt. She could actually see the enemy. Now she understood why she worried about money all the time. Now she knew why she was always working, but never had any money. Now she knew why she could not sleep at night. There it was in plain sight—a mountain of debt. Every chain was a debt and every link was a payment she had to make. Now she understood why she was financially frustrated and miserable. This was her trigger event that made her aware that she was doing the wrong behaviors when it came to credit card debt.

The debt chain exercise can help you see the enemy, and that will help you defeat the enemy. It will also help you change your behavior and create good financial habits. It will help you stop using credit to make purchases, because every time you charge items, you will have to add a new link to the chain. You will not want the chains to get any bigger. The debt chains will also give you encouragement because you can see your progress! Every time you make a payment, you get to take a link off of the chain and you can see it getting smaller and smaller until it totally disappears.

The debt chain exercise is a very powerful activity. It can even be life-changing. It can be scary and even a little depressing to see the enemy, but seeing the enemy can be the first step in defeating the enemy and preventing it from threatening you again. The three steps included in this chapter will help you defeat the enemy of debt once and for all!

Another great way to make the enemy of debt visible is to use the credit card cascade form found later in this chapter. It will allow you to list all of your debts and remaining payments on one sheet of paper so you can see the enemy.

Note: I encourage you to do the debt chain activity and use the credit card cascade. If you do both, you will have a very clear picture of the enemy and you can see your progress as you begin to defeat it.

WHY DOES IT HAPPEN?
REASON #2: IT HAPPENS SLOWLY.

The second big reason people get into a lot of credit card debt is what I call the frog principle. It happens so slowly that they do not notice it. Have you heard the story of the frog and the pot of boiling water? If you throw a frog into a pot of boiling water, it will immediately jump out because it is too hot. It makes sense! If you put the same frog into a pot of water that is room temperature, the frog will not jump out. If you slowly turn up the temperature one degree at a time over a period of time, the frog will stay in the pot of water until it is boiled to death. It does not notice the slow change over time, and that kills it.

I believe the same thing happens to many people with credit card debt. They jump into their first credit card and the temperature seems pretty good, but slowly over time they charge more and more and do not notice that their financial situation is reaching a boiling point. Twenty dollars here, $45 there, $525 charged for a car repair, one degree at a time the water gets hotter, and they do not even notice it.

The three steps in this chapter will help you get out of the hot water of debt if your situation is boiling and will also help you avoid raising the temperature if your situation is not yet at the boiling point.

WHY DOES IT HAPPEN?
REASON #3: AGGRESSIVE MARKETING

A third reason that so many people fall into credit card holes is because credit cards are so aggressively marketed by the credit card companies. We are constantly bombarded with credit card commercials on television. At stores, you are asked if you would like to apply for a credit card and receive a 10 percent discount on your next purchase. I believe many department stores are in the credit business, not the retail business. They just have to have stuff for you to buy to get you into their credit program. On college campuses credit card companies are aggressively targeting students to get them hooked early in life and provide a steady stream of profits to the card companies. We are constantly receiving credit card offers in the mail.

The credit card companies try to make their products seem important with catchy phrases. They also try to make their products appealing with pictures of cute kittens and dogs or your own custom photos. After all, how dangerous could something possibly be that has a picture of a cute dog on it? This is a marketing ploy designed to get you to associate the use of their product with something you find pleasant, like kittens and puppies, or your favorite sports team. The reality is that the use and particularly the over use of their product can often be anything but pleasant. In some cases it can be an absolute nightmare.

Here are some of the credit cards I would like to see:

- The Misery card - Picture of a depressed guy at a desk with piles of bills
- The Bickerson's card - Picture of a couple fighting over their massive debt level
- The Repo card - Picture of a guy running down the street to catch the tow truck that is repossessing his car
- The Master/Slave card - Picture of the customer in chains

- The Insomnia card - Picture of a couple staring at the ceiling as they lay in bed wondering how they will pay off all of their debt
- The Discomfort card - Picture of a person trying to get comfortable on the sofa, but they cannot because of the constant discomfort caused by credit card debt

HOW MUCH DOES DEBT REALLY COST?

Debt has a great cost for individuals and nations. I believe debt is public enemy #1 when it comes to individuals and nations building and enjoying a strong, stable, and enduring financial future. In my opinion, excessive debt is the number one thing keeping people from reaching their financial dreams.

REASONS TO PAY OFF DEBT
REASON #1: PSYCHOLOGICAL COST

When you have debt, especially excessive debt, it can have a very high psychological cost. How much time have you spent worrying about your level of debt or how you will make the monthly payments? How many times have you been discouraged about your financial future because of the burden of your current debt? How much time have you spent arguing over your debt? Debt can cause stress, worry, arguing and even the breakup of families. Eliminating the heavy psychological cost of debt is one very good reason to pay it all off once and for all.

REASON #2: FINANCIAL COST

Banks understand the basics of money (the Big 3) they also know the basics of behavior (covered in Step 3). They use these basics against you to make more profit.

I challenge you to look at any medium to large city skyline, and I bet you will find that many of the tallest and nicest buildings are banks. They get those wonderful buildings by making profits on their products. Make no mistake, when it comes to credit cards, the banks are selling the product of debt. The more debt they can sell you, and the longer they can keep you in it, the more profit they make. They are using the Big 3 (time, amount, and money) against you. If they can stretch out the time it takes you to pay (using the minimum payment each month) and have high interest rates, they know you will end up paying a lot more in total dollars, and they will make more profit. Credit card companies want you to make only the minimum payment each month because they make more money. The banks are not doing anything illegal, but they are certainly not doing anything that works to your advantage. They are waging a war for your dollars. You need to wage war back and win. Remember the section in Step 3 – The Basics where you learned to fight for your money? Review Step 3 to make sure you are fighting the war for your dollars using every available tool and tactic. *This is a battle you must and can win!*

The simple truth is *when you use credit, you pay more!* If you pay only the minimum payment each month, you pay even more. Consider the following examples:

EXAMPLE #1
How to pay $3,020 for a $2,000 flat-panel TV:

Retail price: $2,000 for a flat-panel TV
Credit card with a 17 percent APR (annual percentage rate)
Pay only the minimum monthly payment

- Payments for **111 months** (more than 9 years)
- Pay interest to the bank of **$1,020**
- Pay a total of **$3,020**

Pay $3,020 for a $2,000 TV. Not a good deal!

EXAMPLE #2
How to pay $4,569 for a $3,000 car repair:

$3,000 auto repair
Credit card with a 17 percent APR
Pay only the minimum monthly payment

- Payments for **127 months** (more than 10 years)
- Pay interest to the bank of **$1,569**
- Pay a total of **$4,569**

Pay $4,569 for a $3,000 auto repair
Not a good deal!

EXAMPLE #3
How to pay $23,250 for a $15,000 vacation:

$15,000 vacation
Credit card with a 17 percent APR
Pay only the minimum monthly payment
- Payments for **188 months** (about 15 years)
- Pay interest to the bank of **$8,150**
- Pay a total of **$23,250**

Pay $23,250 for a $15,000 vacation
A very bad deal!

EXAMPLE #4
Here is an example using the average credit card debt per household: $8,329.

$8,329 balance on a credit card
17 percent APR making only the minimum monthly payment

- Payments for **160 months** (about 13 years)
- Pay interest to the bank of **$4,491**
- Pay a total **$12,820**

You paid $12,820 for $8,329 worth of stuff.
A HORRIBLE deal!

IS THIS MAKING AN IMPACT ON YOUR VIEW OF CREDIT CARD USAGE?

As you can see from these examples, the financial cost of debt can be huge. One of the reasons that you pay so much is because the credit card companies will keep reducing the amount of your minimum monthly payment as your balance gets lower. By doing this, they extend the amount of time it takes you to pay off the debt, and you end up paying more.

RULE OF THUMB
Here is a basic rule of thumb you can use. If you have a credit card with an interest rate around 20 percent, and you only make the minimum monthly payment each month, then you will pay double the amount for everything you buy with that credit card.

$200 item costs	$400
$500 item costs	$1,000
$1,000 item costs	$2,000
$2,500 item costs	$5,000
$5,000 item costs	$10,000

Why would you pay double the price for everything you buy? The next time you are tempted to use your credit card, remember, it can easily cost you double the price.

PAY CREDIT CARDS OFF 5 TIMES FASTER

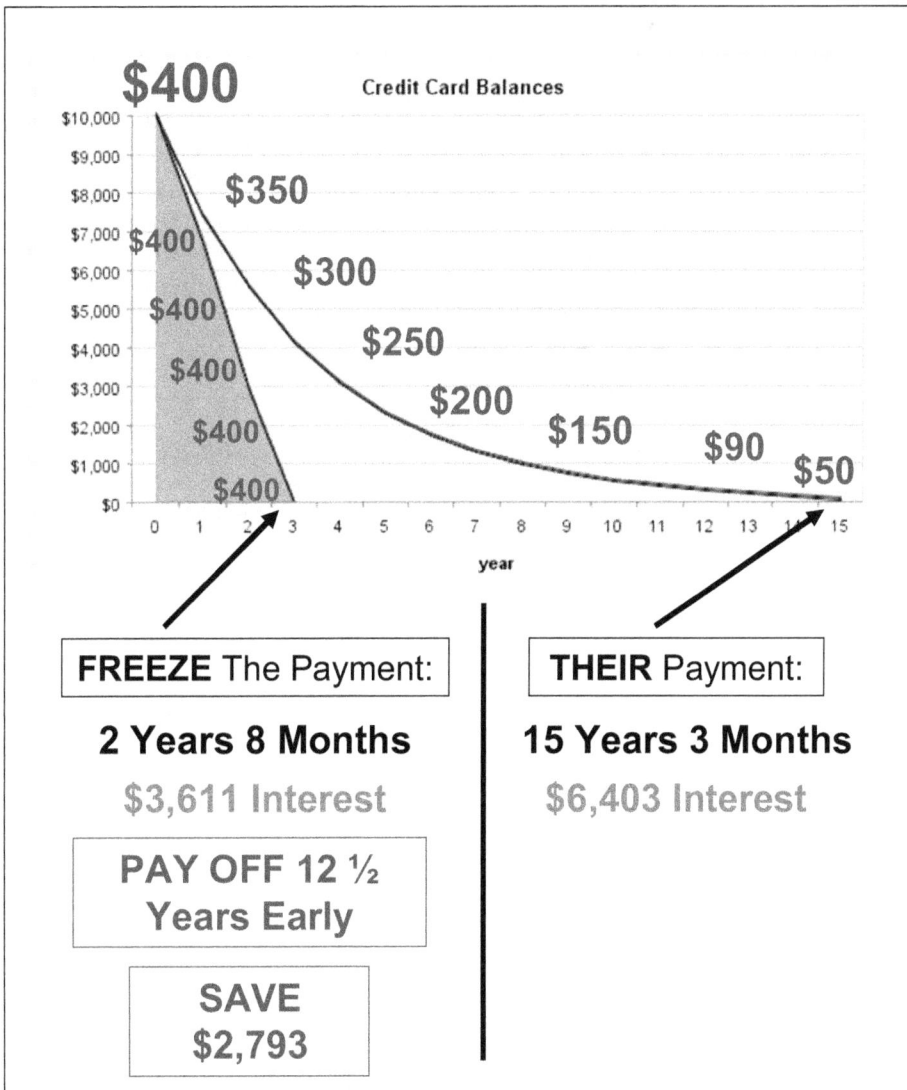

$400 Credit Card Balances

FREEZE The Payment:

2 Years 8 Months

$3,611 Interest

PAY OFF 12 ½ Years Early

SAVE $2,793

THEIR Payment:

15 Years 3 Months

$6,403 Interest

In the illustration above you can see an example of how to pay off a credit card five times faster without increasing your monthly payment or throwing additional money at it. All you have to do is FREEZE the current payment. The illustration represents a credit card with a $10,000 balance with a 19 percent interest rate. The minimum monthly payment on the card is $400. If you follow the credit card company's plan and pay the minimum payment each month, you will end up paying $6,403 in interest, and it will take you 15 years and 3 months to pay it off! The reason you end up paying so much is because the credit card company reduces the minimum amount you need to pay each month in an effort to get you to pay over a longer period of time. That strategy results in you paying much more interest. Remember the Big 3 of money from Step 3 (amount, interest, and time). The credit card company continues to reduce the monthly payment amount, and that increases the amount of time to pay it back. That allows interest to work against you for a longer time period. If you freeze your current monthly payment ($400 in the example) and keep paying that same amount each month regardless of what the credit card company tells you is the minimum payment, you will pay the credit card off in 2 years and 8 months instead of 15 years and 3 months, and you will only pay $3,611 in interest instead of $6,403 in interest. You will pay this credit card off 12 years sooner and save $2,792 in interest. By freezing the monthly payment amount, you reduce the amount of time it takes to pay off the credit card. That reduces the amount of time interest has to work against you. I highly recommend that you freeze the monthly payment amount of your credit cards and resist the temptation to follow the credit cards company's invitation to reduce the minimum monthly payment as the balance goes down. If you freeze the monthly payment amount, you will pay the credit cards off five times faster and save thousands of dollars in interest payments. Freeze the monthly payments and get free sooner.

I believe the following statements about debt are true:

You can't build a foundation on borrowed bricks.

Do not be among those who give pledges, among those who become guarantors for debt.
Proverbs 22:26

You are not borrowing from the bank. You are borrowing from your future.

Some debts are fun when you are acquiring them, but none are fun when you set about retiring them.
Ogden Nash

The more time there is between purchase and payment, the more you will pay.

QUICK REVIEW
Now might be a great time to do a quick review of Step 2 - Work Together and Step 3 – The Basics. You will definitely need to work together on this one, and you will definitely need the marketing self-defense tools and tactics.

THE ACTION ITEMS
There is a particular sequence to accomplishing these three action items.

ACTION 1
DRIVE THE STAKE.
MAKE A FULL COMMITMENT TO PAY OFF YOUR CREDIT CARD DEBT.

Remember the story in Step 3 about the farmer who drove the wooden stake at the end of his field and plowed toward it no matter what? He never quit driving toward that stake. It was his goal no matter what, and he was going to reach it!

You need to make the same type of commitment to pay off your credit card debt and never let it become a problem again. When you pay off all your credit card debt, you will feel a freedom, a power that is absolutely wonderful. You will also be free to build wealth and reach Financial Success faster than ever. Any money you are currently spending on your debt reduction will be freed up to work and build your wealth. This money can become a financial snowball that grows huge. Make the commitment that you will pay off your debt and stay with it until that very last payment is made and you are free.

Also, plan a fun, inexpensive celebration for each card you pay off and a celebration for when you have paid all of them off.

You may not feel any relief during the time you are paying off your debt, but when you reach that last day, there will be sudden and complete relief from the burden of this debt. The money that has been going toward debt each month will be freed up to build your wealth.

Drive the stake and make a firm commitment to pay off all of your debt!

ACTION 2
CUT UP YOUR CREDIT CARDS.
APPLY RULE #2 OF HOLES AND STOP DIGGING

The only way to stop digging is to stop using your credit cards. The best way to stop using your credit cards is to cut them up. I am so serious about this step that I provide a pair of scissors in the Financial Success in a Box Kit.

BURN YOUR SHIPS

The phrase *Burn your ships* comes from the Spanish Conquistador Hernando Cortez. In 1519, Cortez sailed from Spain to Mexico with 11 ships, more than 500 soldiers, and 100 sailors to seize the great treasures held by the Aztec empire. One of the main reasons such a small group was able to overthrow the Aztec empire, which had been in power for over six centuries, was because Cortez decided that he would either be victorious or die.

After they landed, Cortez gathered his men and ordered them to "burn the ships." By doing this, he created a situation where they had to be victorious or die. Retreat was no longer an option. Cortez said, "If we are going home, we are going home in *their* ships."
After they burned their ships, they had a whole new level of commitment. They knew they had to succeed. They had removed all temptations of giving up or giving it less than their best. They had a very simple choice: succeed or die.

Cortez and his men did conquer the Aztecs and succeeded where others had failed for six centuries. That is the kind of commitment I want you to have to pay off your credit card debt and be free.

Cutting up your credit cards is your form of burning your ships. When you cut up your credit cards, you are making the same total commitment to success that Cortez and his men made. You are removing any temptation to retreat or give up. You are saying that failure is not an option. You are saying, "I will be successful; I am fully committed". It is simple math.

$$\begin{aligned} &\text{Freeze the balances. (Cut up your cards.)} \\ +\ &\underline{\text{Reduce the balance.}\quad \text{(Continue to make payments.)}} \\ =\ &\text{Totally debt free.}\quad\ \ \text{(You will be debt free.)} \end{aligned}$$

If you cut up your credit cards, you will only have to slay the credit card beast once. You do not want to do this again in a few years. I strongly encourage you: Make the same commitment as Cortez:

Burn your ships = Cut up your credit cards!

Note: You can use *debit* cards for the things you need to purchase for the convenience of a card without the temptation of going into debt.

Why would you continue to feed a dragon you are trying to slay?
Cut up the credit cards!

When asked what advice he would give children, during a CNBC
special interview, Warren Buffet said:
Stay away from credit cards.
Invest in yourself.

Warren Buffet

Sometimes, to get out of a rut, you have to make a pretty hard turn.
Cut up the credit cards!

ACTION 3
USE THE CREDIT CARD CASCADE TO PAY OFF ALL OF YOUR DEBT IN A SYSTEMATIC, ORGANIZED WAY

CREDIT CARD CASCADE
Now that we have explored some of the reasons people get into debt holes and the high cost of debt, let me share with you the tool to get you out of the debt hole. The simple tool that can get you out of the debt hole and make sure you never get back in is called the credit card cascade. Even if a person wants to eliminate all of their credit card debt, they often do not know where to begin, and they do not have a clear step-by-step plan they can follow all the way through to the end and pay off every last cent of credit card debt. The Credit card cascade (CCC) is a simple tool that will help you eliminate all of your credit card debt in a systematic, powerful, and effective way. The CCC tells you where to start and will take you step-by-step all the way to the end: that glorious day that you make your last payment on your last credit card debt and you are free to build a strong financial future.

WHAT IS IT
The CCC is a tool that will allow you to organize and list all of your credit card debt on one sheet of paper so you know your status, and you can begin to attack it. It will help you pay off credit card debt faster. It also reduces your stress and gives you hope because you know what is going on. You are making progress every month, and an end is in sight. The CCC is the tool that can help you get out of the hole and stay out.

HOW IT WORKS
The CCC allows you to take control of your situation and begin making the monthly credit card payments according to the cascade amount and not the amount the credit card companies determine. You control the amount you will pay each month, and you determine when you will be out of debt, not the credit card companies.

The CCC allows you to focus the power of your monthly payments and pay your debt off faster. When you pay off one credit card, you move that monthly payment to the next card. When you pay off the next card, you apply the monthly payment amounts from the first two cards that are now paid off toward the next card. You continue to do that until all of your credit cards are paid off.

The CCC is a very simple and fast way to eliminate all of your credit card debt once and for all.

HOW TO USE THE CREDIT CARD CASCADE
First, list all of your credit card debts and any other debts (school loan, computer loan, etc.) on the form. List the cards in order from the lowest remaining balance at the top of the form to the largest balance at the bottom. Fill in all of the information for each account on the form: name, remaining balance, minimum payment, and the totals at the bottom of the column. Make sure they are listed in order with the smallest balance on the top to the largest balance on the bottom of the form.

CREDIT CARD CASCADE FORM

CREDIT CARD CASCADE FORM						
NAME	TOTAL BALANCE	MINIMUM PAYMENT	CASCADE PAYMENT		CARD CUT UP	PAID OFF
VISA 1	$100	$25		=		
VISA 2	$250	$25		=		
MASTER CARD	$1000	$30		=		
DISCOVER	$1000	$30		=		
AMERICAN EXPRESS	$1500	$45		=		
CITI BANK	$1600	$50		=		
MACY'S	$2000	$60		=		
SEARS	$5500	$165		=		
				=		
TOTAL	$12,950	$430				

This step is important because it allows you to see all of your debt in one place so you know what you are up against! You may not want to do this step because you are afraid of what you might see on the form. You may be afraid that it will be very ugly. The credit card debt that you are going to see may be very large and very scary. Even if it is large and scary, you simply must face it. The fact that it is or is not written on paper does not change the reality of it. Remember, seeing the invisible enemy may be scary, but it is essential if you are to defeat it. I have given you a powerful weapon. The credit card cascade will help you defeat it and make sure it never rears its ugly head again.

Note: Some advisors would tell you that it makes sense to list your debts so that you are paying off the highest interest rates first. From a strictly financial point of view, this does make sense, but from a human behavior point of view it makes better sense to list your debts from smallest to largest balance. This is because I want you to have victories as soon as possible, and create momentum and success as soon as possible. If you have successes early and often, you will build the confidence and determination you need to complete the task.

The next step is to fill in the cascade payment amounts on the form.

CREDIT CARD CASCADE FORM

NAME	TOTAL BALANCE	MINIMUM PAYMENT	CASCADE PAYMENT		CARD CUT UP	PAID OFF
VISA 1	$100	$25	$25	=		
VISA 2	$250	$25	$50	=		
MASTER CARD	$1000	$30	$80	=		
DISCOVER	$1000	$30	$110	=		
AMERICAN EXPRESS	$1500	$45	$155	=		
CITI BANK	$1600	$50	$205	=		
MACY'S	$2000	$60	$265	=		
SEARS	$5500	$165	$430	=		
				=		
TOTAL	$12,950	$430	$430			

As you can see in the illustration, it is fairly simple to calculate the cascade payment amounts. The first debt listed (Visa 1) has a minimum monthly payment of $25 dollars. When you pay off Visa 1, you will take the $25 you were paying on Visa 1 and add it to the $25 minimum monthly payment on the next debt (Visa 2). So your new monthly cascade payment for Visa 2 is now $50. When you pay off Visa 2, you will take the $50 you were paying on Visa 2 and add it to the $30 minimum monthly payment on the next debt (MasterCard). Your new monthly cascade payment for MasterCard will be $80. As you pay off each debt, the monthly payments that had gone to those debts are now cascaded down to the next debt and pay off each additional debt faster and faster.

You will notice that the total in the minimum payment column and the total in the cascade payment column are equal. That is because you are committing to pay $430 every month to eliminate your debt. So instead of letting the $25 monthly payment for Visa 1 dissipate into the financial abyss once you pay it off, you are harnessing its power to carry all the way through until you pay off your very last debt. The accumulated momentum created by the credit card cascade is amazing.

Once you have all of your debt listed on the form, you can begin to attack it. You will be encouraged every month as the debt gets smaller and smaller. You can see your progress. The form will also help you avoid additional debt because you will not want to add any more debt to the form.

Note: The credit card cascade form has a "card cut up" column and a "paid off" column. Simply put a check mark in the appropriate box to indicate that you have cut up a card or paid off a card. Hopefully you can place a check mark for each credit card in the cut up card column. If you have not yet cut up your credit cards, I highly encourage you to do it **now**! Remember to *burn your ships*.

EXAMPLE:
The example on the next page illustrates what a cascade form would look like after the first three cards have been paid off. Visa 1, Visa 2 and MasterCard have now been paid off, and the minimum monthly payment amounts have cascaded down to help pay off the Discover card. One hundred ten dollars is going toward the Discover card each month. In this example all credit cards have been cut up and the first three credit cards have a check mark in the paid off column. Every month this person gets closer and closer to being debt free.

CREDIT CARD CASCADE FORM

NAME	TOTAL BALANCE	MINIMUM PAYMENT	CASCADE PAYMENT		CARD CUT UP	PAID OFF
VISA 1	$100	$25	$25	=	X	X
VISA 2	$250	$25	$50	=	X	X
MASTER CARD	$1000	$30	$80	=	X	X
DISCOVER	$1000	$30	$110	=	X	
AMERICAN EXPRESS	$1500	$45	$155	=	X	
CITI BANK	$1600	$50	$205	=	X	
MACY'S	$2000	$60	$265	=	X	
SEARS	$5500	$165	$430	=	X	
				=		
TOTAL	$12,950	$430	$430			

Gather the most recent statements from your credit cards, student loans, furniture loans, and every other debt to list on the cascade form. List them in order from smallest balance to largest balance. Transfer the appropriate information to the Credit card cascade form.

Starting this month, you will pay the minimum payment on all accounts listed on the cascade form. If you want to contribute extra money, it will be contributed to the account with the smallest balance until that account is paid off. As each card is paid, cascade all payments that were going to previous cards to the next card. It picks up amazing power as it cascades to each level.

Commit to completing the cascade. I want you to commit that you will stay with it until the very last dollar of the very last debt on the cascade form is paid off. Do not get distracted; and do not ever give up. You can make it—you just need to keep moving forward.

As you commit to complete this credit card cascade, take comfort in the following facts:
- You have money in a financial snowball growing larger everyday. (Step 5)
- You have an emergency fund to protect you. (Step 6)
- The money you have been spending every month on debt will soon be freed up and can be put to work as a financial snowball that will grow and grow and grow as you move toward a great financial life.

KILL THE BEAR
There is a movie called *The Edge* starring Anthony Hopkins and Alec Baldwin. The movie is about a billionaire who gets stranded in the wilderness with two other survivors when their small plane crashes. The three survivors of the plane crash decide to hike out of the wilderness because they do not believe anyone will be able to find them. As they make their way through the wooded mountains, they come across a large Kodiak bear. The bear starts chasing them through the woods, and they barely escape by crossing a river. The bear begins to stalk them as they continue their journey out of the frozen wilderness. The three men are constantly looking over their shoulders and watching out for the bear. In one scene, the bear catches up with them and attacks their camp. One of the men is killed by the bear, and the other two make a narrow escape. From that point on the bear stalks them even more aggressively. In one scene the bear chases the remaining two survivors into a thickly wooded area at night. The two men quickly build small fires to encircle them in hopes that the fire would keep the bear away from them. Finally, one of the men says we have to *kill the bear*! He won't let us sleep, he won't let us eat, and he is harassing us 24 hours a day. If we don't kill him, he is going to kill us. The two men decide that the only way they are going to survive is to *kill the bear*! In the next few scenes you watch as the two men lure the bear into a trap they have set and engage in a very dramatic battle in which they finally kill the bear. In the very next scene, the two men are wearing bear skin coats, sitting by a camp fire, and cooking bear meat. The same bear that had previously been threatening their lives was now the very thing that was going to help them survive and escape from the frozen wilderness. They had turned their biggest threat into their biggest asset. They did it by making a stand. They did it by facing the bear and killing it.

This story reminds me of the situation many people find themselves in with their credit card debt. The credit card debt is like the vicious bear that stalks them 24 hours a day. It doesn't let them sleep, it doesn't let them eat, and it harasses them all day every day. It is the biggest threat to their financial life. They eventually reach the same point the two men in the story reached. If they don't kill the bear it is going to kill them! If they will make the same decision the two men made and face and kill the bear, they can not only survive, they can use the bear to build the rest of their great financial life. If a person is currently making a $430 monthly payment on credit card debt, that $430 is the bear that is making their life miserable day and night. As long as the credit card debt exists it will continue to harass them. If they will make a stand and *kill the bear* (pay off the debt) they will then be able to use the $430 a month to build a great financial life. The $430 dollars a month that was a threat to their financial life before is now an asset that can be used to build a survival fund, a retirement fund, and pay off their house early. The $430 paid in minimum monthly payments invested in a 401(k) or IRA at a 10 percent annual return compounded will grow to **$1,032,711** in 31 years, **$2,066,311** in 38 years, and **$4,080,504** in 45 years. Instead of paying the money to banks in interest, they will become a multi-millionaire.

The credit card debt (bear) you currently have can be turned around to work for you, but you must first *kill the bear*!

TURBOCHARGE IT!

Here are several tips that will help you turbo charge your credit card cascade and pay off your debt even faster:

- Call the credit card companies and negotiate a lower interest rate.
- Have a garage sale and put the money toward credit card debt.
- Work some overtime.

Use the list you created in Step 6 – Emergency Fund on how to raise additional money. Throw everything you have at this. You will not regret it. Nothing is like the feeling of being free of debt. Imagine how great it will feel to be debt free. Imagine having no monthly debt payments. Imagine how much wealth you will be able to build by putting the money you have been spending on debt each month to work building your fortune.

Note: Once you have reached your goal and you are free of debt, remember Rule #1 of Holes – Do Not Fall Into One. Make the commitment that you will never again get near the hole of debt.

CELEBRATE

Remember to celebrate when you pay off each level of the credit cascade and have a big freedom party when you pay off the last debt!

CONGRATULATIONS!

YOU ARE CONTINUING TO MAKE GREAT PROGRESS!

- You have completed Step 1 – 10-Step Plan for Success, and you are following the simple 10-step plan.
- You have completed Step 2 – Work Together, and you are working together toward the same financial goals and using each other's strengths.
- You have completed Step 3 – The Basics, and you are familiar with the basics of how money works, how behavior works, and how to win the marketing battle for your dollars.
- You have completed Step 4 – Giving, and you know how to be a powerful giver.
- You have completed Step 5 – Put Money to Work, and you have the Big 3 working for you 24 hours a day, 365 days a year as your financial snowball grows bigger every time it rolls over.
- You have completed Step 6 – Emergency Fund and you have a strong emergency fund or outer wall to protect you from emergencies as you move toward your goal of a great financial life.
- You have completed Step 7 – Pay Off Debt, and you are free from the oppressive slavery of being in debt. You have freed money (that was going toward debt) to go to work for you building a strong and stable financial future.

You can now move your dot on Step 7 of the scoreboard form to a score of 10.

SCOREBOARD

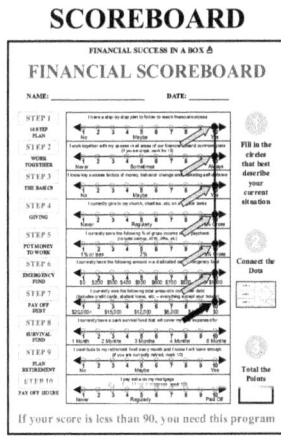

Now it is time for Step 8 – Survival Fund

What does survival fund mean? It means building a cash survival fund that will protect you from major emergencies such as an illness or the loss of a job. It means building the inner wall we discussed in Step 6 that protects your castle.

Move forward and conquer Step 8.

CREDIT CARD CASCADE FORM

NAME	TOTAL BALANCE	MINIMUM PAYMENT	CASCADE PAYMENT		CARD CUT UP	PAID OFF
				=		
				=		
				=		
				=		
				=		
				=		
				=		
				=		
				=		
TOTAL						

PAY OFF DEBT
To Do List

ITEM	COMPLETED
Complete Cascade Form	
Celebrate	

_____   _____
Signature   *Date*

_____   _____
Signature   *Date*

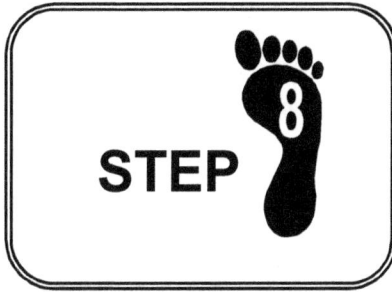

STEP 8

SURVIVAL FUND

SCOREBOARD

FINANCIAL SUCCESS IN A BOX

FINANCIAL SCOREBOARD

NAME: _____   DATE: _____

STEP 1
10 STEP PLAN
I have a step-by-step plan to follow to reach financial success
1 No 2 3 4 5 Maybe 6 7 8 9 10 Yes

STEP 2
WORK TOGETHER
I work together with my spouse in all areas of our finances toward common goals
(If you are single, mark the 10)
1 Never 2 3 4 5 Sometimes 6 7 8 9 10 Always

STEP 3
THE BASICS
I know key success factors of money, behavior change and marketing self-defense
1 No 2 3 4 5 Maybe 6 7 8 9 10 Yes

STEP 4
GIVING
I currently give to my church, charities, etc. on a regular basis
1 Never 2 3 4 5 Regularly 6 7 8 9 10 10% Gross

STEP 5
PUT MONEY TO WORK
I currently save the following % of gross income every paycheck
(Includes savings, 401K, IRAs, etc)
1 1% or less 2 3 4 5 2% 6 7 8 9 10 3% Gross

STEP 6
EMERGENCY FUND
I currently have the following amount in a dedicated cash emergency fund
1 $0 2 $200 3 $300 4 $400 5 $500 6 $600 7 $700 8 $800 9 $900 10 $1000

STEP 7
PAY OFF DEBT
I currently owe the following total amount in consumer debt
(Includes credit cards, student loans, etc. – everything except your house)
1 $20,000+ 3 $16,000 5 $12,000 8 $8,000 9 $4,000 10 $0

STEP 8
SURVIVAL FUND
I currently have a cash survival fund that will cover my total expenses for
1 1 Month 2 2 Months 3 4 3 Months 5 6 7 4 Months 8 9 10 6 Months

STEP 9
PLAN RETIREMENT
I contribute to my retirement fund every month and know I will have enough
(If you are currently retired, mark 10)
1 No 2 3 4 5 Maybe 6 7 8 9 10 Yes

STEP 10
PAY OFF HOUSE
I pay extra on my mortgage
(If you do not have a mortgage, mark 10)
1 Never 2 3 4 5 Regularly 6 7 8 9 10 Paid Off

Fill in the circles that best describe your current situation

Connect the Dots

Total the Points

If your score is less than 90, you need this program

Copyright © 2010

A prudent man sees danger and takes refuge, but the simple keep going and suffer for it.

Proverbs 22:3

IMAGINE

Imagine having a 3- to 6-month cash survival fund dedicated to protect you and your loved ones from unexpected major emergencies such as illnesses or the loss of a job.

Imagine:
- Not stressing out when you hear rumors of layoffs at work
- Not having to go deeper into credit card debt every time an emergency comes up
- Not having to be in a panic or rush to take a bad job because you have plenty of money in the survival fund
- Being able to pursue your life dream after a major interruption in income
- Being able to sleep peacefully because you know you have enough cash stashed away to take care of you and your loved ones for 3, 6, even 12 months even if all of your income stops.

Imagine the comfort you will experience knowing that you are protecting you and your loved ones from the negative impacts of major emergencies.

PURPOSE

BUILD A 3- to 6-MONTH SURVIVAL FUND

The purpose of this step is to show you a simple five-step process that will help you build a cash survival fund that will protect you and your loved ones from major emergencies that will threaten your Financial Success.

This step is very similar to Step 6 – Emergency Fund. We will use the same five action items we used in Step 6, but this time we will use them to build an even bigger protective wall. In Step 6 we built the outer wall. In this step we will build the inner wall to add further protection to your financial castle. The inner wall provides more protection. It is much bigger and gives you maximum defense against attackers. It is important that you maintain both of these protective walls. They have two separate purposes. The outer wall (emergency fund) is to protect you from small emergencies such as car breakdowns, small medical bills, etc. The inner wall (survival fund) will support you and help you survive major emergencies such as the loss of a job that may last for an extended period of time.

SURVIVAL FUND

ACTION 1 → Decide How Much

ACTION 2 → Brainstorm List of Ways

ACTION 3 → Open Dedicated Account

ACTION 4 → Get The Money

ACTION 5 → Use for Major Emergencies

Always bear in mind that your own resolution to succeed is more important than any one thing.
Abraham Lincoln

GOOD NEWS

The first piece of good news is that when you have all of your consumer debt paid off in Step 7 – Pay Off Debt, all of the money you were spending each month on credit card payments can go toward building your Inner Wall - Survival fund. If you were spending $430 each month on credit card payments, you will be able to put that $430 toward building your Survival fund. This will help build your Inner Wall much faster.

Once you have completed Step 7 – Pay Off Debt, I recommend that you put the total amount listed on your Credit card cascade in the Cascade Payment Column toward building your Inner Wall.

The second piece of good news is that you have already built one wall - Your outer wall - emergency fund. So, now that you know how to do it, building a second wall should be easy.

THE INNER WALL

In medieval times, the castle inner wall was even more massive and foreboding than the outer wall. The inner wall would often stand 40 feet tall and the protective towers could rise as high as 70 feet. The inner wall was the single biggest weapon that protected the castle and the people who lived there. It had to be impenetrable. The outer wall was important because it was the first line of defense. The inner wall was important because it was the last line of defense. If the inner wall were breached, then the enemy could reach the castle and its inhabitants.

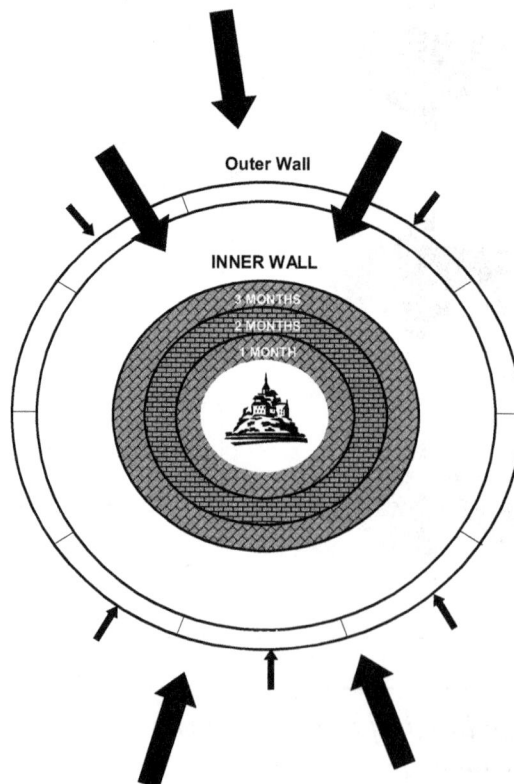

This inner wall (survival fund) is very important because it is the biggest single defense you will have to protect your financial castle and protect your family from large attacks.

When you are prepared with inner and outer walls you can handle just about anything that comes your way.

You need to build an inner wall (survival fund) that will protect your financial castle from the attack of large enemies that the outer wall (emergency fund) will not withstand. The loss of a job, an injury that prevents you from working for a while, or anything that substantially decreases your income could threaten your financial future. If you build a strong inner wall, you will be able to endure those attacks and continue the journey to Financial Success.

WHAT COULD POSSIBLY HAPPEN?
You may be thinking, "What could possibly happen to me? Why would I need a survival fund?" Most every person, sooner or later, goes through a major financial emergency in life. It may be the loss of a job, or it may be a major illness. Whatever it is, this step will get you prepared for it. You need a cash survival fund!

NO CREDIT CARDS
Do you remember what we said in Step 6 – Emergency Fund? Using a credit card for an emergency fund is like using a lead life jacket. It only makes things worse. Do not use debt for emergencies. Have a cash survival fund and be able to take care of financial emergencies without making your financial situation worse.

> *Attitude is a little thing that makes a big difference.*
> *Winston Churchill*

THE ACTION ITEMS
Remember, these five action items are identical to the five action items we used in Step 6 to build your outer wall (emergency fund). The only difference is that in this step we will use the five action items to build a much bigger and stronger wall. We will use them to build the inner wall (survival fund).

ACTION 1
DECIDE HOW MUCH MONEY YOU NEED FOR YOUR SURVIVAL FUND
How strong should your inner wall be? How high and how thick should you build it? The answer is however high and thick it needs to be for you to sleep peacefully in the castle at night, knowing that you and your family are protected if you are attacked by a large enemy (if you go to work tomorrow and are laid off).

Let me give you some guidelines to get you started. The inner wall (survival fund) should be large enough to allow you to survive at least three months if all income stops. I recommend a survival fund to survive six months! Some even recommend the inner wall (survival fund) be large enough to allow you to survive for 12 to 24 months.

It should be at least large enough to allow you to survive 3 to 6 months without any income. If all of your income were cut off, and your monthly expenses were $3000, then you would need a survival fund of $9,000 to survive 3 months and $18,000 to survive 6 months.

The decision to make it 3 or 6 months depends on your comfort level and how long you think it would take to secure another job if something happened to your current income. This may seem like a large amount, but just think how great it will feel when you have that large amount protecting you. You will know that if something happens, you and your family will be taken care of because of protection built in advance. Every bad economic rumor at work will not cause you to panic. If something does happen to your current income, then it could be a great time to pursue your dream or another career field instead of a desperate lunge to another boat before you drown. This step is one of the major foundational pieces that provides the stability in Financial Success.

Note: Use the form at the end of this section to calculate the amount you will need in your survival fund. The form will also help you track your progress as you build.

> *Some people want it to happen, some wish it would happen, others make it happen.*
> *Michael Jordan*

ACTION 2
MAKE A LIST OF THE WAYS TO GENERATE THE MONEY FOR YOUR SURVIVAL FUND.

Use the form at the end of this section to list different ways to generate the money for your survival fund.

- Use the money you were paying each month on credit card debt.
- Have a garage sale.
- Sell things you never use.
- Sell the boat you never use.
- Reduce your monthly bills and put the extra toward the survival fund.
- Cancel unused memberships.
- Work some overtime.
- Work a part-time job for awhile.

There are many ways to raise the money you need for your survival fund. Use the list at the end of this section and see how many ways you can identify. You can also use the list you generated in Step 6 to build your emergency fund.

ACTION 3
OPEN A SEPARATE, ACCESSIBLE, AND DEDICATED ACCOUNT.

Your survival fund should be kept separate from all of your other money. Just like your emergency fund, if you try to keep your Survival fund in your checking or savings account with your other money, I guarantee you will not be able to keep it separate. Keep your survival fund in a separate account dedicated only to survival protection.

You need to keep your survival fund in an account that is easily accessible. If you have a major emergency, you need to be able to get to the funds. Do not put your survival funds in a CD (certificate of deposit) or other accounts that would be difficult to access or charge penalties for withdrawal. The survival fund is not designed to generate large amounts of wealth like the money you are putting in your 401(k) or IRA. The survival fund is designed to protect you, and it needs to be accessible.

A money market savings account can be appropriate. Find one that has low or no fees and pays the highest interest rate available. This account is where you will keep your survival fund - separate from your other money and accessible if needed.

ACTION 4
GET THE MONEY

Use the survival fund chart at the end of this section to track your progress. Make a copy of the chart, and put it on your refrigerator so you can see your positive progress.

The tools and techniques we are going to use in this step are the same ones we used in Step 6 – emergency fund. They will work just as effectively as they worked before.

LET'S GO HUNTING!

Now it is time to actually find the money. You may not know exactly where the money will come from to build your survival fund, but I believe the money is there. You can find it.

Use the list you generated of ways to raise your $1,000 in Step 6 for your emergency fund. Choose the best ideas from the list and get going. Have that garage sale, advertise the boat for sale, or work a little overtime this month.

Here are several additional ways to raise the money for your inner wall that are the same as building the outer wall:

- The change round up
- Monkey traps
- Track spending for a week

ACTION 5
USE SURVIVAL FUND ONLY FOR *MAJOR* EMERGENCIES

The definition of a major emergency would be an unexpected and sudden *major* event that must be dealt with urgently.

You need to make sure that you use your survival fund for major emergencies such as the loss of a job or a major illness and not on things that could and should be planned for in advance.

NOTE: If you use some of the money in your survival fund to pay for a major emergency, replenish the funds as soon as possible. Keep your inner wall at full strength.

CONGRATULATIONS!

YOU ARE MAKING GREAT PROGRESS!

- You have completed Step 1 – 10-Step Plan, and you are following the simple 10-step plan.
- You have completed Step 2 – Work Together, and you are working together toward the same financial goals and using each other's strengths.
- You have completed Step 3 – The Basics, and you are familiar with the basics of how money works, how behavior works, and how to win the marketing battle for your dollars.
- You have completed Step 4 – Giving, and you know how to be a powerful giver.
- You have completed Step 5 – Put Money to Work, and you have the Big 3 working for you 24 hours a day, 365 days a year as your financial snowball grows bigger every time it rolls over.
- You have completed Step 6 – Emergency Fund, and you have a strong emergency fund or outer wall to protect you from emergencies as you move toward your goal of a great financial life.
- You have completed Step 7 – Pay Off Debt, and you are free from the oppressive slavery of being in debt. You have freed money that was going toward debt to work for you building a strong and stable financial future.
- You have completed Step 8 – Survival Fund, and you have a strong inner wall (survival fund) that will provide for your family for 3 to 6 months even if all income is cut off.

You can now move your dot on Step 8 of the scoreboard form to a score of 10.

SCOREBOARD

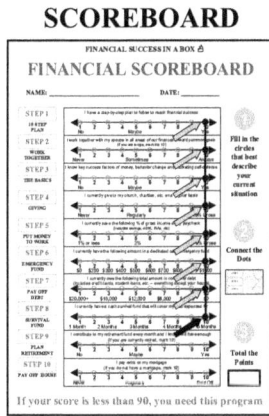

Now it is time for Step 9 – Plan Retirement. What does plan retirement mean?
It means creating a simple, automatic retirement plan that will be large enough to provide you a great retirement.

Move forward and conquer Step 9.

SURVIVAL FUND

3 – 6 Month Expenses

Monthly Expenses = $ $3,000 _____

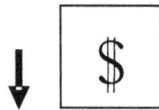

↓ | $ | Fill in Dollar Amounts

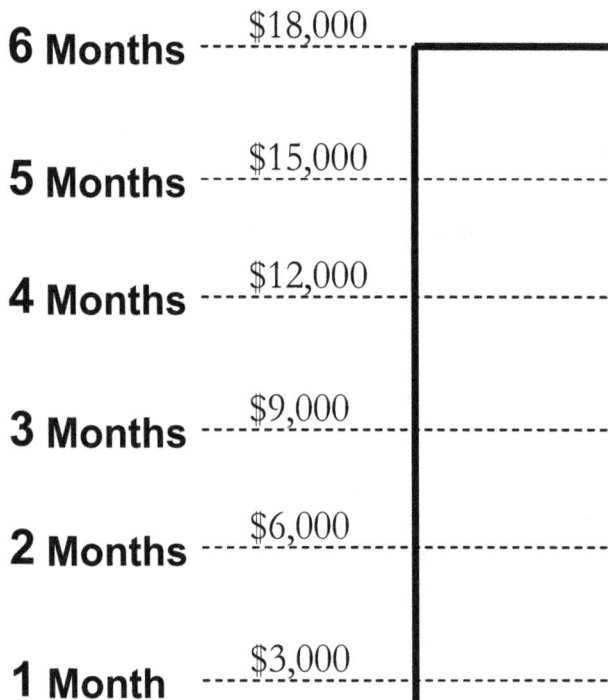

6 Months ----- $18,000

Example: If monthly expenses are $3,000 per month, then you would fill in these numbers.

5 Months ----- $15,000

4 Months ----- $12,000

3 Months ----- $9,000

2 Months ----- $6,000

1 Month ----- $3,000

EXAMPLE

SURVIVAL FUND

3 – 6 Month Expenses

Monthly Expenses = $ _____

$ Fill in Dollar Amounts

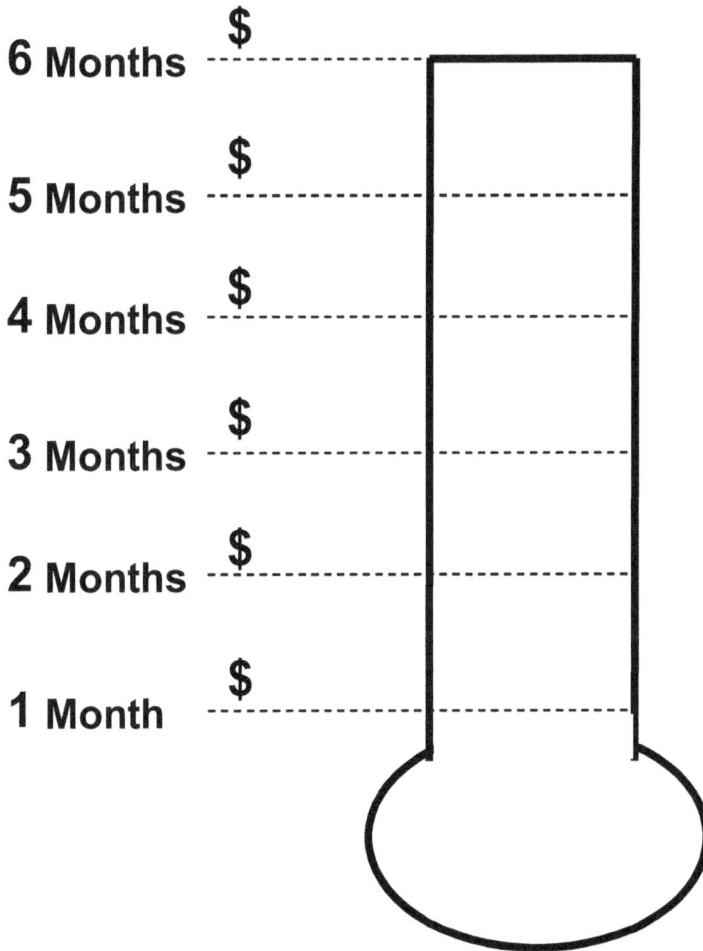

$
6 Months

$
5 Months

$
4 Months

$
3 Months

$
2 Months

$
1 Month

WAYS TO RAISE MONEY

SURVIVAL FUND
To Do List

ITEM	COMPLETED
Complete Survival Fund	
Celebrate	

_____   _____
Signature   *Date*

_____   _____
Signature   *Date*

PLAN RETIREMENT

SCOREBOARD

FINANCIAL SUCCESS IN A BOX

FINANCIAL SCOREBOARD

NAME: _____   DATE: _____

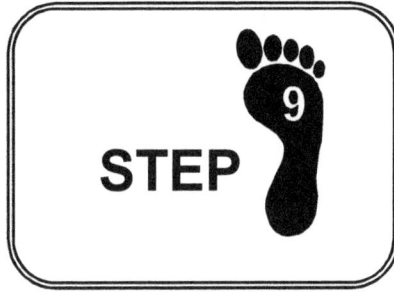

STEP		Statement	Scale
STEP 1	10 STEP PLAN	I have a step-by-step plan to follow to reach financial success	1 No — 2 3 4 5 Maybe 6 7 8 9 10 Yes
STEP 2	WORK TOGETHER	I work together with my spouse in all areas of our finances toward common goals (If you are single, mark the 10)	1 Never — 2 3 4 5 Sometimes 6 7 8 9 10 Always
STEP 3	THE BASICS	I know key success factors of money, behavior change and marketing self-defense	1 No — 2 3 4 5 Maybe 6 7 8 9 10 Yes
STEP 4	GIVING	I currently give to my church, charities, etc. on a regular basis	1 Never — 2 3 4 5 Regularly 6 7 8 9 10 10% Gross
STEP 5	PUT MONEY TO WORK	I currently save the following % of gross income every paycheck (includes savings, 401K, IRAs, etc)	1 1% or less 2 3 4 5 2% 6 7 8 9 10 3% Gross
STEP 6	EMERGENCY FUND	I currently have the following amount in a dedicated cash emergency fund	1 $0 2 $200 3 $300 4 $400 5 $500 6 $600 7 $700 8 $800 9 $900 10 $1000
STEP 7	PAY OFF DEBT	I currently owe the following total amount in consumer debt (Includes credit cards, student loans, etc. – everything except your house)	1 $20,000+ 2 3 $16,000 4 5 $12,000 6 7 $8,000 8 9 $4,000 10 $0
STEP 8	SURVIVAL FUND	I currently have a cash survival fund that will cover my total expenses for	1 Month 2 Months 3 Months 4 Months 5 Months 6 Months
STEP 9	PLAN RETIREMENT	I contribute to my retirement fund every month and I know I will have enough (If you are currently retired, mark 10)	1 No — 2 3 4 5 Maybe 6 7 8 9 10 Yes
STEP 10	PAY OFF HOUSE	(If you do not have a mortgage, mark 10)	1 Never — 2 3 4 5 Regularly 6 7 8 9 10 Paid Off

1 Fill in the circles that best describe your current situation

2 Connect the Dots

3 Total the Points

[_____]

If your score is less than 90, you need this program

Copyright © 2010

Steady plodding brings prosperity.

Proverbs 21:5

IMAGINE

Imagine having a simple, automatic retirement plan that would provide you with a great retirement.

Imagine:

- Having a retirement plan that is so simple anyone can understand it
- Having your retirement contributions happen automatically each month
- Taking the uncertainty out of retirement
- Being able to retire years early
- Being able to calculate how much money you need to retire in less than five seconds
- Being able to calculate how much you need to save per month to retire in less than 15 seconds
- Being able to retire with the same income or more than you have now
- Putting the right amount in the right account every month automatically, and having confidence that it will be enough to support you when you retire

Imagine the comfort you will experience knowing that you are providing a great retirement for you and your loved ones.

PURPOSE

CREATE A SIMPLE AUTOMATIC RETIREMENT PLAN

The purpose of this step is to show you three simple action items that will help you build a simple automatic retirement plan that will provide for you and your loved ones when you retire.

This step takes the mystery out of planning for retirement. With the three simple action items you will be able to determine how much money you will need to retire, determine how much you need to save each month to reach your goal, and adjust your monthly contribution to make sure you are on track. This step is the completion of what you started in Step 5 – Put Money to Work. In this step we will simply increase the amount you put to work in Step 5 to the appropriate amount to build a strong retirement fund.

RETIREMENT PLAN

ACTION 1 → Total Amount Needed

ACTION 2 → Monthly Amount Needed

ACTION 3 → Adjust Monthly Amount

YOU HAVE A HEAD START

The first piece of good news is that you have already completed the first part of this step. In Step 5 – Put Money to Work, you put a certain percentage of your income to work in a 401(k), 403(b), 457, IRA, or some other retirement account. You have already completed the most difficult part: getting started. All we have to do in this step is adjust your monthly contribution amount if necessary, to make sure you are contributing the appropriate amount to reach your goal.

THE MONEY MAY ALREADY BE THERE

The second piece of good news is that the money you spent each month on credit card debt before you completed Step 7 – Pay off Debt and then used to build your survival fund, is now available to use to build your retirement plan. If you paid $430 a month on credit card debt, now that you have pitched your debt and built your survival fund, that $430 a month is free to build your retirement plan.

The same dollars that paid off your credit card debt and built your survival fund will now be given the job of building a retirement fund that will provide for you after retirement.
Note: If you have not completed Step 5 – Put Money to Work, go back and do it or review it.

MONEY - NOT AGE

Before we get into the actual steps in this section, I want to challenge you to think a little differently about the concept of retirement.

When most people think of retirement, they think about it in relation to age. They say, "I want to retire at the age of 65," or "I want to retire early at the age of 55." Most people think of retirement as a function of age. When you think of retirement as a function of age, then you let age determine when you will retire. I want to challenge you to think of retirement differently.

Retirement is not a function of age; it is a function of money. You do not retire because you have reached a certain age; you retire because you have enough money to support retirement. If you are 65 years old but have no money, you will not be able to retire. If you are 40 years old and you have enough money to support you without working, then you can retire. Retirement is a function of money, not age.

This distinction is important because it will determine how dedicated you will be in your savings, and it will determine when you will be able to retire. For example, if you say, "I want to retire at the age of 65," and you determine that you will need $1,000,000 to retire, then you will calculate the amount you will need to save each month to have the $1,000,000 at the age of 65. If all goes well, you will save each month and retire at the age of 65 with $1,000,000. What if you approached it the other way, as a function of money instead of age? In this case you say, "I need $1,000,000 to retire," then you calculate how fast you could possibly accumulate the $1,000,000 at various levels of monthly contributions. You see that if you decide to be aggressive, you can possibly have the $1,000,000 way before you reach the age of 65. Using this approach you may find that you can retire years earlier than you would if you used age as a guide.

My point is that if you use age to determine your retirement, you will probably be less dedicated and less aggressive than if you use the amount of money as the determining factor. You can have some control over the speed of the accumulation of money. You cannot speed the aging process, and you would not want to. It is the amount of money that determines when you can retire, not your age.

KEEP IT SIMPLE

I want to keep this section simple. There are many complicated techniques you can use when planning your retirement. The goal of this section is for you to use very simple steps that will allow you to create a simple automatic retirement plan. You can explore more sophisticated tools once you have the basics completed.

NOBODY CAN PREDICT THE FUTURE

The truth is that nobody can predict the future. Nobody can tell you what interest rates will be 5, 10, 20, or 30 years from now or even tomorrow, but you can use reasonable numbers based on historical data to make projections and start planning for your retirement.

The numbers used in the following examples are not guaranteed. They are simply reasonable numbers used to make projections. The examples are used to help you make plans in a simple, effective way. If you believe the numbers in the examples are too high or too low, then simply make appropriate adjustments when you make your personal retirement plans.

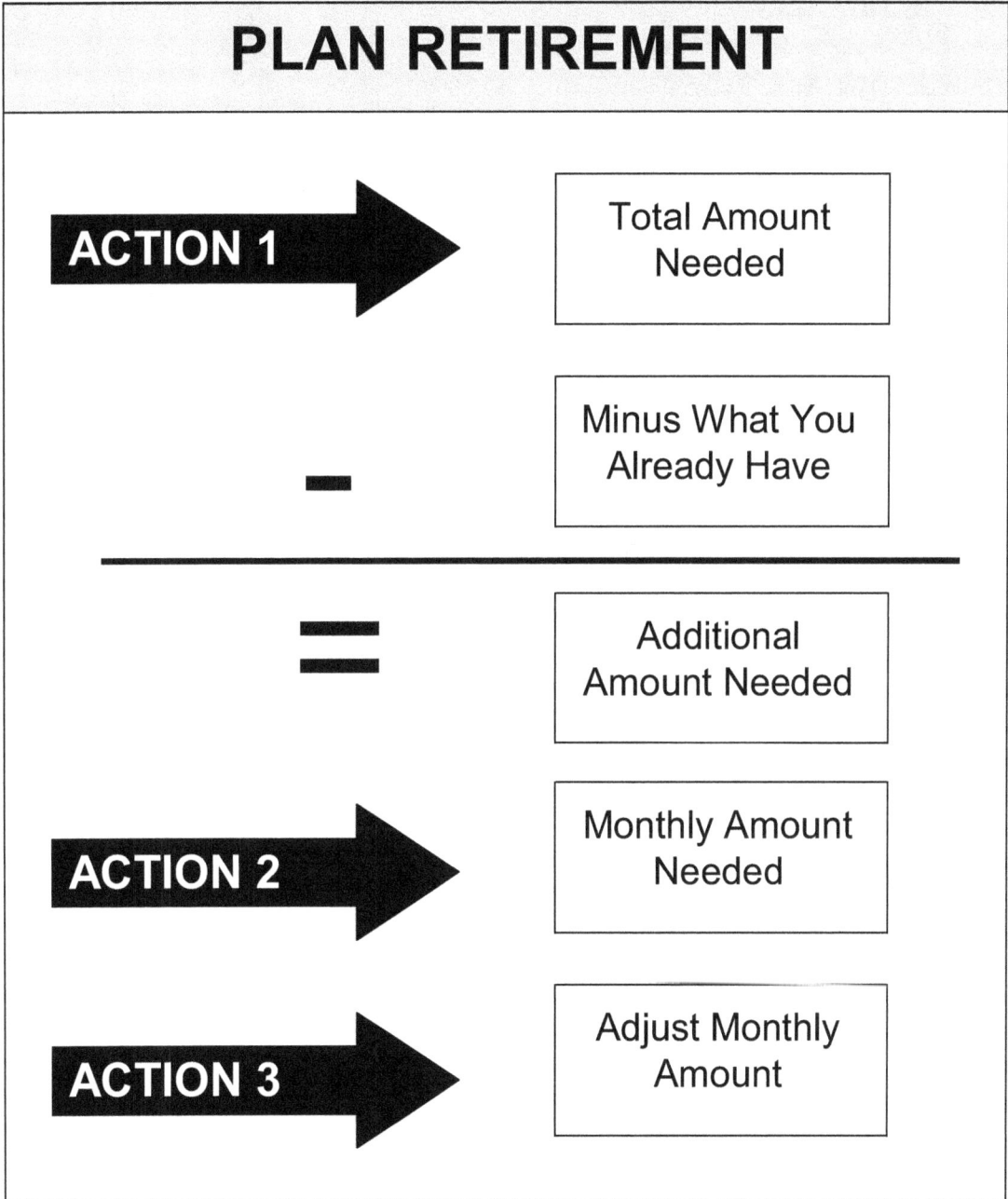

ACTION ITEMS

PLAN RETIREMENT

ACTION 1 → Total Amount Needed

− Minus What You Already Have

_____

= Additional Amount Needed

ACTION 2 → Monthly Amount Needed

ACTION 3 → Adjust Monthly Amount

ACTION 1
DETERMINE TOTAL AMOUNT NEEDED

Believe it or not, this is a very simple step. It will only take about 5 seconds to do. All you have to do is determine how much you want your annual income to be in retirement and multiply it by 10 (add a zero).

Desired annual retirement income:	$75,000
Amount needed to retire:	$750,000

Desired annual retirement income:	$100,000
Amount needed to retire:	$1,000,000

This method is based on a return rate of 10 percent annually. If you have $750,000 in a retirement account, and it is earning a 10 percent return annually, then you will have an annual income of $75,000. If you have $1,000,000 in a retirement account and it is earning a 10 percent return annually, then you will have an annual income of $100,000.

Note: This simple calculation method does not account for the effects of inflation. To account for inflation, increase the total amount needed to retire. There are many retirement calculators online to calculate an amount that considers the effects of inflation.

Once you have calculated the total amount needed to retire, the next part of this step is to subtract the amount you have already saved in retirement accounts from the total amount needed.

Desired annual retirement income:	$ 100,000
Amount needed to retire:	1,000,000
Amount already in retirement account:	50,000
Amount needed to retire:	950,000

Subtract the $50,000 from the $1,000,000 to determine the additional amount needed ($950,000) to reach your retirement goal. The diagram on the next page shows an example of how to do this calculation.

> *Your job is to transfer the responsibility of generating income*
> *from YOU to your MONEY!*

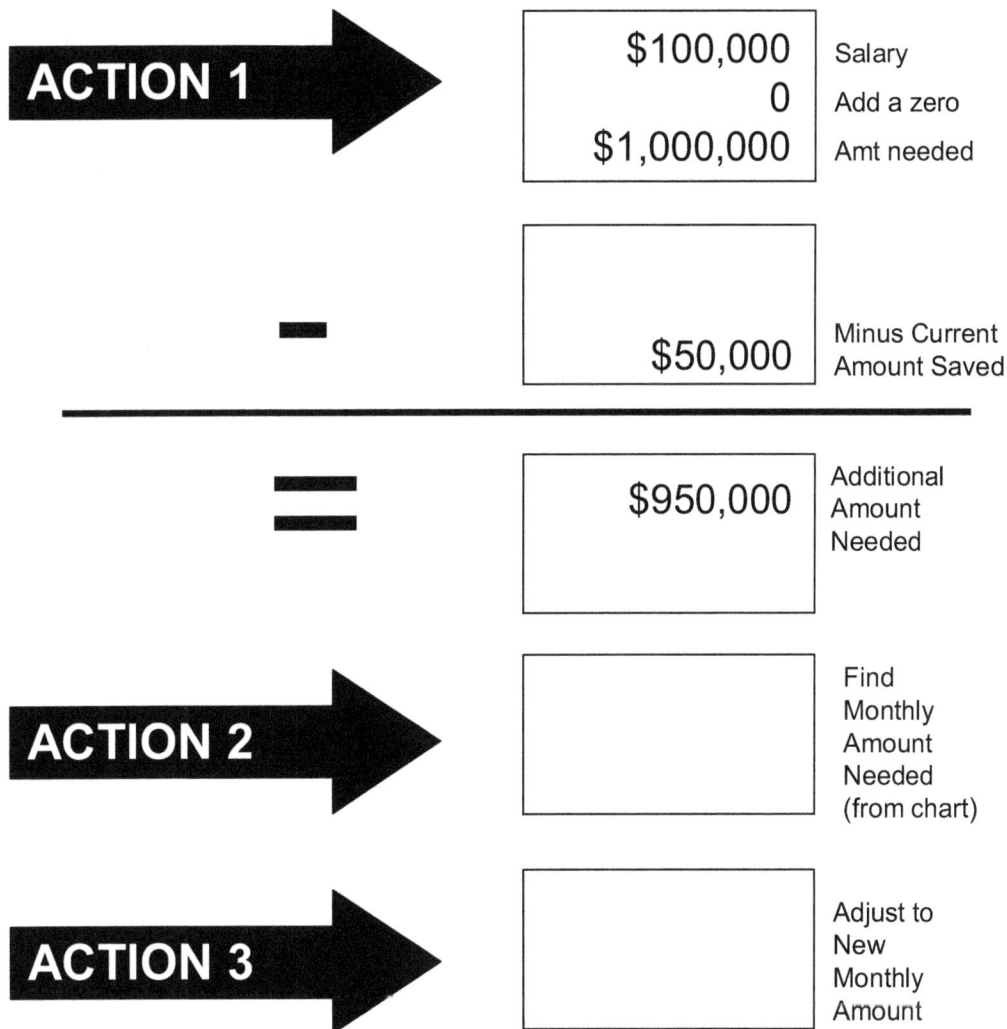

PLAN RETIREMENT
Example

ACTION 1

$100,000	Salary
0	Add a zero
$1,000,000	Amt needed

−

| $50,000 | Minus Current Amount Saved |

=

| $950,000 | Additional Amount Needed |

ACTION 2 — Find Monthly Amount Needed (from chart)

ACTION 3 — Adjust to New Monthly Amount

ACTION 2
DETERMINE MONTHLY AMOUNT NEEDED
Once you have determined the additional amount needed, the next step is to determine the monthly amount needed to reach your retirement goal. This action item is simple. It will only take about 15 seconds to do. Use the chart in the following example on the next page to determine your monthly amount needed.

EXAMPLE

- In column 1 locate the row that represents how many years until you want to retire. Example: If you are 30 years from retirement then you would scan down to the row labeled "30 years."

- Then scan across that row until you find the amount closest to your additional amount needed of $950,000 (column 4). The amount on the chart closest to your $950,000 amount is $1,085,661. It does not have to be an exact match.

- Then go to the top of that column and you will find the monthly amount needed ($500) that you will need to save each month to reach your retirement goal.

- Write this monthly amount needed in the proper box on the calculation form.

The chart shows how different monthly contributions will grow over time. Column 2 shows you how big $150 monthly contributions will grow from 1 through 45 years. Column 2 illustrates how big $250 monthly contributions will grow from 1 through 45 years. All of the projections on the chart assume a 10 percent return compounded annually. This number is used based on historical data.

A lotto ticket a day keeps retirement away.

DETERMINE MONTHLY AMOUNT NEEDED

Column1	Column2	Column3	Column4	Column5	Column6	Column7	Column8
Per Month	$150	$250	$500	$750	1,000	1,500	$2,000
1 Year	$1,980	$3,300	$6,600	$9,900	$13,200	$19,800	$26,400
	$4,158	$6,930	$13,860	$20,790	$27,720	$41,580	$55,440
	$6,554	$10,923	$21,846	$32,769	$43,692	$65,538	$87,384
	$9,189	$15,315	$30,631	$45,946	$61,261	$91,892	$122,522
5 Years	$12,088	$20,147	$40,294	$60,440	$80,587	$120,881	$161,175
	$15,277	$25,462	$50,923	$76,385	$101,846	$152,769	$203,692
	$18,785	$31,308	$62,615	$93,923	$125,231	$187,846	$250,461
	$22,643	$37,738	$75,477	$113,215	$150,954	$226,431	$301,907
	$26,887	$44,812	$89,625	$134,437	$179,249	$268,874	$358,498
10 Years	$31,556	$52,594	$105,187	$157,781	$210,374	$315,561	$420,748
	$36,692	$61,153	$122,306	$183,459	$244,611	$366,917	$489,223
	$42,341	$70,568	$141,136	$211,704	$282,273	$423,409	$564,545
	$48,555	$80,925	$161,850	$242,775	$323,700	$485,550	$647,400
	$55,390	$92,317	$184,635	$276,952	$369,270	$553,905	$738,540
15 Years	$62,910	$104,849	$209,698	$314,548	$419,397	$629,095	$838,794
	$71,180	$118,634	$237,268	$355,902	$474,536	$711,805	$949,073
	$80,279	$133,798	$267,595	$401,393	$535,190	$802,785	$1,070,380
	$90,286	$150,477	$300,955	$451,432	$601,909	$902,864	$1,203,818
	$101,295	$168,825	$337,650	$506,475	$675,300	$1,012,950	$1,350,600
20 Years	$113,404	$189,007	$378,015	$567,022	$756,030	$1,134,045	$1,512,060
	$126,725	$211,208	$422,416	$633,625	$844,833	$1,267,249	$1,689,666
	$141,377	$235,629	$471,258	$706,887	$942,516	$1,413,774	$1,885,033
	$157,495	$262,492	$524,984	$787,476	$1,049,968	$1,574,952	$2,099,936
	$175,225	$292,041	$584,082	$876,124	$1,168,165	$1,752,247	$2,336,329
25 Years	$194,727	$324,545	$649,091	$973,636	$1,298,181	$1,947,272	$2,596,362
	$216,180	$360,300	$720,600	$1,080,899	$1,441,199	$2,161,799	$2,882,399
	$239,778	$399,630	$799,260	$1,198,889	$1,598,519	$2,397,779	$3,197,038
	$265,736	$442,893	$885,786	$1,328,678	$1,771,571	$2,657,357	$3,543,142
	$294,289	$490,482	$980,964	$1,471,446	$1,961,928	$2,942,892	$3,923,857
30 Years	$325,698	$542,830	$1,085,661	$1,628,491	$2,171,321	$3,256,982	$4,342,642
	$360,248	$600,413	$1,200,827	$1,801,240	$2,401,653	$3,602,480	$4,803,306
	$398,253	$663,755	$1,327,509	$1,991,264	$2,655,019	$3,982,528	$5,310,037
	$440,058	$733,430	$1,466,860	$2,200,290	$2,933,720	$4,400,581	$5,867,441
	$486,044	$810,073	$1,620,146	$2,430,219	$3,240,292	$4,860,439	$6,480,585
35 Years	$536,628	$894,380	$1,788,761	$2,683,141	$3,577,522	$5,366,282	$7,155,043
	$592,271	$987,118	$1,974,237	$2,961,355	$3,948,474	$5,922,711	$7,896,948
	$653,478	$1,089,130	$2,178,261	$3,267,391	$4,356,521	$6,534,782	$8,713,042
	$720,806	$1,201,343	$2,402,687	$3,604,030	$4,805,373	$7,208,060	$9,610,747
	$794,867	$1,324,778	$2,649,555	$3,974,333	$5,299,111	$7,948,666	$10,598,221
40 Years	$876,333	$1,460,555	$2,921,111	$4,381,666	$5,842,222	$8,763,333	$11,684,443
	$965,947	$1,609,911	$3,219,822	$4,829,733	$6,439,644	$9,659,466	$12,879,288
	$1,064,521	$1,774,202	$3,548,404	$5,322,606	$7,096,808	$10,645,212	$14,193,617
	$1,172,953	$1,954,922	$3,909,845	$5,864,767	$7,819,689	$11,729,534	$15,639,378
	$1,292,229	$2,153,715	$4,307,429	$6,461,144	$8,614,858	$12,922,287	$17,229,716
45 Years	$1,423,432	$2,372,386	$4,744,772	$7,117,158	$9,489,544	$14,234,316	$18,979,088

Note: The new monthly amount needed includes the total amount contributed to your retirement accounts including any company matched dollars.

PLAN RETIREMENT
Example

ACTION 1		
	$100,000	Salary
	0	Add a zero
	$1,000,000	Amt needed

−	$50,000	Minus Current Amount Saved

=	$950,000	Additional Amount Needed

ACTION 2	$500	Find Monthly Amount Needed (from chart)

ACTION 3		Adjust to New Monthly Amount

ACTION 3
ADJUST MONTHLY AMOUNT

Action item 3 is also a very simple step. In this step you will be adjusting, if necessary, your monthly contribution amount to your retirement accounts. For example, if the chart identified the monthly contribution amount you need to make of $500 and you are currently contributing $350 per month then increase your monthly contribution amount to your 401(k), 403b, IRA from $350 to $500 per month.

Note: Select a percentage of your income that will result in the $500 amount being contributed. Do not choose the fixed amount of $500. The lesson from Step 5 – Put Your Money to Work shows that you need to choose a percent contribution, not a fixed amount, because a percent contribution will grow as your income grows; a fixed amount will not.

If you are already making a monthly contribution that is equal to or higher than the monthly amount needed from the chart, then just continue to make the same monthly contribution. *DO NOT LOWER IT!*

The more money you put to work, the more money you will have at retirement.

Continuous effort—not strength or intelligence—is the key to unlocking your potential.

Winston Churchill

PLAN RETIREMENT
Example

ACTION 1 →	$100,000	Salary
	0	Add a zero
	$1,000,000	Amt needed
–		
	$50,000	Minus Current Amount Saved
=	$950,000	Additional Amount Needed
ACTION 2 →	$500	Find Monthly Amount Needed (from chart)
ACTION 3 →	Current Monthly $350	Adjust to New Monthly Amount
	+ 150	
	New Monthly 500	

As illustrated in Step 5 – Put Money to Work, if you are using pre-tax dollars, your spendable income will not go down as much as you raise your contribution.

You will absolutely love the feeling of Financial Success when you have a fully funded retirement plan!

CONGRATULATIONS!

You are now on track to a simple, automatic, and stable retirement.

YOU HAVE COME A LONG WAY!

- You have completed Step 1 – 10-Step Plan, and you are following the simple 10-step plan.
- You have completed Step 2 – Work Together, and you are working together toward the same financial goals and using each other's strengths.
- You have completed Step 3 – The Basics, and you are familiar with the basics of how money works, how behavior works, and how to win the marketing battle for your dollars.
- You have completed Step 4 – Giving, and you know how to be a powerful giver.
- You have completed Step 5 – Put Money to Work, and you have the Big 3 working for you 24 hours a day, 365 days a year as your financial snowball grows bigger every time it rolls over.
- You have completed Step 6 – emergency fund and you have a strong emergency fund or outer wall to protect you from emergencies as you move toward your goal of Financial Success.
- You have completed Step 7 – Pay Off Debt, and you are free from the oppressive slavery of being in debt. You have freed money that was going toward debt to go to work for you building a strong and stable financial future.
- You have completed Step 8 – survival fund, and you have a strong survival fund or inner wall that will provide for your family for 3 to 6 months even if all income is cut off.
- Now you have completed Step 9 - Plan Retirement, and you are on your way to a great retirement.

> *The path to success is to take massive, determined action.*
> *Anthony Robbins*

You can now move your dot on Step 9 of the scoreboard to a score of 10.

SCOREBOARD

Now it is time for Step 10 – Pay Off House

What does pay off house mean? It means creating a simple, automatic plan that will help you pay your house off years early and save thousands and thousands of dollars.

Move forward and conquer Step 10 – Pay Off House.

> *You are never too old to set another goal or to dream a new dream.*
>
> *C.S. Lewis*

PLAN RETIREMENT
Example

ACTION 1 ➡️ [ ] Salary
Add a zero
Amt needed

− [ ] Minus Current
Amount Saved

———————————————

= [ ] Additional
Amount
Needed

ACTION 2 ➡️ [ ] Find
Monthly
Amount
Needed
(from chart)

ACTION 3 ➡️ Current Monthly
+
New Monthly

Adjust to
New
Monthly
Amount

PLAN RETIREMENT
To Do List

ITEM	COMPLETED
Complete 3 Actions Form	
Celebrate	

_____   _____

Signature   *Date*

_____   _____

Signature   *Date*

PAY OFF HOUSE

SCOREBOARD

FINANCIAL SUCCESS IN A BOX

FINANCIAL SCOREBOARD

NAME: _____   DATE: _____

STEP 1
10 STEP PLAN
I have a step-by-step plan to follow to reach financial success

| 1 No | 2 | 3 | 4 | 5 Maybe | 6 | 7 | 8 | 9 | 10 Yes |

STEP 2
WORK TOGETHER
I work together with my spouse in all areas of our finances toward common goals
(if you are single, mark the 10)

| 1 Never | 2 | 3 | 4 | 5 Sometimes | 6 | 7 | 8 | 9 | 10 Always |

STEP 3
THE BASICS
I know key success factors of money, behavior change and marketing self-defense

| 1 No | 2 | 3 | 4 | 5 Maybe | 6 | 7 | 8 | 9 | 10 Yes |

STEP 4
GIVING
I currently give to my church, charities, etc. on a regular basis

| 1 Never | 2 | 3 | 4 | 5 Regularly | 6 | 7 | 8 | 9 | 10 10% Gross |

STEP 5
PUT MONEY TO WORK
I currently save the following % of gross income every paycheck
(includes savings, 401K, IRAs, etc)

| 1 1% or less | 2 | 3 | 4 | 5 2% | 6 | 7 | 8 | 9 | 10 3% Gross |

STEP 6
EMERGENCY FUND
I currently have the following amount in a dedicated cash emergency fund

| 1 $0 | 2 $200 | 3 $300 | $400 | 5 $500 | 6 $600 | $700 | 8 $800 | $900 | 10 $1000 |

STEP 7
PAY OFF DEBT
I currently owe the following total amount in consumer debt
(includes credit cards, student loans, etc. – everything except your house)

| 1 $20,000+ | 2 | 3 $16,000 | 4 | 5 $12,000 | 6 | 7 $8,000 | 8 | 9 $4,000 | 10 $0 |

STEP 8
SURVIVAL FUND
I currently have a cash survival fund that will cover my total expenses for

| 1 1 Month | 2 | 3 2 Months | 4 | 5 3 Months | 6 | 7 4 Months | 8 | 9 | 10 6 Months |

STEP 9
PLAN RETIREMENT
I contribute to my retirement fund every month and I know I will have enough
(if you are currently retired, mark 10)

| 1 No | 2 | 3 | 4 | 5 Maybe | 6 | 7 | 8 | 9 | 10 Yes |

STEP 10
PAY OFF HOUSE
I pay extra on my mortgage
(If you do not have a mortgage, mark 10)

| 1 Never | 2 | 3 | 4 | 5 Regularly | 6 | 7 | 8 | 9 | 10 Paid Off |

Fill in the circles that best describe your current situation

Connect the Dots

Total the Points

If your score is less than 90, you need this program

Copyright © 2010

The best nights' sleep happens in a paid-for house.

- 297 -

IMAGINE

Imagine how nice it would be to have your house completely paid for—to have no monthly house payment.

Imagine:
- How much extra money you would have if you did not have a house payment
- How much less stress you would have
- The great stuff you could buy
- The places you could travel
- How much you could help others with the extra money you would have
- How secure you would feel in tough economic times
- How free you would be to do whatever you want financially
- How much you could give

Imagine the awesome feeling you will experience when you make that last payment on your house. The money you spent every month on a house payment will then be free for you to use however you want.

PURPOSE

PAY HOUSE OFF EARLY

The purpose of this step is to get you to the wonderful place described above. I will show you 3 simple action items that will help you pay your house off years early and save thousands and thousands of dollars.

This step shows how easy it is to make extra payments toward your house and pay it off years early. The 3 simple action items will show how you can save tens of thousands of dollars by adding a little extra money to your monthly house payment. Much of the money you would have given to the bank in interest payments now can be kept.

ACTION ITEMS

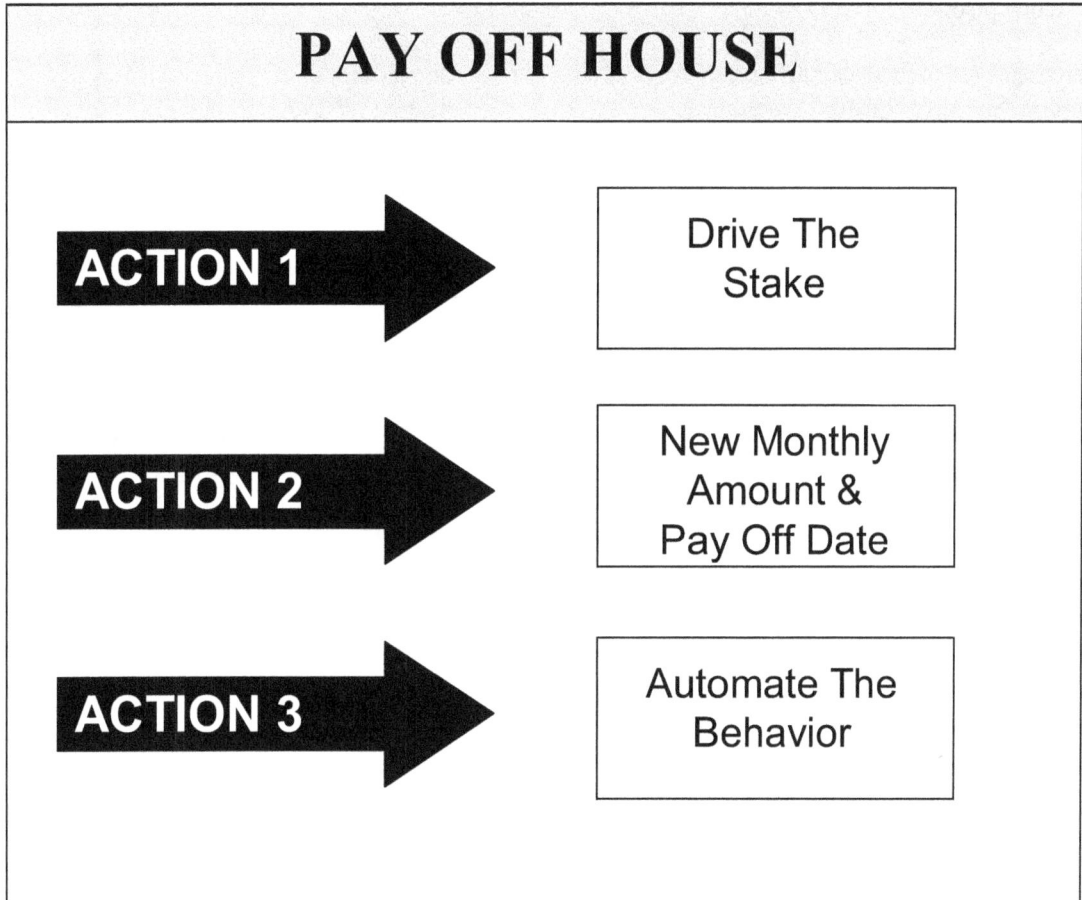

IT CAN BE DONE!
You may be thinking that it is impossible to pay off your house. *IT IS POSSIBLE!* I will show the simple steps. Make the commitment and stick with it.

I had a friend who made the decision to pay off her house. She knew how great it would be not to have a monthly house payment. She knew how strong it would make her financially to be free of it. She made the commitment and stuck to it. She put extra money toward her house payment each month and ended up paying it off years early and saving tons of money. She even created an incentive for herself to help stay committed. She decided to reward herself with a mink coat when she reached her goal. She stuck with the plan, reached her goal of paying the house off in full and bought herself a mink coat.

One of the reasons I remember this story is because it happened during a time when I was working at a large bank that was experiencing layoffs. My friend also worked at the bank. While the other employees were stressed out by the possibility of losing their job, she was totally calm. That really impressed me. If she lost her job, she would be fine. It is much easier to survive economic setbacks and emergencies when you do not have a monthly house payment. She had no credit card or consumer debt. Having no credit card payments and no house payment creates a very strong financial position.

My friend did not have a particularly high-paying job, and she did not come from a wealthy family. She simply made a commitment, stuck to it, and was a steady plodder until she reached her goal.

You can do this step, too! You may be surprised when you read this chapter at how fast you can reach this goal and how much progress you can make without contributing a lot of extra money each month.

Note: Some financial experts will advise you not to pay off your house. They say to take that same money and put it to work making 10 to 12 percent, and since you are only paying about 6 percent on your mortgage you will come out ahead. Technically, they are correct, but when you factor in human behavior you realize that while their argument is logical, most people will not have the discipline to actually do it. As you will see in this section, there are many great benefits to paying your house off early. I believe these benefits far out weigh the benefits of continuing to remain in debt and paying the bank exorbitant amounts of interest.

WHY YOU SHOULD PAY YOUR HOUSE OFF EARLY

REASON #1
YOU ARE PAYING TOO MUCH.
How much will your house really cost?

House FOR SALE $100,000	YOU PAY $215,838

If you bought a house for $100,000 with a 6 percent mortgage for 30 years, you would really pay $215,838.
If the house you found, liked, and were willing to pay $100,000 for had a sign on it with the price of $215,838, you would have walked away and thought, "They are crazy!" The truth is that you really are willing to pay that much as long as it is spread over a long period of time. Do not be fooled—you are not paying the sticker price for your house.

If you pay for your house on the bank's schedule, you will end up paying as much as 2½ times the sale price, depending on the interest rate. The bank is using the Big 3 of money (time, interest, and amount) against you. Just as I illustrated that they do in Pay Off Debt, they are stretching out your repayment schedule and only requiring minimum payments, and that ensures that you will pay more.

WHAT IS REALLY GOING ON?
If you end up paying $215,838 for a $100,000 house, you are really paying 115 percent not 6 percent. Mortgages are money machines for banks.

WHEN YOU OWE MONEY, THE BIG 3 ARE WORKING AGAINST YOU!
THE SHELL GAME
A shell game is when a pea is placed under one of three shells. It is obvious under which shell the pea has been placed. Then swift hands switch the shells around so that you lose track of the pea. You try to keep your eye on the shell, but it becomes a blur. Buying a house is like playing a shell game with the bank. The mortgage companies have figured out a way to make the Big 3 work *against* you and *for* them. It is business. They know that the typical person thinks in terms of monthly amount paid (M.A.P) and not in terms of total amount paid (T.A.P). So while you are focused on the shell with the monthly amount on it, they are moving the shell with the time on it so far out that you end up paying 2½ times more. It is all written out in the truth in lending disclosure when you sign the loan, but how many truly comprehend the true consequences of it?

It boils down to the basics—the Big 3 working *for* or *against* you.

REASON #2
YOU ARE PAYING THE BANK FIRST.
When the bank gives you a mortgage, they front load it heavily in their favor. What I mean is that they load their interest payments at the front of the mortgage so that you pay them more in interest than you pay yourself in principle. Look at the table on the next page, and you will see what I mean. This table illustrates a $100,000 mortgage loan at a 6 percent interest rate paid over a 30-year period. In year 1, you will pay $5,966 in interest to the bank and only $1,228 in principal to yourself. That means that out of $7,194 paid, you paid $5,966 to the bank and only $1,228 to yourself. In year 1, 83 percent of the money you paid went to the bank and only 17 percent went to you. That is horrible!

> *Beware of little expenses. A small leak will sink a great ship.*
> *Benjamin Franklin*

In year 2, you will pay the bank $5,890 and pay yourself only $1,303. If you pay according to this schedule, you will pay the bank more in interest than you pay yourself in principal every year for the first 18 years of the loan. That is not acceptable! Do you really want to pay the bank more than you pay yourself for 18 years? I do not think so. Year 19 is the first year when you pay yourself more than you pay the bank. Using the bank's payment schedule, it will take you 21 years to pay off *half* of the $100,000 loan. You are 21 years into a 30-year loan before you reach the halfway point.

\$100,000 MORTGAGE AT 6 PERCENT INTEREST FOR 30 YEARS			
Year	Principle	Interest	Balance
1	\$1,228.01	\$5,966.59	\$98,771.99
2	\$1,303.75	\$5,890.85	\$97,468.24
3	\$1,384.17	\$5,810.44	\$96,084.07
4	\$1,469.54	\$5,725.07	\$94,614.53
5	\$1,560.18	\$5,634.43	\$93,054.36
6	\$1,656.40	\$5,538.20	\$91,397.95
7	\$1,758.57	\$5,436.04	\$89,639.39
8	\$1,867.03	\$5,327.57	\$87,772.35
9	\$1,982.19	\$5,212.42	\$85,790.17
10	\$2,104.44	\$5,090.16	\$83,685.72
11	\$2,234.24	\$4,960.37	\$81,451.48
12	\$2,372.04	\$4,822.56	\$79,079.44
13	\$2,518.35	\$4,676.26	\$76,561.09
14	\$2,673.67	\$4,520.93	\$73,887.42
15	\$2,838.58	\$4,356.03	\$71,048.84
16	\$3,013.66	\$4,180.95	\$68,035.19
17	\$3,199.53	\$3,995.07	\$64,835.66
18	\$3,396.87	\$3,797.73	\$61,438.79
19	\$3,606.38	\$3,588.22	\$57,832.40
20	\$3,828.82	\$3,365.79	\$54,003.59
21	\$4,064.97	\$3,129.64	\$49,938.62
22	\$4,315.69	\$2,878.92	\$45,622.93
23	\$4,581.87	\$2,612.74	\$41,041.06
24	\$4,864.47	\$2,330.14	\$36,176.59
25	\$5,164.50	\$2,030.11	\$31,012.09
26	\$5,483.04	\$1,711.57	\$25,529.05
27	\$5,821.22	\$1,373.39	\$19,707.84
28	\$6,180.26	\$1,014.35	\$13,527.58
29	\$6,561.44	\$633.16	\$6,966.14
30	\$6,966.14	\$228.47	\$0.00

Below is a graph of the previous table. It shows the yearly amount of interest and principal paid. The interest paid to the bank is loaded heavily to the front of the loan so you end up paying the bank much more than you pay yourself. Year 19 is the first year that you pay yourself more than you pay the bank.

$100,000 MORTGAGE AT 6% INTEREST FOR 30 YEARS
YEARLY INTEREST VS. YEARLY PRINCIPAL

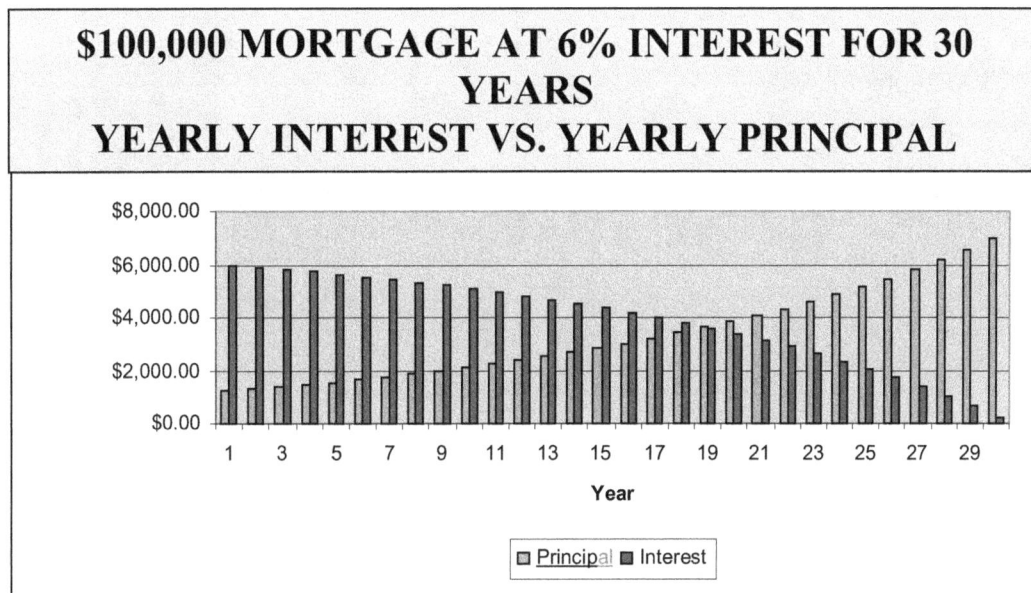

On the next page is another graph of the above illustration. It shows the total amount of interest and principal paid at the end of each year. As you can see, an extremely high percentage of the money you pay goes toward interest in the early years of the loan. In year 14, you have paid a total of $100,724. That is more than the original $100,000 price of the house, but $74,611 (74 percent) of that went to the bank and only $26,112 (26 percent) went toward paying off your house. At the end of 30 years, you have paid $215,000 for a $100,000 house. You have paid $115,000 of that to the bank, and you paid the bank first. There is not one single time during this 30-year relationship that the total amount you have paid yourself is higher than the total amount you have paid the bank. I hope these illustrations make you angry enough to take control of your own situation by taking the actions in this section.

$100,000 MORTGAGE AT 6 PERCENT INTEREST FOR 30 YEARS
TOTAL INTEREST VS. TOTAL PRINCIPAL

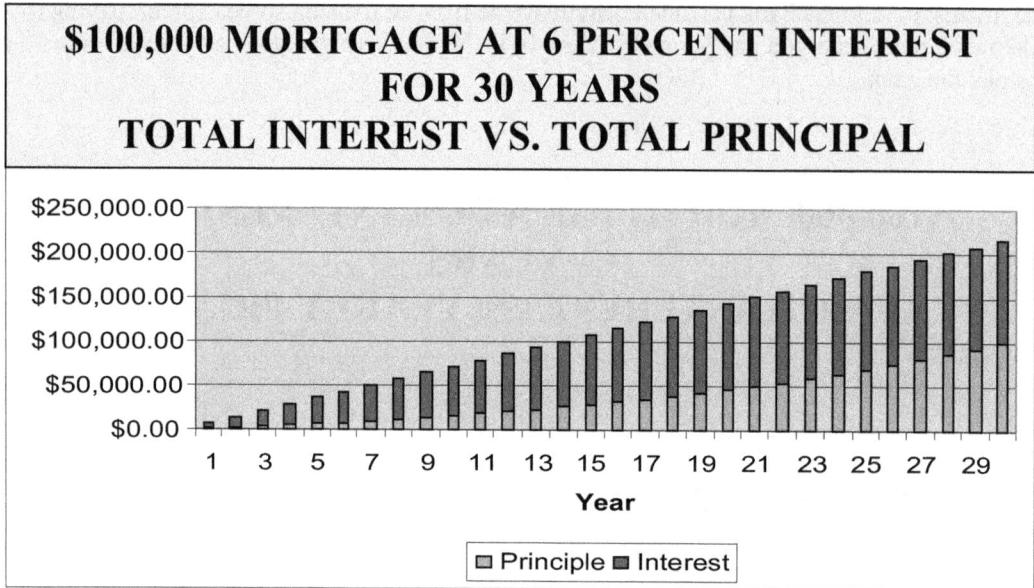

REASON #3
YOU SHOULD BUILD YOUR WEALTH, NOT THE BANK'S WEALTH.

OPPORTUNITY COST
There is a principal called opportunity cost. Opportunity cost simply means that when you spend money on one thing you no longer have the opportunity to do other things with that money. For example, if you spend $10,000 on interest payments to the bank each year, then you are missing out on the opportunity to put that $10,000 to work for you in a high-yield mutual fund. The money you are giving to the bank each month in interest payments has a very high opportunity cost. If you can pay your house off early and put the money you would have given the bank in interest payments to work, you can build wealth for you and your family. Just think how great it will be to have your house paid off. Your retirement money will go much further, your survival fund will go much further, and you will be able to do wonderful things with the money you would have paid to the bank. Do not make the bank rich; build your wealth instead by paying off your house.

This is where T.A.P. (total amount paid) is critical. Ask yourself what the T.A.P. is on your house.

The money you are giving to the bank in interest could go to work for you and your family for generations and generations. The way to solve this problem is to increase the amount you pay each month, and that will reduce the time it takes to pay your house off, and that will lower the total amount you will pay for your house.

YOU ARE IN A WAR

Remember the 3 fastest ways to lose a war from Step 3.

- Do not realize you are in one.
- Let the enemy decide the rules.
- Obey the enemy's rules.

Good news: You do not have to play by the bank's rules. You can take control of this situation by paying extra toward your mortgage each month.

It is time for you to take control and win this battle. You will now set your own rules. You, not the bank, will now decide how much you will pay each month and when the mortgage will be paid in full.

ACTION 1
DRIVE THE STAKE
Make a full commitment to pay off your house early.

Once again I ask you to remember the story about the farmer who drove the wooden stake at the end of his field and plowed toward it. No matter what happened, he never quit driving toward that stake. It was his goal, and no matter what, he was going to reach it!

You need to make the same type of commitment that you will pay off your house and never again take out any loans against it. When you pay off your house, you will feel a freedom, a power that you cannot even imagine. You will also be free to build wealth and reach a great financial life faster than ever. Any money you are currently spending on your house payment will be freed up to work and build your wealth. This money can become a powerful financial snowball that can build wealth for generations to come.

Make the commitment that you will pay off your house, and stick with it until you make that very last payment.

Plan a fun, inexpensive celebration for the day you make that last house payment and become mortgage payment free.

You may not feel any relief during the time you are paying off your house, but when you reach that last day, there will be sudden and complete relief from the burden of this debt. The money that has been going toward your house payment each month will be freed up to build your wealth.

Teach your children to start saving for a house with their very first dime. They have time on their side. Imagine if they saved a percentage of all their money for a home. They may not ever even go into debt for a house. What a wonderful thing!

So, drive the stake and make a firm commitment to pay off your house!

> *It has been my observation that most people get ahead during the time that others waste.*
>
> *Henry Ford*

ACTION 2
DECIDE EXTRA AMOUNT TO PAY
Determine the extra amount you will pay toward your house payment each month.

The next form gives examples of how much you can save by paying extra on your mortgage payment each month. It also shows you how much faster you can pay off your house.

Add $10 to monthly payment.
Save $5,744 and knock 1.3 years off of your loan.

Add $50 to your monthly payment.
Save $24,738 and knock 5.5 years off of the loan

Add $250 to your monthly payment.
Save $64,588 and knock 15.2 years off of your loan.

Think of what you could do with those monthly mortgage payments during the last 15 years of the 30-year loan.

PAY OFF HOUSE
EXAMPLES

Based on a $100,000 Loan at 6% interest for 30 Year term

Extra Amount To Principal Each Month		Amount Saved On T.A.P.	Years Knocked Off Loan
$10	SAVES YOU	$ 5,744	1.3 Yrs
$25	SAVES YOU	$ 14,041	3.1 Yrs
$50	SAVES YOU	$ 24,738	5.5 Yrs
$75	SAVES YOU	$ 33,022	7.4 Yrs
$100	SAVES YOU	$ 40,076	9.1 Yrs
$250	SAVES YOU	$ 64,588	15.2 Yrs
$500	SAVES YOU	$ 82,014	19.8 Yrs

When does $100 dollars equal more than $40,000 dollars?
When you add it to your regular mortgage payment every month!

YOU DO NOT HAVE TO DOUBLE YOUR PAYMENT
In the example on the next page, the 30-year loan requires a monthly payment of $599.55.
The 15-year loan requires a payment of $843.86—only $244.31 more than the 30-year loan. You do not have to double your payment to pay your house off in half the time. If you increase your monthly payment by only $245 dollars, your house will be paid off 15 years early.

PAY OFF HOUSE

T.A.P. PRICE

Sale Price	Terms	T.A.P. Price	Extra Paid
$100,000	6% @ 30 Years	$215,838	$115,838
$100,000	6% @ 15 Years	$151,894	$51,894
$100,000	Pay Cash	$100,000	$0

The entire difference goes directly to the bank in the form of interest payments.

You are sending your dollars (employees) to work for the bank instead of you.

There are several ways you can increase the amount of your monthly payment.

#1: ADD A SPECIFIC DOLLAR AMOUNT.

The first way to increase your monthly payment amount is to simply choose a fixed amount and add it to your payment each month. For example, add $10, $25, $250, or $500 extra to your monthly payment. Go to a financial site with mortgage calculators such as Bankrate.com to help you determine the results of adding an extra amount to your mortgage payment. Go to bankrate.com and click on the calculator section. Go to the mortgage calculator section and choose the mortgage calculator. It will allow you to run different scenarios to see how much you will save and how much faster you can pay off your mortgage. Simply fill in the information, and click the calculate button. Be sure you input the remaining balance on your mortgage, not the original amount. Plug in different extra amounts, and review the results. Record the numbers on the estimates form at the end of this section. Choose the extra amount that gives you the results you want, and starting with your next payment, add it to the regular amount you pay. Also, make sure you fill in the commitment form at the end of this section.

I recommend that you put at least 10 percent additional money toward each monthly payment. For example, if your monthly payment is $600 then I recommend you put at least $60 extra toward your monthly payment each month. In our previous example of a $100,000 mortgage at 6 percent for 30 years, you would knock 6 years off of the loan and pay tens of thousands of dollars less.

#2 MAKE BIWEEKLY PAYMENTS

Another way to increase the amount of your payment is to make biweekly payments. You pay the same amount each month, but because you make half of the payment every two weeks, you end up making an extra payment each year. You end up making 26 half payments which equals 13 full payments. This pays your loan off faster and reduces the amount of interest you pay on the loan. Bankrate.com has a biweekly mortgage calculator to use to figure out if this is a good option for you. Many banks have biweekly mortgage programs that you can join. There is typically a charge of several hundred dollars to get it set up, but the money you save will greatly outweigh the money it costs to set it up. You will need to join the bank's biweekly payment program. If you send in payments every two weeks on your own, the bank may not know what to do with the payments and things may get mixed up. Call your bank and ask if they have a biweekly payment program.

Ask them about the costs and also about when the payments will be credited to your mortgage. This is very important because you do not want the money to be held and applied at a later date. You want each payment applied as soon as possible. Also, make sure there are no early payoff penalties.

Note: You could also make one extra monthly payment each year. For example, you could make one extra monthly payment when you get your tax return. Just make sure that the bank credits the payment to the principal immediately and does not hold the funds. This practice will save you thousands of dollars and knock years off of your mortgage.

ACTION 3
AUTOMATE IT
Remember in Step 3 – The Basics, we discussed the basics of behavior. One of the principles we discussed was automating your right behaviors—behaviors that have a positive effect on your financial health. If you automate right behaviors, then you are ensuring that they will continue to happen. When you automate a right behavior, you are removing the requirement for you to be diligent and disciplined enough to keep doing it. If you want to pay your house off early by paying an additional amount on top of your regular monthly payment or by making biweekly payments, then you need to automate it. Do not rely on the fact that you will have the long-term willpower to do it. If you rely on your willpower, sooner or later you will be tempted to skip the right behavior and then your progress will stop. Trust me—automate it!

ADD A SPECIFIC DOLLAR AMOUNT
If you are going to contribute an extra dollar amount to your payment each month, I recommend that you sign up to have your monthly mortgage payment made automatically from your checking or savings account. Contact your mortgage company and ask them the best way to do it. You can either have the new, larger amount deducted each month, or they may advise you to have the regular payment amount in one automatic payment and the extra amount you are contributing in a separate automatic payment. Make sure that the extra money is applied to your principal as soon as possible. You do not want the extra payment to be held and applied later. It should be applied immediately. Also, check your mortgage account each month to make sure things are posting properly.

MAKE BIWEEKLY PAYMENTS
If you are going to make biweekly mortgage payments, then I highly recommend that you join the formal plan offered by your bank. You may be tempted to avoid the cost (probably several hundred dollars) and commit to making the payments every two weeks yourself. Resist the temptation. The money you will save by doing this will be thousands if not tens of thousands of dollars more than the small amount you will spend to automate it. Pay the fee, automate it, forget about , and save tons of money!
REMEMBER, THE BEST WAY TO ENSURE A RIGHT BEHAVIOR CONTINUES IS TO AUTOMATE IT.

Complete the items listed on the to do list at the end of this section.

CONGRATULATIONS!

You are now on track to pay your house off years early and save thousands and thousands of dollars.

YOU HAVE COME A LONG WAY!

- You have completed Step 1 – 10-Step Plan, and you are following the simple 10-step plan.
- You have completed Step 2 – Work Together, and you are working together toward the same financial goals and using each other's strengths.
- You have completed Step 3 – The Basics, and you are familiar with the basics of how money works, how behavior works, and how to win the marketing battle for your dollars.
- You have completed Step 4 – Giving, and you know how to be a powerful giver.
- You have completed Step 5 – Put Money to Work, and you have the Big 3 working for you 24 hours a day, 365 days a year as your financial snowball grows bigger every time it rolls over.
- You have completed Step 6 – Emergency Fund, and you have a strong emergency fund or outer wall to protect you from emergencies as you move toward your goal of Financial Success.
- You have completed Step 7 – Pay Off Debt, and you are free from the oppressive slavery of being in debt. You have freed money that was going toward debt to go to work for you building a strong and stable financial future.
- You have completed Step 8 – Survival Fund, and you have a strong survival fund or inner wall that will provide for your family for 3 to 6 months even if all income is cut off.
- You have completed Step 9 - Plan Retirement, and you are on your way to a great retirement.
- And now you have completed Step 10 – Pay Off House, and you are on your way to saving tons of money and paying your house off years early.

> *That some achieve great success, is proof to all that others can achieve it as well.*
>
> *Abraham Lincoln*

PAY OFF HOUSE

You can now move your dot on Step 10 of the scoreboard form to a score of 10.

SCOREBOARD

FINANCIAL SUCCESS IN A BOX

FINANCIAL SCOREBOARD

NAME: _____   DATE: _____

STEP 1
10 STEP PLAN
I have a step-by-step plan to follow to reach financial success
1 2 3 4 5 6 7 8 9 10
No   Maybe   Yes

STEP 2
WORK TOGETHER
I work together with my spouse in all areas of our finances toward common goals
(if you are single, mark the 10)
1 2 3 4 5 6 7 8 9 10
Never   Sometimes   Always

STEP 3
THE BASICS
I know key success factors of money, behavior change and marketing self-defense
1 2 3 4 5 6 7 8 9 10
No   Maybe   Yes

STEP 4
GIVING
I currently give to my church, charities, etc. on a regular basis
1 2 3 4 5 6 7 8 9 10
Never   Regularly   10% Gross

STEP 5
PUT MONEY TO WORK
I currently save the following % of gross income every paycheck
(includes savings, 401K, IRAs, etc)
1 2 3 4 5 6 7 8 9 10
1% or less   2%   10% Gross

STEP 6
EMERGENCY FUND
I currently have the following amount in a dedicated cash emergency fund
1 2 3 4 5 6 7 8 9 10
$0 $200 $300 $400 $500 $600 $700 $800 $900 $1000

STEP 7
PAY OFF DEBT
I currently owe the following total amount in consumer debt
(includes credit cards, student loans, etc. – everything except your house)
1 2 3 4 5 6 7 8 9 10
$20,000+ $16,000 $12,000 $8,000 $ $0

STEP 8
SURVIVAL FUND
I currently have a cash survival fund that will cover my total expenses for
1 2 3 4 5 6 7 8 9 10
1 Month 2 Months 3 Months 4 Months   6 Months

STEP 9
PLAN RETIREMENT
I contribute to my retirement fund every month and I know I will have enough
(if you are currently retired, mark 10)
1 2 3 4 5 6 7 8 9 10
No   Maybe   Yes

STEP 10
PAY OFF HOUSE
I pay extra on my mortgage
(if you do not have a mortgage, mark 10)
1 2 3 4 5 6 7 8 9 10
Never   Regularly   Paid Off

Fill in the circles that best describe your current situation

Connect the Dots

Total the Points

If your score is less than 90, you need this program

Copyright © 2010

CONGRATULATIONS!

You have completed all 10 steps of the program. Now your goal is to stay financially successful in all of the 10 categories. I recommend that you fill out a new scoreboard every couple of months to make sure your scores in each of the 10 categories are staying high. If a score starts to go lower than you are happy with, simply repeat that step of the program and bring your score back to the higher level. I also recommend that you continue to use the dashboard each month and the other powerful tools in this program.

WELCOME TO THE WONDERFUL WORLD OF FINANCIAL SUCCESS!

PAY OFF HOUSE
PAY MORE ESTIMATES

Based on a $_____ Loan at ___% interest for ___-Year Term

Extra Amount To Principal Each Month		Amount Saved On T.A.P.	Years Knocked Off Loan
$10	**SAVES YOU**	$_____	____Yrs
$25	**SAVES YOU**	$_____	____Yrs
$50	**SAVES YOU**	$_____	____Yrs
$75	**SAVES YOU**	$_____	____Yrs
$100	**SAVES YOU**	$_____	____Yrs
$250	**SAVES YOU**	$_____	____Yrs
$500	**SAVES YOU**	$_____	____Yrs

PAY OFF HOUSE

I COMMIT TO PAY THE EXTRA AMOUNT BELOW ON MY MORTGAGE PAYMENT EACH MONTH.

Extra Amount To Principal Each Month		Amount Saved On T.A.P.	Years Knocked Off Loan

$ _____   **SAVES YOU** $ _____   _____Yrs

My new pay off date is: __ / __ / __

NAME: _____   DATE: _____

PAY OFF HOUSE
To Do List

ITEM	COMPLETED
Complete 3 Actions Form	
Complete Estimates Form	
Complete Commitment Form	
Celebrate	

_____   _____
Signature   *Date*

_____   _____
Signature   *Date*